From Mines and Wells to Well-Built Minds

DIRECTIONS IN DEVELOPMENT
Human Development

From Mines and Wells to Well-Built Minds

Turning Sub-Saharan Africa's Natural Resource Wealth into Human Capital

Bénédicte de la Brière, Deon Filmer, Dena Ringold, Dominic Rohner, Karelle Samuda, and Anastasiya Denisova

Contents

Boxes

Figures

Map

Tables

Foreword

Sub-Saharan African countries are endowed with a rich and varied array of natural resources that all contribute to the continent's wealth. Over the past 15 years or so, the revenues from oil, gas, and minerals have driven a remarkable growth story. However, recent commodity price declines have highlighted the inherent risks and potential fragility of this growth.

Leveraging oil, gas, and minerals for development is a challenge for many countries around the world. It has underpinned dramatic positive transformation in some countries but has fueled dependence and inefficiency and has even stymied economic growth and poverty reduction in others—the so-called *natural resource curse*. Managing the downturn and protecting the right expenditures will help countries to make the most of the sector, which will remain key to the continent's development.

African governments need to address some key issues as they seek to make the most out of their endowments. These include questions such as how to facilitate exploration and how to ensure that the interests of local communities, firms, and governments are aligned without irreversibly damaging the natural and social environment.

This book focuses on one specific issue—how to ensure that the stream of revenues that flow into the public purse are used most effectively to promote a growth strategy that all segments of society share. It makes the case that investing in people—in their health and education to ensure that their minds are as powerful as possible—will be an important part of any strategy to transform finite resources into long-run development.

Resource-rich countries in Sub-Saharan Africa do not do well in terms of health and education outcomes, especially when compared with similarly wealthy countries outside the region. Resource-rich countries in Sub-Saharan Africa spend less on human development as a share of national income and get less for what they spend. The book shows why investments in human capital make sense as part of the portfolio allocation of wealth derived from natural resources, alongside investments in infrastructure and savings, especially in potentially fragile and conflict-affected situations. The book highlights how the volatility and volume of natural resource rents can exacerbate some of the service delivery challenges that make it hard for public investments to improve human capital—and points to ways to mitigate those constraints. The book also emphasizes the critical issues related to improving the quality of health and education services and the potential of direct cash transfers to relieve poverty and vulnerability and increase demand for health and education. It highlights the somewhat neglected role that investing effectively in early child development—both at the earliest ages and in the preschool years—can play in laying the foundations for greater skills and successful human development and in breaking the intergenerational cycle of conflict and poverty.

This book is a reminder that Africa's greatest wealth is its people. Policies to transform the revenues from oil, natural gas, and minerals into smart investments in Africa's people will be the foundation for the continent's long-run prosperity in an increasingly volatile environment.

Makhtar Diop
Vice President, Africa Region

Acknowledgments

This report was prepared by a core team led by Bénédicte de la Brière and Deon Filmer and included Dena Ringold, Dominic Rohner, Karelle Samuda, and Anastasiya Denisova. David Evans, Anna Popova, and Quentin Wodon provided additional contributions to chapter 4. Antonia Doncheva and Anca Rusu provided research assistance. The initial directors of the team were Francisco H. G. Ferreira and Ritva Reinikka and later Punam Chuhan-Pole and Albert Zeufack. Mapi Buitano provided invaluable support in implementing this work. Several World Bank staff, as well as policy makers, academics, and other stakeholders, provided comments at various stages, in particular during authors' workshops, midterm reviews, and decision meetings. Hana Brixi and Ezequiel Molina provided feedback on chapter 3. Sébastien Dessus, Margaret Grosh, Anand Rajnaram, Albert Zeufack, and an anonymous reviewer carefully peer-reviewed draft versions. Anne Grant copyedited the book. Any errors and omissions are the responsibility of the team.

About the Authors

Bénédicte de la Brière is a lead economist in the Gender Cross-Cutting Solutions Area group at the World Bank. She was previously in the Human Development group of the Africa region, and the focal point for Governance and Service Delivery in the Office of the Chief Economist for Human Development. At the World Bank, she has worked on social assistance in the Middle East and North Africa, Latin America and the Caribbean, and Sub-Saharan Africa regions. She has previously served at the Food and Agriculture Organization of the United Nations, leading research about the productive impacts of social cash transfers in Africa. In addition, she was a U.K. Department for International Development adviser to the Ministry of Social Development in Brazil during the first Lula government. She holds a PhD in agriculture and resource economics from the University of California, Berkeley and undertook postdoctoral research at the International Food Policy Research Institute on intrahousehold impacts of rural development and social interventions.

Anastasiya Denisova is an economist with the Social Protection and Labor Global Practice in the South Asia region of the World Bank. Before joining the World Bank, she worked with the International Finance Corporation, studying the impacts of private sector interventions on job creation. She was also engaged in research on the political economy of migration and international trade, with a particular focus on the effects of lobbying on migration and international trade laws. She holds a PhD in economics from Georgetown University and a BA with high honors in economics and political science from the University of California, Berkeley.

Deon Filmer works on issues of education, youth employment and skills, service delivery, and the study of policies and programs to improve human development outcomes. His research spans the areas of education, health, social protection, and poverty and inequality. His publications include articles on the impact of demand-side programs on schooling outcomes; the roles of poverty, gender, orphanhood, and disability in explaining education inequalities; the determinants of effective service delivery and the evaluation of interventions aimed at improving it; the determinants of fertility behavior; and trends in adult mortality around the world. He is currently the codirector of the World Development Report

2018 on education. He has recently coauthored books on *Making Schools Work: New Evidence from Accountability Reforms* and *Youth Employment in Sub-Saharan Africa* and was a core team member of the World Development Report in 1995 (*Workers in an Integrating World*) and 2004 (*Making Services Work for Poor People*). He holds a PhD in economics from Brown University in Providence, Rhode Island.

Dena Ringold is a practice manager for the Social Protection and Labor Global Practice, covering East and Southern Africa at the World Bank. Throughout her career, she has worked on operations and analytical work covering social protection and human development. Dena was a core team member of the *World Development Report* 2013 on jobs and worked in the Office of the Chief Economist for Human Development, where she focused on the governance of service delivery. She began working at the World Bank in the Europe and Central Asia region, where she helped to initiate the World Bank's involvement on Roma inclusion and set up the Roma Education Fund.

Dominic Rohner is a professor of economics at the University of Lausanne. He is an associate editor of the *Journal of the European Economic Association* and a research fellow of the Center for Economic and Policy Research, CESifo, OxCarre, and the Households in Conflict Network. His research on political and development economics has won several prizes and grants and has been published in journals such as the *Quarterly Journal of Economics*, the *Journal of Political Economy, Review of Economic Studies*, the *Journal of Public Economics*, the *Journal of the European Economic Association*, the *Journal of Development Economics*, and the *Journal of Economic Growth*. He holds a PhD in economics from the University of Cambridge.

Karelle Samuda is a PhD candidate in public policy at the Schar School of Policy and Government at George Mason University in Fairfax, Virginia. She received her BA from Washington and Lee University in Lexington, Virginia, and an MPP from the McCourt School of Public Policy at Georgetown University in Washington, DC. In 2014, she was selected to be part of the first cohort of Africa Junior Fellows at the World Bank. Her major research areas are on the political economy of distributive politics in the Caribbean and Africa and on the relation between African countries and international financial institutions.

Abbreviations

BDP	Botswana Democratic Party
CCT	conditional cash transfer
CDJP	Commission Diocésaine de Justice et Paix
CERDI	Centre d'Etudes et de Recherches sur le Développement International
DDP	direct dividend payment
DHS	Demographic Health Surveys
DSGE	Dynamic Stochastic General Equilibrium
EITI	Extractive Industry Transparency Initiative
ESSF	Economic and Social Stabilization Fund
GNI	gross national income
GUT	Grand Unified Theory
HDI	Human Development Index
HIV	human immunodeficiency virus
ICT	information communication technology
IMF	International Monetary Fund
IMR	infant mortality rate
IYCF	infant and young child feeding
LSMS	Living Standards Measurement Study
MICS	Multiple Indicator Cluster Surveys
NDP	National Development Plan
NGO	nongovernmental organization
OAP	old-age pension
PER	Public Expenditure Review
PIM	public investment management
PISA	Programme for International Student Assessment
PPP	public-private partnership
PRF	Pension Reserves Fund
PTA	parent-teacher association

RBA	results-based aid
RBF	results- or performance-based financing
RCT	randomized control trial
SCT	social cash transfer
SDI	Service Delivery Indicator
SGA	small-for-gestational-age
SSA	Sub-Saharan Africa
SWF	Sovereign Wealth Fund
TIMSS	Trends in International Mathematics and Science Study
TVET	Technical Vocational Education and Training
UCT	unconditional cash transfer
WDR	World Development Report

Overview

Sub-Saharan Africa's natural-resource-rich countries—those endowed with minerals or hydrocarbons such as oil and natural gas—have poor human development. Children in these countries are more likely to die before their first birthday, more likely to be stunted, and less likely to attend school than are children in other countries with similar national income. Resource-rich countries in Sub-Saharan Africa (SSA) spend less on education and health than other countries in the region and less than resource-rich countries in other regions. And their spending is also less effective; in these countries, additional spending on education and health yields poorer outcomes than elsewhere.

Recent commodity price declines have highlighted the risks inherent in relying on natural resources for development. Just a few years ago, the issue in SSA was how to manage the wealth created; today, the challenge is how to protect the right expenditures during the necessary fiscal adjustment. Despite the current downturn, the extractives sector remains, and is likely to remain, an important part of SSA's growth story. Managing the resource flows and using rents optimally remain a long-term challenge facing many countries in the region.

There is a strong case for government involvement in improving human capital. Families underinvest relative to the socially optimal level because of the cash and credit constraints they face and because additional benefits accrue to societies over and above what families receive themselves. Rents from natural resources can potentially relieve governments of their own constraints and enable them to ratchet up investments in the education and health of their people.

Governments face a choice of how best to allocate resource rents between spending, investing in human or physical capital, and investing in global financial assets (through a sovereign wealth fund, for example). The optimal choice will vary across countries, depending on the relative rate of return to each choice. Rates of return to investing in physical and human capital will be high in countries where the capital stock is low. Moreover, higher levels of human capital make investments in physical capital more productive, and vice versa, which suggests that the optimal portfolio will involve investing in both. Human capital should be prioritized in many of Sub-Saharan Africa's resource-rich countries because of their low starting point. Human capital also has an additional advantage: it is embodied in people and hard to expropriate, which is all the more important in conflict-prone resource-rich countries.

Investing effectively in human capital is hard because it ultimately involves delivering services, which entails coordinating a large number of actors and activities. Using resource rents to fund this investment exacerbates the difficulties for three main reasons. First, resource rents tend to be subject to less accountability than are other public funds. Second, resource rents are (relatively) large in volume, and it is hard for weak public financial systems to absorb them. Third, they are volatile, which makes optimal investment strategies difficult.

This book focuses on three dimensions of governance to address these challenges: institutions, incentives, and information. Institutional structures govern the management of the resource rents themselves and shape the allocation of revenues to areas of government: decentralization and leveraging the private sector are key entry points. Incentives affect the way provider organizations, managers, and staff are held accountable for their behaviors and ability to deliver services with quality and efficiency. Revenues from natural resources can fund financial incentives to strengthen either performance (that is, linking rewards to measurable actions or achievements) or demand (that is, conditional or unconditional cash transfers to potential beneficiaries of services). Lack of information hampers citizens' ability to understand their rights and to hold governments and providers accountable. Producing information, making it available, and increasing social accountability offer potential ways to address this challenge.

Improving the quality of education and health services will be central to improving human capital outcomes. In addition to smart investments and policy reforms in those sectors, this book identifies two foundational areas that are critical for the effective development of human capital. First, early child development—including both mother and newborn health as well as early childhood nutrition, care, and education—significantly improves outcomes in childhood and later on in life. Second, cash transfers—either conditional or unconditional—significantly reduce poverty, and increase household investments in child education, nutrition, and health, as well as increase the investment in productive assets that foster further income generation.

Across the world, natural resource wealth has not always translated into good economic outcomes. Countries that have avoided the so-called resource curse and set a course for long-run development have pursued a balanced approach that has included investing in people. In SSA countries, where the education and health needs are great, governments should pursue effective investments in human capital and undertake reforms to maximize the positive effects of those investments.

Resource-Rich Countries Have Higher National Incomes, but Their Populations Are Not Less Poor, and Their Human Development Is Low

The Resource Curse Is Not a Given

A natural resources boom has occurred in Sub-Saharan Africa—nearly all countries in the region are exploring new oil, natural gas, or mineral reserves. SSA exports of oil alone are nearly triple the aid receipts (van der Ploeg and Venables 2011). Countries that had never before been considered resource-rich have seen a windfall of resource rents. Ghana's Jubilee oil field, which entered production in 2010, averages more than 85,000 barrels per day, and Uganda's Lake Albert rift fields target production of 200,000 barrels per day. Natural gas findings are expected to return billions of dollars to Mozambique and Tanzania. Recent declines in oil prices highlight the risks inherent in natural resource dependence (figure O.1). For countries to realize the potential wealth revealed through the identification and exploitation of natural resources, they have to manage the rents flowing from those endowments through the vagaries of the markets. If they do so well, Africa's natural resource wealth could be a boon to economic growth and individual well-being (Africa Progress Panel 2013).

However, a substantial literature points to the economic as well as the social, political, and institutional challenges that accompany natural resource riches (Venables 2016). The specter of a "resource curse" hangs over the promise. The success of several countries in transforming natural resources into long-run development—Malaysia and Norway, for example—suggests that such a curse is

Figure O.1 The Prices of Natural Resources Are Volatile: Index of Real Prices, 1990–2015 (January 2010 = 100)

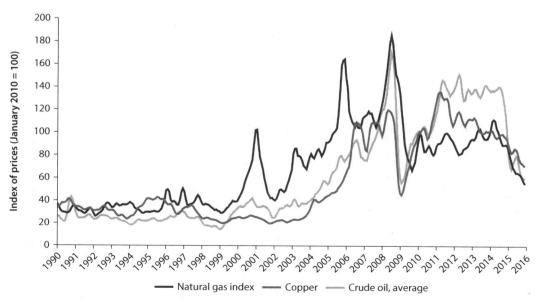

Source: World Bank commodity price data (the Pink Sheet), http://www.worldbank.org/en/research/commodity-markets.

not destiny (Lederman and Maloney 2007). Harnessing the returns from natural resource wealth and channeling them productively can contribute substantially to eradicating extreme poverty and enhancing shared prosperity. Success will depend on good decisions and sound implementation.

Natural Resource Wealth Leads to Higher National Incomes in Sub-Saharan Africa, but Does Little to Reduce Poverty

Mineral wealth—and oil wealth in particular—has stimulated dramatic growth in national incomes in many SSA countries. Between 1995 and 2013, gross national income (GNI) per capita in the region as a whole rose 50 percent, but in oil-rich countries it rose 80 percent (figure O.2; the country classification is described in chapter 1). Countries that were not resource-rich, or not oil-rich, grew only 40 percent. Countries identified as "potentially" resource-rich (with reserves identified but not yet extracted) grew fast as well—70 percent—but this was from a much lower base and translated into smaller annual increases in income.

Figure O.2 In SSA, Oil-Rich Countries Grew Substantially Faster Than Other Countries: Cumulative Growth in GNI per Capita, 1995–2013

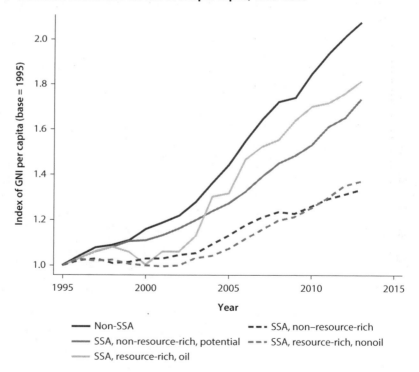

Source: World Development Indicators data.
Note: SSA = Sub-Saharan Africa; GNI = gross national income. See chapter 1 for country classifications. Non-SSA countries include only countries with GNI per capita of less than US$10,000 in 1995 (in 2005 U.S. dollars).

Today, natural-resource-rich countries in SSA have higher GNI per capita than do other countries in the region; average GNI per capita in 2013 was US$4,528 among oil-rich countries, US$2,607 among nonoil resource-rich countries, and only US$1,683 among non–resource-rich countries.

Poverty is only modestly lower in resource-rich countries than in non–resource-rich countries. Taking into account the fact that they are substantially richer, the picture looks much worse; compared with other countries at the same level of income, resource-rich countries have done less to reduce poverty. Figure O.3 shows the difference between poverty rates in non–resource-rich SSA countries and those in various country groupings (for a poverty threshold of US$2.50 a day), after adjusting for GNI per capita. In SSA, poverty rates are higher in the resource-rich countries, whereas in non-SSA countries, poverty rates, on the whole, are lower.

This is consistent with patterns of structural transformation in the region. Growth in Sub-Saharan Africa has been less poverty-reducing than growth in other parts of the world, and growth in resource-rich countries has reduced

Figure O.3 Resource Wealth Is Not Associated with Substantially Lower Poverty: Headcount Poverty Rates Relative to Non–Resource-Rich SSA Countries at a Poverty Threshold of US$2.50 a Day

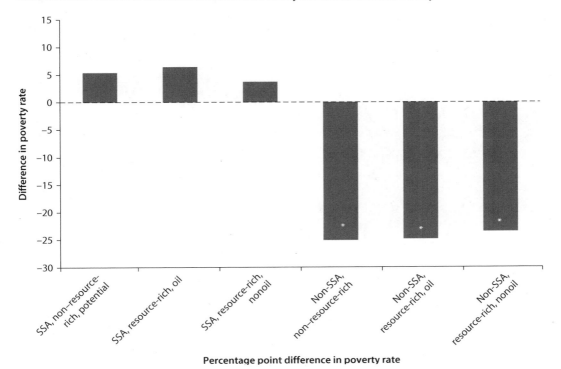

Source: Analysis of data from PovCalNet (latest data available).
Note: SSA = Sub-Saharan Africa. After controlling for GNI per capita. Poverty threshold of US$2.50 per day. Significance level: * = 10 percent.

poverty less than growth in other countries (Chuhan-Pole 2013). Moreover, in SSA, growth in agriculture and services—where most poor people work—tends to result in larger reductions in poverty than growth in industry, which includes mining (Chuhan-Pole 2014; Filmer and Fox 2014).

Natural Resource Wealth Is Not Associated with Better Education and Health

SSA countries that are oil-rich fare poorly on the United Nations' human development index (HDI), which combines national income, life expectancy, educational attainment, and school participation. For each level of GNI per capita, oil-rich SSA countries have consistently lower HDIs than other SSA and non-SSA countries (figure O.4).[1]

Controlling for national income, education outcomes are systematically worse in oil-rich SSA countries than in non–resource-rich SSA countries. The proportions of children ages 6–15 years currently attending school and the proportions of adolescents ages 15–19 years who have completed grade 6 are at least 7 percentage points lower in resource-rich than in non–resource-rich countries compared with what would be expected for their level of income (figure O.5).

Figure O.4   Resource-Rich Countries in SSA Fare Poorly on the Human Development Index: HDI and GNI per Capita in 2013

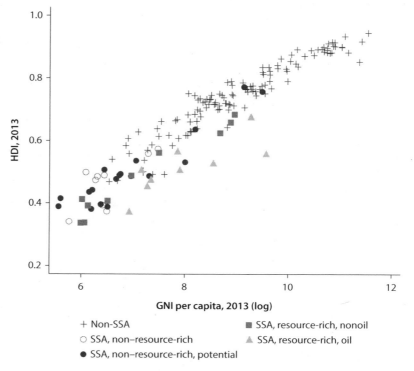

Sources: World Bank 2013; World Development Indicators data.
Note: SSA = Sub-Saharan Africa; HDI = human development index; GNI = gross national income.

Figure O.5 Resource-Rich Countries in SSA Have Low School Participation and High Infant Mortality: Indicators Relative to Non–Resource-Rich SSA Countries, Controlling for GNI per Capita

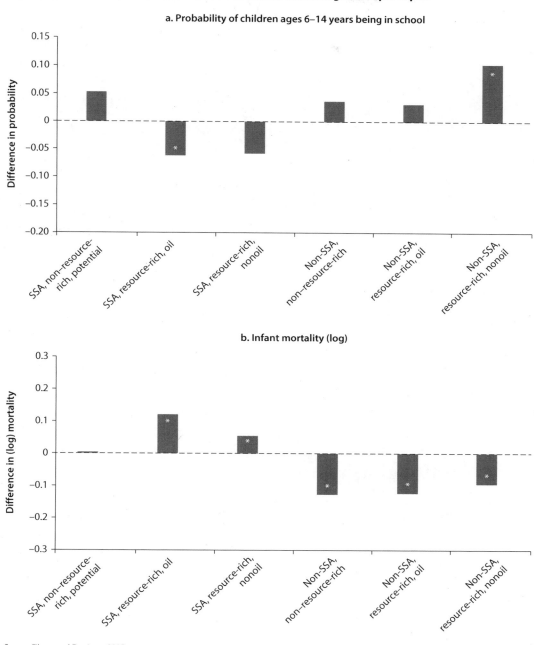

a. Probability of children ages 6–14 years being in school

b. Infant mortality (log)

Source: Filmer and Denisova 2015.

Note: SSA = Sub-Saharan Africa; GNI = gross national income. Figures report coefficients from regression models. Models control for per capita GNI and its square. Reference category is non–resource-rich SSA countries. Significance level: * = 10 percent.

This pattern is even more pronounced among the poor: for children and youth in the poorest quintile, the shortfall is 15–20 percentage points. The pattern is similar but more muted in nonoil resource-rich countries. They perform like non–resource-rich countries in school completion but systematically worse (though not statistically significantly so) in school participation.

The education shortfall in resource-rich countries in Africa is all the more striking because there is no shortfall in resource-rich countries in other parts of the world. In countries outside of Sub-Saharan Africa, grade 6 completion is systematically higher in resource-rich than in non–resource-rich countries. The enrollment rate is also similar in both oil-rich and non–resource-rich countries and is significantly higher in nonoil resource-rich countries.

Cross-country patterns for health are similar to those for education. Africa's oil-rich countries have infant mortality rates that are 30 percent higher than rates in non–resource-rich countries (figure O.5), again factoring in that national income is higher in those countries and mortality would therefore be expected to be lower. Nonoil resource-rich countries in SSA have infant mortality rates 14 percent higher. Other indicators show consistent results. In oil-rich SSA countries, vaccination rates are lower: the proportion of infants age 12–13 months who have had their full course of vaccinations is more than 30 percentage points lower than in non–resource-rich SSA countries after controlling for national income; and nonoil resource-rich countries have vaccination coverage that is about 15 percentage points lower. In addition, the proportion of children who are stunted is significantly higher in oil-rich countries.

For each indicator, the shortfall in resource-rich countries is most pronounced for children in the poorest quintile. Indeed, inequalities, as measured by the gap between the richest and poorest quintiles, are largest in resource-rich SSA countries, especially those that are oil-rich (figure O.6).

While There Are Compelling Reasons for Resource-Rich Countries to Invest in Human Capital, Their Investment Is Paltry and Ineffective

Investment in Human Capital Development Is Often Overlooked in SSA Resource-Rich Countries

Governments and other stakeholders must grapple with (at least) four central questions when they seek to transform a finite amount of natural resources into lasting development (Barma and others 2012; van der Ploeg and Venables 2011; Venables 2016):

1. What is the optimal contract between government and entities that extract natural resources to balance public benefits with incentives to the private sector?
2. What is the optimal timing of extraction to ensure the maximum stream of benefits from reserves?

Figure O.6 Rich-Poor Gaps in Education and Health Are Largest in SSA Resource-Rich Countries: Differences between the Richest and Poorest Quintiles on Outcome Indicators

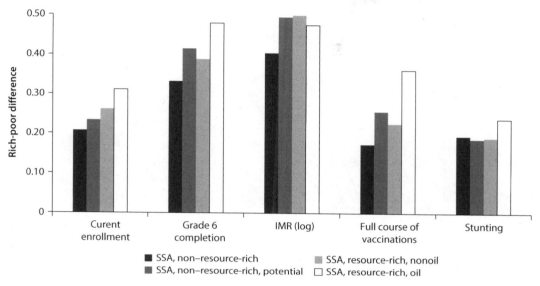

Source: Filmer and Denisova 2015.

Note: SSA = Sub-Saharan Africa; IMR = infant mortality rate. See chapter 1 for the definition of variables. Difference is reversed (that is, it is poorest to richest quintile) for IMR (log) and stunting, since more of each is worse.

3. What is the optimal portfolio allocation of mineral revenues between consumption, savings, and investment? And what should be the profile of investments in terms of financial assets, physical capital (for example, infrastructure), and human capital?

4. How can resource revenue be spent most effectively and efficiently? And what complementary activities or reforms are required to ensure effectiveness and efficiency?

Answers to these questions are critical to harnessing the benefits of natural resource extraction for long-term benefits. This book focuses on the third and fourth questions, with emphasis on the role that investing in human capital—understood broadly to include education, capabilities, and health—should play in the investment portfolio, in part because investments in human capital are often overlooked in these countries.

Investment

In cash terms, public spending on both education and health tends to be higher in resource-rich countries than in other countries in the SSA region. Governments in oil-rich SSA countries spend US$69 per capita on education, and nonoil

Table O.1 In SSA, Resource-Rich Countries Spend Relatively Less on Education and
Health Than Other Countries: Public Spending on Education and Health per Capita and
as a Share of GDP, 2000–13

Indicator and country category	Health (average 2000–13)		Education (average 2000–13)	
	SSA	Non-SSA	SSA	Non-SSA
Spending per capita				
Resource-rich, oil	50	73	69	125
Resource-rich, nonoil	62	102	116	99
Non–resource-rich, potential	12	—	19	—
Non–resource-rich	29	158	49	170
All	37	137	62	157
Spending as a share of GDP				
Resource-rich, oil	1.7	2.4	2.9	4.7
Resource-rich, nonoil	2.9	3.0	4.3	4.5
Non–resource-rich, potential	2.7	—	4.1	—
Non–resource-rich	3.0	4.1	5.0	4.9
All	2.6	3.7	4.3	4.8

Source: World Development Indicators data.
Note: SSA = Sub-Saharan Africa; GDP = gross domestic product; — = not available. Data are calculated as an average of
nonmissing values for 2000–13. Spending per capita is expressed in constant 2005 U.S. dollars.

resource-rich countries spend, on average, US$116. In contrast, non–resource-
rich countries spend, on average, US$49, and countries "with potential" resources
spend even less (table O.1). The pattern for public health spending per capita is
similar: on average, resource-rich SSA countries spend almost double what non–
resource-rich countries do.

The pattern is dramatically reversed, however, when public spending is considered as a share of gross domestic product (GDP). The percentage of GDP
devoted to education and health in oil-rich SSA countries is not quite half the
amount allocated by non–resource-rich countries in the region. This is not the
pattern outside of Sub-Saharan Africa, where government spending on education
in nonoil resource-rich countries is lower and spending on health is similar to
spending in non–resource-rich countries.

Return on Spending

Simply increasing government spending on education and health does not guarantee better outcomes (Dreher, Nunnenkamp, and Thiele 2008; Filmer and
Pritchett 1999; World Bank 2003). Resource-rich SSA countries that spend more
on education or health have little to show for it. Grade 6 completion is not
responsive to more spending on education, and infant mortality rates are not
responsive to more spending on health (figure O.7).

The average association between spending and outcomes, however, potentially
masks several factors. Research has shown that spending has more of an impact

Figure O.7 Increased Public Spending Is Not Associated with Improved Outcomes in Oil-Rich Countries: Association between Public Spending and Outcomes, Controlling for Other Factors

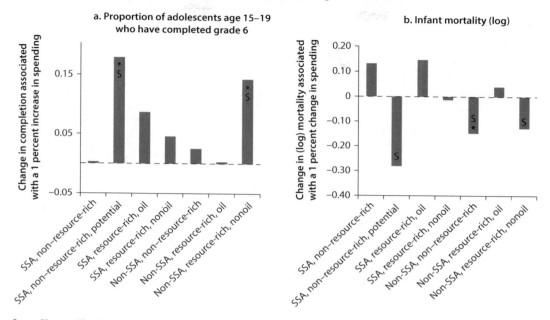

Source: Filmer and Denisova 2015.
Note: SSA = Sub-Saharan Africa; GNI = gross national income. Figure reports coefficients from cross-country regression model of outcome on log of public spending on education (2000–13) in each country subgroup. Model controls for per capita GNI and its square, and additional country-level variables (see text). Significance level: * = 10 percent. "S" indicates that the coefficient is significantly different from that in non–resource-rich Sub-Saharan Africa.

on the poor (Bidani and Ravallion 1997) or when it is done in a context of better overall governance (Rajkumar and Swaroop 2008). Strategically targeted investments—especially those that establish a solid foundation of human capital on which to build further skills—and careful attention to factors that enhance the effectiveness of spending are important for turning the additional investments enabled by resource wealth into human capital.

Investing in Human Capital Is Complementary to Investing in Infrastructure

Should countries prioritize one type of investment over another? When an initial stock of capital, whether human or physical, is low, investing in it will have high returns (Venables 2016). As stocks of capital accumulate, the return on further investment decreases. In contrast, the marginal returns of a sovereign wealth fund (SWF) are fixed by international capital markets. The basic logic of building a portfolio composed of a variety of assets suggests that the marginal returns to all investment options should be equalized in equilibrium. Hence, all types of investments should take place as long as the returns are higher than the alternatives. Figure O.8, panel a, illustrates this basic logic. The horizontal axis shows the amount of resource windfalls available to invest, and the vertical axis

Figure O.8 An Optimal Public Investment Portfolio Is Likely to Be Balanced: Positive Complementarities Suggest Higher Levels of Investment

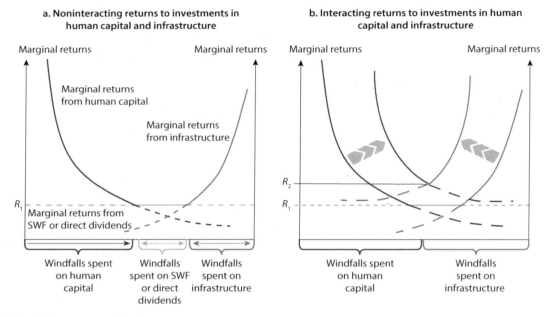

Note: SWF = sovereign wealth fund.

shows the marginal returns on various investment options. The marginal returns to human capital investments are plotted from left to right, and those from infrastructure investments are plotted from right to left. In the case illustrated, a country should invest part of its windfall in human capital, part in infrastructure, and part in an SWF. The rate of return on all would be the return given by international markets (R_1).

But the returns to investing in either type of capital are not independent of each other. Physical capital (infrastructure) is more productive when there is more human capital, and human capital is more productive when there is more physical capital. Figure O.8, panel b, illustrates a case where human and physical capital interact to produce greater output. In the figure, the marginal return curves shift upward. In this example, the country should only invest in human capital and infrastructure (but not in an SWF), because doing so would produce a rate of return higher (R_2) than what international markets offer.

The share of natural resource rents that should be invested in the various options (human capital, infrastructure, international markets) will depend on several factors. Key will be the relative shape of the marginal returns to investments in each option (which, in the case of human capital and infrastructure, will also depend on their initial levels)—as well as the size of the resource rents. Although the mix of investments may vary between physical capital and human capital, the analysis undertaken for this report suggests that, at lower levels of resource wealth, countries should prioritize human capital, while at higher levels of resource wealth, countries should diversify the mix of investments, notably in infrastructure.

The point here is not that countries should not invest in an SWF; indeed, such funds may serve useful functions (for example, stabilization) complementary to investments in capital accumulation (Venables 2016). Rather, the point is that the optimal portfolio for any given country will depend on its current stock of different types of capital, the marginal return to additional investments (which may depend on the complementarities between investments), the rate obtained on international markets, and the volume of funds made available by resource rents. This balance will vary by country, depending on the investment climate and other policy factors that affect the relative returns to different investments. What is clear is that the optimal portfolio will include a mix of investments.

Investing in Human Capital Also Helps to Reduce the Risks of Conflict

Abundance of natural resources has been linked to outbreaks of conflict and to longer durations for those conflicts. Resources increase the contested "pie" that is up for appropriation; they undermine state capacity because the state has less incentive to invest in building legal and fiscal capacity; capturing resource rents makes armed rebellion financially feasible for rebels; and the unequal geographic distribution of natural resource deposits fuels secessionism and interstate wars.

Studies have found that human capital may potentially reduce the risk of civil war and violent conflict.[2] These protective effects of human capital may work through three types of pathways:

1. Human capital investments are difficult to appropriate. It is much harder to appropriate human capital than liquid assets like those in an SWF (Acemoglu and Wolitzky 2011). The human capital of future generations is also hard to appropriate. The human capital of both present and future generations has little "scrap value" compared with most infrastructure.
2. Human capital investments (through proper nutrition, nurturing care, and schooling) make work more attractive and raise the opportunity cost of giving up productive work to engage in fighting.
3. Education increases the moral costs of fighting. Schooling transmits knowledge, social norms, and, potentially, values of cooperation and tolerance. The enlightenment and capacity for self-reflection may raise the moral costs of fighting. In multiethnic societies, schools may help to foster tolerance, intercultural exchange, and ultimately interethnic trust.

While there are compelling reasons for resource-rich countries to invest more in building human capital, doing so is hard, as natural resource abundance exacerbates governance challenges. Conflict is an extreme manifestation of those challenges, but less acute problems are pervasive.

From Mines and Wells to Well-Built Minds • http://dx.doi.org/10.1596/978-1-4648-1005-3

Resource Rents Exacerbate Governance Challenges: Tackling Them Requires Strengthening Institutions, Incentives, and Information

Resource-Rich Environments Are More Governance Challenged: The Role of Rents, Volume, and Volatility

More money is not sufficient to transform resource revenues into human capital: the quality of public spending on social services matters. Effectively and efficiently allocating resources from natural resources extraction is a first step toward reaping the highest dividends in terms of human development. Municipalities in Brazil that received oil windfalls reported higher spending on a variety of public goods and services, but households benefited far less than expected because the money was spent ineffectively (Caselli and Michaels 2013).

To set up incentives that maximize the human development effects of resource wealth, countries need to ensure that governance and accountability are robust. Many of the studies of the relationship between governance and development outcomes have found that better governance leads to better development outcomes (Gupta, Verhoeven, and Tiongson 2002; Jensen and Wantchekon 2004; Karl 2004; Kaufmann and others 2004; Rajkumar and Swaroop 2008; Ross 1999). The reality is that poor governance—particularly fragile institutions—can undermine service delivery and limit the impact of public spending. Governance in SSA's resource-rich countries is under stress: resource-rich countries stand out for their poor performance across a range of indicators (figure O.9).

Figure O.9 Governance Indicators Are Worse In Resource-Rich Countries

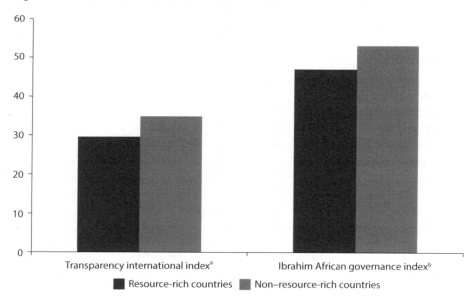

Source: Afrobarometer round 4.
a. Measures perceived levels of public sector corruption on a scale from 0 (highly corrupt) to 100 (very clean).
b. Assesses governance progress on a scale from 0 (weak) to 100 (strong) using data from more than 30 sources.

Governance can be defined as the incentives, rules, and accountability arrangements that affect how policy makers and service providers are held accountable for what they do.[3] Accountability is the relationship between key actors in which five features (delegation, financing, performance, information about performance, and enforcement) are robust (World Bank 2003).

Accountability is particularly challenging in the delivery of social services, such as health and education, for three main reasons. First, because services are *transaction-intensive* and *discretionary* (they involve repeated interactions between actors, and providers need to make decisions about how to handle each situation), monitoring and accountability mechanisms can be overwhelmed if they attempt to micromonitor the daily interactions of service providers with clients, such as teachers with students or health workers with patients. Second, the *multiple principals* (the range of stakeholders in the system, who may have inconsistent objectives) and *multiple tasks* (the range of types of decisions—for example, assessing a situation, taking stock of the resources available, delivering a service, assessing whether it has been effective) may "blunt the precision of incentives" and blur distinctions in roles and responsibilities. Third, *attribution* (the ability to associate changes in outcomes with the specific actions of individuals) is difficult because the complex relationship between inputs and outputs is affected by factors beyond the quality of health care and schooling; this complexity makes monitoring difficult because outcomes are dependent not solely on service providers but also on the recipients of services and their household and community environments.

The challenges are particularly severe in resource-rich countries. The rents, volume, and volatility that characterize resource-rich environments exacerbate the challenges of service delivery.

Rents

Resource rents create a sense of "free money" that can distort spending decisions. Rents—the difference between the revenues from and the extraction costs of natural resources—differ from other forms of government revenue, such as revenue from taxation. They can induce rent-seeking behavior with perverse effects, including unequal fiscal distribution, inefficient and unproductive ventures ("white elephants"), and poor governance and corruption (Arezki and Gylfason 2013; Karl 2004; Robinson and Torvik 2005). The rents create pseudo-entrepreneurs who enjoy umbilical relationships with the state and are intertwined in the capturing of resource rents (Barma and others 2012). Since the government has less need to generate other forms of revenue, its administrative and institutional capacity may wither. Since citizens do not have to pay for the services though taxes, their demand—especially for quality—may be lower.

Volume

Large inflows of capital from resource windfalls can overwhelm sectors by temporarily inflating prices. To transform resource wealth into human capital, the institutional environment needs to support sound public investment management (PIM) systems in sectors like health and education. Resource-rich countries need to assess the capacity of their PIM systems to maximize the effectiveness of their spending. Administrative capacity is central to the optimal allocation of funds and the types of public investments. However, PIM is often weak in resource-rich countries (Arezki and Gylafson 2013; Dabla-Norris and others 2010).

Volatility

Resource-rich countries are vulnerable to revenue volatility because of commodity price fluctuations, as highlighted by the recent fall in commodity prices. Volatility can impede economic growth by creating uncertainty about the future (Ross 2012). It also puts pressure on public investment decisions. Because public investment is discretionary, capital that is typically used for investment projects is more sensitive to cuts than are recurrent expenditures, such as public sector wages and transfer programs (Bacon and Kojima 2008; Barma and others 2012). Between June 2014 and January 2015, oil prices fell about 57 percent. For oil exporters like Angola, Chad, Equatorial Guinea, and Nigeria, this put tremendous pressure on fiscal revenues. For example, while oil accounts for about 13 percent of Nigeria's GDP, it supports 65 percent of government revenues (World Bank 2015). Countries like Nigeria have had to adjust their budgets, particularly capital spending, because of the plunge in oil prices.

Tackling Governance Challenges Requires Leveraging Institutions, Incentives, and Information

Tackling governance challenges is an essential part of making the most of natural resources—and not only in Sub-Saharan Africa. A recent study of resource-rich Eurasian countries concluded that, while these countries are "heavy in tangible assets such as oil and [natural] gas, road and rail, and schools and hospitals," they are "light in intangibles such as the institutions for managing volatile resource earnings, providing high-quality social services, and even-handedly regulating enterprise," and it is the latter that distinguish successful resource-rich countries (Gill and others 2014). Improving governance in resource-rich countries requires activating levers in institutions, incentives, and information (figure O.10). While the political economy of natural resource–led investment in human development is country-specific, the discussion that follows provides a framework for addressing specific governance issues and building up service delivery in resource-rich SSA countries.

Institutions

Institutions shape human interaction. They can be formal, through rules and regulations, such as a country's constitution and laws. They can also be informal, with conventional, often unwritten, codes of behavior. Formal institutions include laws related to natural resource sectors and revenue allocation and rules that shape the allocation of resource rents to various levels of government (Barma and others 2012). As a potentially resource-rich country, Ghana passed the Petroleum Revenue Management Act (2011), which set out rules and

Figure O.10 Accountability Framework for Service Delivery

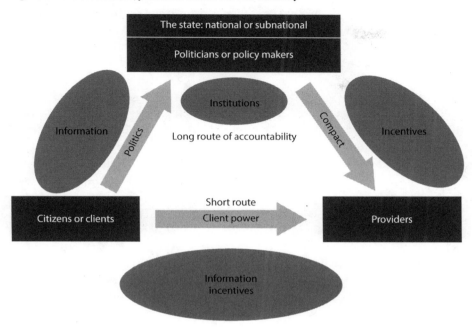

regulations related to governance, sustainability, and the allocation of oil revenues. Angola (2002), Guinea (2010), and Liberia (2010) all have passed freedom-of-information or access-to-information laws that create a pathway for citizens and other entities to obtain information related to natural resource allocation and service delivery.

Incentives

Incentives affect the way in which provider organizations, their managers, and staff are held accountable for their behavior and are able to deliver services with quality and efficiency. From this vantage point, what is of interest is how providers are selected, paid, monitored, and held accountable for their performance, notably in delivering human development services. Revenues from natural resources can fund financial incentives to strengthen either (a) performance, also known as results-based financing (RBF) or performance-based financing (PBF), often through cash or nonmonetary benefits provided in response to measurable actions or achievement; and (b) demand, through cash transfers (conditional or unconditional) provided to potential beneficiaries of services. Zambia's RBF program, launched in 2012, paid facilities a base transfer according to the quantity of health services delivered and a premium for quality scores over 50 percent. The services covered infant immunization, facility-based delivery, and antenatal and postnatal care. Initial comparisons of the RBF program with two other modes of service delivery found that the number of facility-based deliveries

From Mines and Wells to Well-Built Minds • http://dx.doi.org/10.1596/978-1-4648-1005-3

and prenatal visits increased more in RBF facilities than in non-RBF facilities (World Bank 2014). For resource-rich countries, during resource wealth booms, there is fiscal space to engage in developing and implementing the types of incentive structures that can affect service delivery. During resource busts, these programs, if well-targeted, provide an efficient way to spend public resources.

Information

Information opens channels of redress and monitoring and also opens the door to action, particularly by citizens, but imperfect information is pervasive and has serious implications for service delivery. Citizens are often unaware of their entitlements, the standards they should expect, and the performance of both politicians and providers in relation to service delivery. For example, studies of local service provision and allocation of funds in Uganda found that substantial portions of school grants to local authorities were not distributed to the intended schools. However, the creation and availability of user-friendly public information on how these grants were disbursed led to a significant reduction in their capturing (Reinikka and Svensson 2004, 2005, 2011). Such information interventions give citizens tools to influence the quality of service delivery by holding politicians and providers accountable, and new research suggests specific ways to deploy such tools (box O.1). While information alone is not sufficient to improve governance and accountability in service delivery, it is certainly necessary. The stakes for social accountability in resource-rich countries are especially high because access to information on resource revenues and their allocation is often restricted. Many resource-rich countries have started to

---

Box O.1 Transparency to Improve the Quality of Political Engagement

According to a recent World Bank policy research report (Khemani 2016), sustainable improvements in governance can happen when two forces—transparency and political engagement—interact to strengthen institutions. The study showed that targeted information that enables citizens to select and sanction leaders on the basis of performance in delivering public goods can strengthen institutions by shaping how leaders behave in office—when disciplined by the threat of challengers. The study offered four key policy recommendations:

1. Policies should support the generation of reliable and impartial evidence on the performance of leaders tasked with the delivery of public policies, and this evidence should include information on the consequences of policy actions for public goods outcomes.

2. Policies should promote healthy competition in media markets, complemented by regulations to support public interest programming. Sponsorship of appealing programs, or so-called "infotainment," to communicate the findings of technical evidence, holds potential to change norms and persuade citizens to shift political beliefs in ways that strengthen the demand for good policies.

box continues next page

Box O.1 Transparency to Improve the Quality of Political Engagement *(continued)*

3. Information on public goods provision at the local level is more relevant to voters' decisions in local elections than information at the national level. Performance assessments of
both current incumbents and challengers, delivered regularly during a term in office but
also at the time of elections, can make it easier for citizens to use information when they
are actively engaged in holding leaders accountable.

4. Governments should experiment with the design of public sector institutions to take
advantage of the interaction between growing political engagement and transparency
and should do so in crosscutting ways. Models of individual citizen engagement should
not rest on organized groups within each school or health clinic. Rather, they should
target individual domains of citizen action, such as a local administration with a range of
service delivery responsibilities.

Source: Adapted from Khemani 2016.

---

address the information deficit by joining campaigns such as the Extractive
Industries Transparency Initiative (EITI) and passing access-to-information
laws. However, because transparency, oversight, and participation are minimal
in resource-rich African countries, social accountability approaches there face
particularly challenging environments.

Table O.2 presents possible entry points within the framework of institutions,
incentives, and information to strengthen the link between governance and service delivery in resource-rich SSA countries.

Decentralization arrangements may play a role in addressing how governments allocate resource wealth and in improving the delivery of human development services. It is important for the fiscal regime of a resource-rich country to
have the capacity to collect resource revenues, prioritize their allocation and
spending, and minimize capturing. Decentralized service delivery may improve
services through a better fit with local needs, more responsive providers, and
more citizen participation. However, for it to work, several conditions need to
be in place:

- Responsibilities of the different levels of government are clearly defined based
on an understanding of which roles are best undertaken at which levels, factoring in the capacity at each level.
- Local agencies have the authority and resources to fulfill their responsibilities.
- The fiscal rules take into account the size of the rents and price volatility and
ensure that distribution across government levels is equitable and efficient.

Building the capacity of PIM systems is the key to managing resource rents,
which are subject to price and volume volatility. Public investment strategies in
resource-rich countries must contend with the boom-and-bust cycles that are

Table O.2 Guiding Principles for Improving the Governance of Service Delivery in Resource-Rich Countries

Indicator	Institutions	Incentives	Information
Rents	Draft and reinforce the formal rules and structures that shape allocation of rents. For example, • A fiscal regime that maximizes broad-based allocation of rents • Decentralized arrangements to allow for subnational transfer of rents • Rules to guide private provision of services	Consider incentive-based interventions that link allocation of rents to service delivery outcomes and use	Reduce information asymmetries to stimulate citizens' monitoring of government spending and service provision: • Disclose contract terms and support third-party monitoring of bundled contracts • Improve the flow of information about resource rents • Use analytical and diagnostic tools such as public expenditure tracking to determine allocation of resources
Volume	Strengthen public investment management to make PIM more efficient	Establish clear PIM rules to guide capital versus recurrent spending	Provide quality-of-service information to assess the efficiency and effectiveness of sectors that maximize social welfare
Volatility	Establish and adhere to fiscal rules that help to smooth spending-related decisions during booms and busts; promote countercyclical spending; separate regulatory from service provision agencies	Consider earmarks to protect social spending; provide matching grants and performance-based transfers	Disseminate information on countercyclical mechanisms to protect social spending; provide clarity on budget assumptions related to resource rents and allocation

Note: PIM = public investment management.

peculiar to natural resources. High public investment in some sectors can strain their absorptive capacity, particularly where project management capabilities are inadequate. Price volatility affects the financing of the public investment portfolio: during bust cycles, capital spending is typically among the first to be cut or eliminated. Strengthening PIM systems allows for clear rules to smooth expenditure-related decisions, such as capital and current spending during booms and busts.

Incentives on both the supply and demand sides of service delivery can be effective in mitigating information and motivation asymmetries among policy makers, service providers, and citizens. RBF, as a supply-side incentive intervention, makes financing contingent on results. Where service is low or quality is poor, RBF is a promising mechanism for tackling these challenges. Cash transfers are demand-side incentive programs that seek both to stimulate citizens' use of services that contribute to human capital formation and to create spaces where participation and accountability are possible for a wide cross section of social groups.

The lack or inadequate availability of information on mining contracts, resource revenues, and public spending of these revenues weakens governance that enables service delivery. Using right-to-information and access-to-information laws can help to lower the information asymmetries and stimulate citizens' and third-party monitoring of government expenditures and service provision.

Getting Things Rights Takes Time, But Time Can Run Out

Establishing a governance regime that underpins smart investments of resource wealth in human capital takes time. However, in many countries that are resource-rich but have significant numbers of poor citizens and weak institutions, governments face considerable pressure to demonstrate quick results from resource rents. This reduces the political space they have to tackle governance-enhancing interventions.

This problem is exacerbated by the high expectations raised by resource windfalls. In Tanzania, the prospects of future revenues from exploiting natural gas reserves have already stimulated pressure for increased spending. According to a 2014 International Monetary Fund report, "The authorities' 'Big Results Now' initiative envisages ambitious infrastructure investment that … needs to be fully integrated into the budget process, while safeguarding critical social expenditures" (IMF 2014, 4).

The experience of successful countries suggests that putting in place the right elements early is possible; Botswana, Chile, Malaysia, and other countries have developed governance regimes that have enabled them to invest smartly in human capital (box O.2).

Box O.2 Malaysia: Managing Mineral Resources Revenues for Human Development

The first discovery of oil in Malaysia dates to 1910. Today oil and natural gas account for 12.5 percent of exports, and tin and ore account for another 20 percent. In 1988, Malaysia set up the National Trust Fund to conserve its natural resource wealth and invest it in development projects. The central bank manages the fund, which held more than US$1.8 billion in 2011.

Malaysia has emphasized the importance of investing in human capital for a healthy and productive population and to ensure social stability. Its HDI ranking for 2013 was 0.769, in the "high" human development category. The relevant indicators have been rising steadily since 1980: life expectancy rose from 68 years in 1980 to 74.8 years in 2012; in the same period, under 5-mortality dropped from 30.8 to 8.5 deaths per 1,000. Between 1991 and 2012, the literacy rate rose from 83 to 93 percent. Poverty has been drastically reduced. Currently, just 1.7 percent of Malaysians live under the national poverty line, down from 49.3 percent in 1970. People living in extreme poverty (less than US$1.25 a day) account for 0.5 percent of the population.

The Malaysian government has consistently invested in education. Its spending on education amounted to almost 6 percent of GDP in 2014. Primary education is compulsory, and both primary and secondary schooling are free, with the government providing more than 95 percent of the funding. Early childhood education programs are well used: in 2012, 88 percent of children age 6 years and 73 percent of children age 5 years were enrolled in a preprimary program (World Bank 2013a). Enrollment in tertiary education has increased. Yet, learning

box continues next page

Box O.2 Malaysia: Managing Mineral Resources Revenues for Human Development *(continued)*

outcomes are low, and skilled workers to fill job vacancies are still scarce. Two major problems are the low numbers of qualified teachers and the centralization of the school system.

The health care system in Malaysia is highly successful in providing universal primary care, with a solid record of delivering services even in rural areas. Total government health expenditures rose steadily, from 3 to 4 percent of GDP between 1997 and 2012. Although more than 80 percent of Malaysians rely on public health care, private services are growing, especially in urban areas, and out-of-pocket costs have risen. A review of the health system found that spending needs to increase in order to improve the quality of care provided, the availability of hospital beds (currently 1.9 per 1,000 people), and the ratio of doctor to patients (1.2 per 1,000 in 2010).

The state wants to focus on the poorest 40 percent of the population and thus to expand social safety nets and poverty reduction programs. Cash transfer initiatives, introduced in 2012, now benefit about 55 percent of households (IMF 2014). A national minimum wage was put in place in 2013.

Malaysia has no access-to-information law. It ranks 53 of 177 countries on the corruption perceptions index and 39 of 100 on the open budget index in 2012, indicating that it provides "minimal" information to the public about budget documents. The legislature has some oversight powers with respect to the budget process, and there are few provisions for public involvement. Malaysia ranked 34th among 58 countries on the resource governance index in 2013, with a "weak" score of 46 out of 100. The country does not participate in the EITI.

The Returns to Making Smart Investments in Human Capital Are High

Investment in human capital yields direct private returns in terms of better health, education, skills, and jobs. There are also compelling economic arguments for governments to invest in the human capital of their people, since limited access to credit, information failures, and spillover effects may all lead to families investing suboptimally. Investments in human capital also have indirect effects in reducing violent conflicts because they provide people with better social and noncognitive skills and raise the opportunity costs of not being productive. This effect is especially important in resource-rich countries. However, credit constraints at the national level and bad governance may also result in government investments that are less than optimal.

Human Capital Investments Pay Off

Human development underpins shared prosperity at the micro and macro levels. Private returns to human capital are high across the board. Evidence is accumulating on the very high returns to early investments in health, nutrition, and early childhood development. The cost-benefit ratios for behavioral interventions range from 5:1 to 67:1 for promotion of breastfeeding, from 4:1 to 43:1 for vitamin A supplementation, from 3:1 to 60:1 for deworming, and around 30:1 for salt iodization (Horton, Alderman, and Rivera 2008). Increasing preschool enrollment has a benefit-cost ratio of 17.6:1 (Engle and others 2011). New evidence on the long-term benefits of better nutrition in utero and in the first two years of life may mean that the returns are larger still. And the high returns to education have long been documented: Psacharopoulos and Patrinos (2004) reported that the average rate of return of an additional year of schooling is around 10 percent in terms of earnings.

These investments also have high externalities: they benefit the society beyond the individual in at least four ways: (1) better nutritional status at age 2 years and more education lead to better public health, lower fertility, and lower population growth; (2) education helps to decrease crime rates; (3) education promotes civic values and good citizenship; and (4) the likelihood of civil conflict falls with higher education and better health status.

Human capital investments have lifelong and intergenerational effects. Early life conditions have repercussions throughout an individual's life, laying the foundations for adult human capital—expressed in terms of adult physical stature (height), cognitive and noncognitive skills, and capabilities, such as health and social functioning (Friedman and Sturdy 2011; Victora and others 2008). Cognitive ability, socioemotional competence, and sensory-motor development at very young ages all affect school preparedness, subsequent school performance, and adult earnings. Stunted children (low height-for-age) perform less well in school, which ultimately leads them to lose an estimated 22 to 30 percent of adult income (Grantham-McGregor and others 2007).

Moreover, investing in human capital not only leads to better outcomes for the current generation but also begets further accumulation of human capital in the next generation. Mothers with better education have healthier—and ultimately better educated—children (box O.3). And healthier mothers have healthier babies: fetal growth influences long-term health—children who were

---

Box O.3 The Human Capital of Parents and Offspring

What effect does parents' education have on the education of their offspring? It has long been known that there is a close association between the education level of parents and that of their children. In recent years, a growing literature has been studying the question of whether the association is a simple correlation driven by unobservable confounding factors, such as innate ability, or whether there is a causal effect in which parental education stimulates the educational achievements of their offspring. A review by Holmlund, Lindahl, and Plug (2011) concluded that parents' education has a significant and robust causal effect on the education of their children; for Scandinavian countries, the causal effect was estimated to be about 0.1, suggesting that a parent's additional year of schooling increases their children's schooling by 0.1 additional year.

Do parental nutrition and mental health influence children's health? Similar to education, it has long been known that children in utero during famines are at higher risk of chronic

box continues next page

From Mines and Wells to Well-Built Minds • http://dx.doi.org/10.1596/978-1-4648-1005-3

Box O.3 The Human Capital of Parents and Offspring *(continued)*

diseases (diabetes and hypertension) and mental illness in middle age and have greater loss of attention and cognitive ability than the general population as they age further. One possible explanation is linked with biological adaption to nutritional stress in the womb, which makes children particularly efficient at conserving resources. However, in a resource-rich environment, this maladapted response contributes to overnutrition and higher risk of chronic disease. New evidence on brain development indeed shows that biological pathways may be irremediably modified if key micronutrients are lacking during sensitive phases of brain development. At the other extreme, maternal overweight or obesity may also threaten the welfare of the next generation because maternal hyperglycemia or diabetes increases the risk of diabetes in offspring.

Stress is the biological mechanism that links early adversity and future problems. Maternal depression also leads to higher stress in utero and may increase anxiety in infants. Toxic stress[a] linked to poverty affects the family environment and the quality of nurturing. Prolonged activation of the stress response systems can disrupt the development of brain architecture and other organ systems and increase the risk of stress-related disease, cognitive impairment (concentration, learning, memory), and noncognitive difficulties (impulse control, attention to directions) well into the adult years. Parents, especially mothers, who have had their share of adversity and insecure attachments in early childhood are less likely to establish a secure, nurturing relationship with their own children and may perpetuate a vicious circle of childhood adversity (Snellman, Silva, and Putnam 2015).

a. Toxic stress response can occur when a child experiences strong, frequent, or prolonged adversity—such as physical or emotional abuse, chronic neglect, caregiver substance abuse or mental illness, exposure to violence, and the accumulated burdens of family economic hardship—without adequate adult support.

malnourished in utero and in their early years are also more at risk of chronic diseases, such as type 2 diabetes, abdominal obesity, hypertension, and cardiovascular disease. Long-term undernutrition in infancy is linked with worse marriage matches, and women who were stunted face higher-risk pregnancies. The nurturing environment in which children grow up reflects their parents' experiences and the stresses they face—many of which are linked to poverty and all of which affect the subsequent generation.

Investing Early Is More Cost-Effective

The early years are a period of both great vulnerability and great opportunity to invest in human capital. The acquisition of cognitive and noncognitive skills begins in early childhood, and gaps between children from wealthier and poorer households emerge early (Filmer and Fox 2014; Schady and others 2015; Snellman, Silva, and Putnam 2015). Failure to invest early is difficult—and expensive—to compensate for later (Walker and others 2011). The earlier the intervention, the higher both the probability of preventing or reversing any damage and the long-term payoff. Investing early has higher rates of return and minimizes efficiency trade-offs (figure O.11).

Figure O.11 Early Investments Have the Highest Returns: Indicative Rate of Return to Investments at Each Age

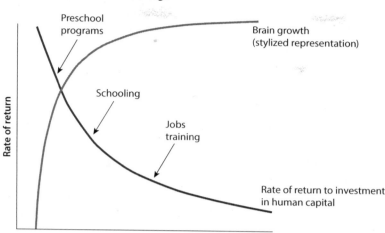

Source: Heckman and Carneiro 2003

The skills that children develop early form the basis for future learning and labor market success (Heckman and Kautz 2013). These skills are both cognitive and noncognitive (also called behavioral or socioemotional). The latter—such as conscientiousness, perseverance, sociability, and curiosity—are as important as pure cognitive skills to succeeding at school and in the workplace; they have been linked to higher educational attainment, more labor market success, better health, and lower criminality. To succeed in society, people need both types of skills.

As an integrated system for human capital formation, interventions in nutrition, health, and early education have mutually reinforcing and cumulative effects. Well-nourished, healthy children who have received adequate care and stimulation are better prepared to enter school and succeed there. The three main priorities for interventions are therefore ensuring that mothers and their children are healthy, that children are prepared for school, and that they learn what they need to succeed in the workplace and beyond. The following are key interventions:

- *Maternal and child health.* Prenatal care during pregnancy and adequate birth and emergency preparedness, skilled care during childbirth and proper care and support in the weeks after childbirth, prevention of teenage pregnancy and safe abortions, promotion of breastfeeding, decrease in low birthweight and support for catch-up growth before age 2 years, and management of childhood illness, in particular diarrhea, acute respiratory infections, and malaria.
- *School preparedness.* Parenting interventions and access to high-quality center-based care and preschool. To ensure quality, curriculum, practice for parents,

training for childcare workers, monitoring, assessment, and supervision (Engle and others 2011).

- *Schooling.* Strong numeracy and literacy skills; teamwork; active learning; links with the labor market to ease the school-to-work transition. To ensure quality, curriculum, information for accountability, school-based management, and incentives for teachers (Bruns, Filmer, and Patrinos 2011).

Paying Attention to the Demand Side Is Important

Given their starting point, many resource-rich countries in SSA have the potential to reap very high marginal rates of return on their investments if they can manage the scale and ensure quality. Even if services are available, however, poor households may face barriers in accessing them. Poverty itself may be such a barrier, as households need to choose between food and other basic needs; other barriers include distance or transportation and cultural and social norms.

In the context of resource-rich countries, cash transfers can play three main roles: (1) they are a way of distributing resource rents; (2) they alleviate poverty in the short run, which can ease poverty-linked stress; and (3) they lift demand-side barriers such as credit and information constraints and enable access to complementary inputs (uniforms, school supplies, transportation).

Building on global lessons (Fiszbein and others 2009), SSA countries such as Ethiopia, Ghana, Kenya, and Tanzania are scaling up cash transfers with innovative delivery arrangements, such as working with communities at the targeting and monitoring stages and leveraging information technology for payments and monitoring.

Alleviating the poverty of poor parents makes space for them to invest in the foundation of their children's human capital through better nutrition, better parenting practices, and better decisions about health and schooling. Because the children will be better prepared to learn in school, they are more likely to acquire the cognitive and noncognitive skills they need to participate fully and productively in society and to reap the benefits of broad-based development. Because the well-being of their children largely depends on their own well-being, girls and mothers will be key agents in breaking the vicious circle of intergenerational poverty.

Conclusion: Invest Early and Smartly

The wealth derived from oil, natural gas and minerals is nonrenewable. The resources will eventually run out. Investing in human capital should be a central part of the strategy for converting natural resources into long-run development. It extends the time horizon of a natural resource windfall by converting a finite resource into a form of capital that is perpetuated through the generations; it helps to promote growth by distributing the wealth broadly; and it helps to lay the foundation for broad-based economic development as natural resource rents taper off.

But investing well in human capital is hard; the track record of turning natural resource wealth into less poverty and better education and health is not encouraging. Moreover, spending on human capital in resource-rich countries tends to be low and only tenuously associated with better outcomes. Spending wisely and confronting the challenges that are unique to natural-resource-rich countries are essential for success.

Emerging resource-rich countries stand at a crossroads. The flow of revenues they expect from mineral wealth may evaporate or be diverted to a few groups before people and economies reap their full benefits. However, sound institutions, coherent incentives for service delivery, and open access to information will help both governments and citizens to channel the resources to investments that sustain broad-based development. Starting at the source, in early childhood, will set the course for better health and education, improve the prospects that youth and adults will be productive, and decrease the risk of civil conflict. Distributing the wealth will also widen the space for the reforms needed for governments to invest in PIM and service delivery. Together with other investments in infrastructure, these elements will enhance the flow of revenues and harness their potential to help form the basis for inclusive and shared prosperity.

Notes

1. Using an instrumental variables strategy, Edwards (2015) shows that the impact of the size of the mining sector on negative human development outcomes is causal.

2. Bodea, Higashijima, and Singh (2016) show more generally that increased welfare expenditures are associated with lower risks of conflict.

3. This book adopts the definition of governance and accountability used in both the 2012 World Bank report on citizens, service delivery, and social accountability (Ringold and others 2012) and *World Development Report 2004: Making Services Work for Poor People* (World Bank 2003).

References

Acemoglu, Daron, and Alexander Wolitzky. 2011. "The Economics of Labor Coercion." *Econometrica* 79 (2): 555–600.

Africa Progress Panel. 2013. "Equity in Extractives: Stewarding Africa's Natural Resources for All." Africa Progress Report. Africa Progress Panel, Geneva, Switzerland.

Arezki, Rabah, and Thorvaldur Gylfason. 2013. "Resource Rents, Democracy, Corruption, and Conflict: Evidence from Sub-Saharan Africa." *Journal of African Economies* 22 (4): 552–69.

Bacon, Robert, and Masami Kojima. 2008. "Coping with Oil Price Volatility." Energy Sector Management Assistance Program Report, World Bank, Washington, DC.

Barma, Naazneen, Kai Kaiser, Tuan Minh Le, and Lorena Vinuela. 2012. *Rents to Riches? The Political Economy of Natural Resource-Led Development.* Washington, DC: World Bank.

Bidani, Benu, and Martin Ravallion. 1997. "Decomposing Social Indicators Using Distributional Data." *Journal of Econometrics* 77 (1): 125–39.

Bodea, Cristina, Masaaki Higashijima, and Raju Jan Singh. 2016. "Oil and Civil Conflict: Can Public Spending Have a Mitigation Effect?" *World Development* 78 (C): 1–12.

Bruns, Barbara, Deon Filmer, and Harry Anthony Patrinos. 2011. *Making Schools Work: New Evidence on Accountability Reforms*. Washington, DC: World Bank.

Caselli, Francesco, and Guy Michaels. 2013. "Do Oil Windfalls Improve Living Standards? Evidence from Brazil." *American Economic Journal: Applied Economics* 5 (1): 208–38.

Chuhan-Pole, Punam. 2013. "Africa's Pulse (April)." World Bank, Washington, DC.

———. 2014. "Africa's Pulse (April)." World Bank, Washington, DC.

Dabla-Norris, Era, Jim Brumby, Annette Kyobe, Zac Mills, and Chris Papageorgiou. 2010. "Investing in Public Investment: An Index of Public Investment Efficiency." IMF Working Paper WP/11/37, International Monetary Fund, Washington, DC.

Dreher, Axel, Peter Nunnenkamp, and Rainer Thiele. 2008. "Does Aid for Education Educate Children? Evidence from Panel Data." *World Bank Economic Review* 22 (2): 291–314.

Edwards, Ryan B. 2015. "Mining away the Preston Curve." *World Development* 78 (February): 22–36.

Engle, Patrice L., Lia Fernald, Harold H. Alderman, Jere R. Behrman, Chloe O'Gara, Aisha Yousafzai, Meena Cabral de Mello, Melissa Hidrobo, Nurper Ulkuer, Ilgi Ertem, and Selim Iltus. 2011. "Strategies for Reducing Inequalities and Improving Developmental Outcomes for Young Children in Low- and Middle-Income Countries." *The Lancet* 378 (9799): 1339–53.

Filmer, Deon, and Anastasiya Denisova. 2015. "Human Capital in Resource-Rich Countries in Sub-Saharan Africa: Levels, Inequalities, and Spending." Background note for this book, World Bank, Washington, DC.

Filmer, Deon, and Louise Fox. 2014. *Youth Employment in Sub-Saharan Africa*. Africa Development Forum. Washington, DC: Agence Française de Développement and World Bank.

Filmer, Deon, and Lant Pritchett. 1999. "The Impact of Public Spending on Health: Does Money Matter?" *Social Science and Medicine* 49 (10): 1309–23.

Fiszbein, Ariel, Norbert Schady, Francisco Ferreira, Margaret Grosh, Niall Keleher, Pedro Olinto, and Emmanuel Skoufias. 2009. *Conditional Cash Transfers: Reducing Present and Future Poverty*. Washington, DC: World Bank.

Friedman, J., and Jennifer Sturdy. 2011. "The Influence of Economic Crisis on Early Childhood Development: A Review of Pathways and Measured Impact." In *No Small Matter: The Impact of Poverty, Shocks, and Human Capital Investments in Early Childhood Development*, edited by Harold Alderman, ch. 2. Washington, DC: World Bank.

Gill, Indermit S., Ivailo Izvorski, Willem van Eeghen, and Donato De Rosa. 2014. *Diversified Development: Making the Most of Natural Resources in Eurasia*. Washington, DC: World Bank.

Grantham-McGregor, Sally, Yin B. Cheung, Santiago Cueto, Paul Glewwe, Linda Richter, Barbara Strupp, and the International Child Development Steering Committee. 2007. "Developmental Potential in the First Five Years for Children in Developing Countries." *The Lancet* 369 (9555): 60–70.

Gupta, Sanjeev, Marijn Verhoeven, and Erwin R. Tiongson. 2002. "The Effectiveness of Government Spending on Education and Health Care in Developing and Transition Economies." *European Journal of Political Economy* 18 (4): 717–37.

Heckman, James J., and Pedro Carneiro. 2003. "Human Capital Policy." IZA Discussion Paper 821, Institute for the Study of Labor, Bonn, Germany. http://ssrn.com /abstract=434544.

Heckman, J. J., and T. Kautz. 2013. "Fostering and Measuring Skills: Interventions That Improve Character and Cognition." NBER Working Paper 19656, National Bureau of Economic Research, Cambridge, MA. http://www.nber.org/papers/w19656.

Holmlund, Helena, Mikael Lindahl, and Erik Plug. 2011. "The Causal Effect of Parents' Schooling on Children's Schooling: A Comparison of Estimation Methods." *Journal of Economic Literature* 49 (3): 615–51.

Horton, Sue, Harold Alderman, and Juan Rivera. 2008. "Hunger and Malnutrition." Copenhagen Consensus 2008 Challenge Paper, Copenhagen Consensus Center, Tewksbury, MA.

IMF (International Monetary Fund). 2014. *IV Consultation for Malaysia*. Washington, DC: IMF.

Jensen, Nathan, and Leonard Wantchekon. 2004. "Resource Wealth and Political Regimes in Africa." *Comparative Political Studies* 37 (7): 816–41.

Karl, Terry. 2004. "The Social and Political Consequences of Oil." In *Encyclopedia of Energy*, edited by Cutler Cleveland, 661–72. San Diego, CA: Elsevier.

Kaufmann, Daniel, Aart Kraay, and Massimo Mastruzzi. 2004. "Governance Matters III: Governance Indicators for 1996, 1998, 2000, and 2002." *World Bank Economic Review*. 18 (2): 253–287.

Khemani, Stuti. 2016. "Making Politics Work for Development." Policy Research Report, World Bank, Washington, DC.

Lederman, Daniel, and William F. Maloney. 2007. *Natural Resources: Neither Curse Nor Destiny*. Stanford, CA: Stanford University Press.

Psacharopoulos, George, and Harry Patrinos. 2004. "Returns to Investment in Education: A Further Update." *Education Economics* 12 (2): 111–34.

Rajkumar, Andrew Sunil, and Vinaya Swaroop. 2008. "Public Spending and Outcomes: Does Governance Matter?" *Journal of Development Economics* 86 (1): 96–111.

Reinikka, Ritva, and Jakob Svensson. 2004. "Local Capture: Evidence from a Central Government Transfer Program in Uganda." *Quarterly Journal of Economics* 119 (2): 679–705.

———. 2005. "Fighting Corruption to Improve Schooling: Evidence from a Newspaper Campaign in Uganda." *Journal of the European Economic Association* 3 (2–3): 259–67.

———. 2011. "The Power of Information in Public Services: Evidence from Education in Uganda." *Journal of Public Economics* 95 (7): 956–66.

Ringold, Dena, Alaka Holla, Margaret Koziol, and Santhosh Srinivasan. 2012. *Citizens and Service Delivery: Assessing the Use of Social Accountability Approaches in the Human Development Sectors*. Washington, DC: World Bank.

Robinson, James A., and Ragnar Torvik. 2005. "White Elephants." *Journal of Public Economics* 89 (2): 197–210.

Ross, Michael. 1999. "The Political Economy of the Resource Curse." *World Politics* 51 (2): 297–322.

———. 2001. "Does Oil Hinder Democracy?" *World Politics* 53 (3): 325–61.

———. 2006. "A Closer Look at Oil, Diamonds, and Civil War." *Annual Review of Political Science* 9 (June): 265–300.

———. 2012. *The Oil Curse: How Petroleum Wealth Shapes the Development of Nations*. Princeton, NJ: Princeton University Press.

Schady, Norbert, Jere Behrman, Maria Caridad Araujo, Rodrigo Azuero, Raquel Bernal, David Bravo, Florencia Lopez-Boo, Karen Macours, Daniela Marshall, Christina Paxson, and Renos Vakis. 2015. "Wealth Gradients in Early Childhood Cognitive Development in Five Latin American Countries." *Journal of Human Resources* 50 (2): 446–63.

Schultz, T. Paul. 2004. "Evidence of Returns to Schooling in Africa from Household Surveys: Monitoring and Restructuring the Market for Education." *Journal of African Economies* 13 (Suppl. 2): ii95–148.

Snellman, K., J. M. Silva, and R. D. Putnam. 2015. "Inequity outside the Classroom: Growing Class Differences in Participation in Extra-Curricular Activities." *Voices in Urban Education* 40: 7–14.

van der Ploeg, Frederick, and Anthony J. Venables. 2011. "Harnessing Windfall Revenues: Optimal Policies for Resource-Rich Developing Economies." *Economic Journal* 121 (551): 1–30.

Venables, Anthony J. 2016. "Using Natural Resources for Development: Why Has It Proven So Difficult?" *Journal of Economic Perspectives* 30 (1): 161–84.

Victora, Cesar, Linda Adair, Caroline Fall, Pedro Hallal, Reynaldo Martorell, Linda Richter, and Harshpal Singh Sachdev. 2008. "Maternal and Child Undernutrition: Consequences for Adult Health and Human Capital." *The Lancet* 371 (9609): 340–57.

Walker, Susan P., Theodore D. Wachs, Sally Grantham-McGregor, Maureen Black, Charles A. Nelson, Sandra L. Huffman, Helen Naker-Henningham, Susan M. Chang, Jena D. Hamadani, Betsy Lozoff, Julie M. Meeks Gardner, Christine A. Powell, Atif Rahman, and Linda Richter. 2011. "Inequality in Early Childhood: Risks and Protective Factors for Early Child Development." *The Lancet* 378 (9799): 1325–38.

World Bank. 2003. *World Development Report 2004: Making Services Work for Poor People*. Washington, DC: Oxford University Press for the World Bank.

———. 2013a. *Malaysia Economic Monitor: High-Performing Education*. Malaysia Economic Monitor. Washington, DC: World Bank.

———. 2013b. *World Development Report 2014: Risk and Opportunity*. Washington, DC: World Bank.

———. 2014. *Education for All Report*. Washington, DC: World Bank.

———. 2015. *Global Economic Prospects: Having Fiscal Space and Using It*. World Bank Flagship Report. Washington, DC: World Bank. http://www.worldbank.org/content/dam/Worldbank/GEP/GEP2015a/pdfs/GEP15a_web_full.pdf.

CHAPTER 1

Human Capital in Resource-Rich Countries

Abstract

Natural resource wealth has helped to drive up national income in many Sub-Saharan African countries. Although modestly lower in resource-rich countries, poverty is higher after factoring in gross national income per capita, suggesting that resource wealth is not generally shared. Countries rich in natural resources fare particularly badly in terms of education and health outcomes—school participation and completion rates are far below those that national income would predict; infant mortality and stunting rates are also higher, and vaccination rates are lower. Resource-rich countries invest less in education and health than their national income would predict, and their investments tend to be only weakly associated with better outcomes.

Introduction

Over the past 15 years, Sub-Saharan Africa (SSA) has experienced a boom in natural resources, and virtually all countries in the region are exploring new oil, natural gas, or mineral reserves. The region's exports of oil alone are nearly triple its aid receipts (van der Ploeg and Venables 2011). Countries that had not previously been considered resource-rich are seeing a windfall of resource rents. Ghana's Jubilee oil field, which entered production in 2010, averages more than 85,000 barrels a day, and Uganda's Lake Albert rift fields target production of 200,000 barrels a day. Natural gas exploitation could potentially bring returns of billions of dollars to Mozambique and Tanzania.

Natural resources hold promise of being a great boon to economic growth and individual well-being, but numerous studies point to the economic as well as the social, political, and institutional challenges that accompany natural resource riches (Africa Progress Panel 2013; Venables 2016). The specter of a "resource curse" shrouds the promise (Sachs and Warner 1999, 2001). But the success of several countries—Chile, Malaysia, and Norway, for example—in transforming natural resources into long-term development suggests that such a curse is not inevitable (Lederman and Maloney 2007). Harnessing the returns from natural resource wealth can contribute substantially to eradicating extreme poverty and enhancing shared prosperity.

Success requires a series of good decisions and sound implementation. Recent declines in oil prices highlight just one of the risks associated with growth driven by natural resource wealth. Revenues from natural resources are volatile, and government strategies for managing these resources need to take into account the possibility of busts as well as booms and to address the challenge of transforming finite, volatile resources into sources of growth (figure 1.1).

Governments and other stakeholders must grapple with (at least) four central questions when they seek to transform a finite amount of natural resources into lasting development (Barma and others 2012; van der Ploeg and Venables 2011; Venables 2016):

1. What is the optimal contract between government and entities that extract natural resources to balance public benefits with incentives to the private sector?
2. What is the optimal timing of extraction to ensure the maximum stream of benefits from reserves?
3. What is the optimal portfolio allocation of mineral revenues between consumption, savings, and investments? And what should be the profile of investments with regard to financial assets, physical capital (for example, infrastructure), and human capital?
4. How can resource revenue be spent most effectively and efficiently, and what complementary activities or reforms are required to ensure effectiveness and efficiency?

Answers to these questions determine whether the benefits of natural resource extraction will last through the long term. This book focuses on questions 3 and 4, exploring, in particular, how long-term benefits can be achieved by investing in human capital—in part because this issue is too often overlooked.

As the book makes clear, investing in human capital—understood broadly to include education, capabilities, and health—should be a central part of the strategy for converting natural resources into long-term development. It extends the time horizon of the natural resource windfall by converting a finite resource into a form of capital that can be preserved through generations, it helps to promote growth by distributing wealth broadly, and it helps to lay the foundation for broad-based economic development as natural resource revenues decline.

However, investing well in human capital is hard; the track record of using natural resource wealth to lessen poverty and promote better education and health outcomes is not good. Moreover, because resource-rich countries tend not to spend much on human capital, and, because the challenges in delivering services

Figure 1.1 Strategies for Managing Resource Rents Need to Account for Booms and Busts: Index of the Real Price of Natural Resources, 1990–2015

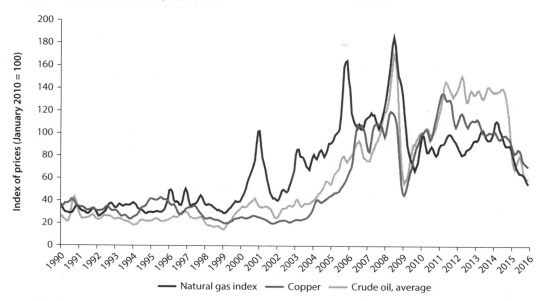

Source: World Bank commodity price data (the Pink Sheet), http://www.worldbank.org/en/research/commodity-markets.

are exacerbated in these countries, the outcomes are not impressive. Spending wisely and directly confronting challenges that are unique to natural-resource-rich countries are both essential for success.

Natural Resource Wealth, National Income, Poverty, and Inequality

Natural resource wealth—and oil wealth in particular—has been supporting dramatic growth in national incomes in SSA countries. Between 1995 and 2013, gross national income (GNI) per capita in the region as a whole rose 50 percent. The gain was 80 percent in oil-rich countries, but substantially lower, at 40 percent, in non–resource-rich countries (figure 1.2). Countries identified as "potentially" resource-rich (with reserves identified but not yet extracted) also grew quickly (70 percent over the period), although this was from a much lower base and annual increases in income were smaller.[1] Box 1.1 presents the country classifications.

This chapter assesses the extent to which the higher national income resulting from this growth is associated with higher human capital outcomes and less inequality in those outcomes. It then assesses patterns of investment in human capital by different types of countries. The chapter uses new databases built from individual and household-level surveys to contrast levels and inequalities in outcomes between resource-rich and non–resource-rich countries, both within and beyond Sub-Saharan Africa.

Natural resource wealth is closely associated with higher national income in Sub-Saharan Africa (figure 1.3). Average GNI per capita in 2013 was US$4,528 in oil-rich countries and US$2,607 in nonoil resource-rich countries, compared with US$1,683 in non–resource-rich countries. In the last group, it is noteworthy that countries identified as potentially resource-rich tend to have substantially

Figure 1.2 In SSA, Oil-Rich Countries Grew Substantially Faster Than Other Countries: Cumulative Growth in GNI per Capita, 1995–2013

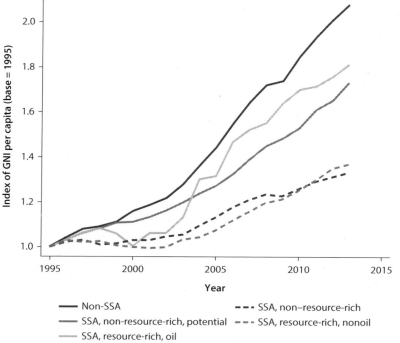

Source: World Development Indicators data.
Note: SSA = Sub-Saharan Africa; GNI = gross national income. Non-SSA countries include only countries with GNI per capita of less than US$10,000 in 1995 (in 2005 U.S. dollars).

Box 1.1 Country Classification

This book classifies countries into subgroups by their resource endowments (table B1.1.1). The classification is based on the analysis described in IMF (2012), which defines countries as resource-rich if they had either natural resource revenue of at least 20 percent of total revenue or natural resource exports of at least 20 percent of total exports for 2006–10. The classification includes some countries for which data are lacking (Côte d'Ivoire, Liberia, Niger, and Uzbekistan) and is augmented by Namibia and South Africa based on later analyses of World Development Indicators data (Filmer and Denisova 2015). Countries identified as potentially resource-rich are those with identified reserves where production has not begun or reached significant levels.

box continues next page

Box 1.1 Country Classification (continued)

Table B1.1.1 Countries Classified as Resource-Rich or Potentially Resource-Rich

SSA						Non-SSA			
Resource-rich				Potentially resource-rich		Resource-rich			
Oil		Nonoil				Oil		Nonoil	
Country	Resource	Country	Resource	Country	Resource	Country	Resource	Country	Resource
Angola	Oil	Botswana	Diamonds	Central African Republic	Diamonds, gold	Albania	Oil, natural gas	Bolivia	Natural gas
Cameroon	Oil	Congo, Dem. Rep.	Minerals, oil	Ghana	Gold, oil	Algeria	Oil	Brunei Darussalam	Natural gas
Chad	Oil	Guinea	Mining products	Madagascar	Oil, natural gas, minerals	Azerbaijan	Oil	Chile	Copper
Congo, Rep.	Oil	Liberia	Gold, diamonds, iron	Mozambique	Natural gas, bauxite, other	Bahrain	Oil	Guyana	Gold, bauxite
Côte d'Ivoire	Oil, natural gas	Mali	Gold	Sierra Leone	Diamonds	Ecuador	Oil	Lao PDR	Copper, gold
Equatorial Guinea	Oil	Mauritania	Iron	Tanzania	Gold, precious stones	Indonesia	Oil	Mongolia	Copper
Gabon	Oil	Namibia	Minerals	Togo	Phosphate	Iran, Islamic Rep.	Oil	Peru	Minerals
Nigeria	Oil	Niger	Uranium	Uganda	Oil	Iraq	Oil	Qatar	Natural gas
Sudan	Oil	South Africa	Minerals			Albania	Oil, natural gas	Suriname	Minerals
		Zambia	Copper			Kazakhstan	Oil	Trinidad and Tobago	Natural gas
		Botswana	Diamonds			Libya	Oil	Uzbekistan	Gold, natural gas
						Mexico	Oil		
						Norway	Oil		
						Oman	Oil		

table continues next page

box continues next page

Box 1.1 Country Classification *(continued)*

Table B1.1.1 Countries Classified as Resource-Rich or Potentially Resource-Rich *(continued)*

SSA					Non-SSA			
Resource-rich				Potentially resource-rich	Resource-rich			
Oil		Nonoil			Oil		Nonoil	
Country	Resource	Country	Resource	Country	Resource	Country	Resource	Country	Resource
						Papua New Guinea	Oil, copper, gold		
						Russian Federation	Oil		
						Saudi Arabia	Oil		
						Syrian Arab Republic	Oil		
						Timor-Leste	Oil		
						Turkmenistan	Oil		
						United Arab Emirates	Oil		
						Venezuela, RB	Oil		
						Vietnam	Oil		
						Yemen, Rep.	Oil		

Source: IMF 2012, except for Namibia and South Africa, which were added based on later analysis.

Note: The non–resource-rich countries in Sub-Saharan Africa (SSA) are Benin, Burkina Faso, Burundi, Cabo Verde, the Comoros, Eritrea, Ethiopia, The Gambia, Guinea-Bissau, Kenya, Lesotho, Malawi, Mauritius, Rwanda, Senegal, the Seychelles, Somalia, South Sudan, Swaziland, and Zimbabwe.

Figure 1.3 Natural Resource Wealth in SSA Generally Translates into Higher GNI per Capita: GNI per Capita, by Country Classification, 2013

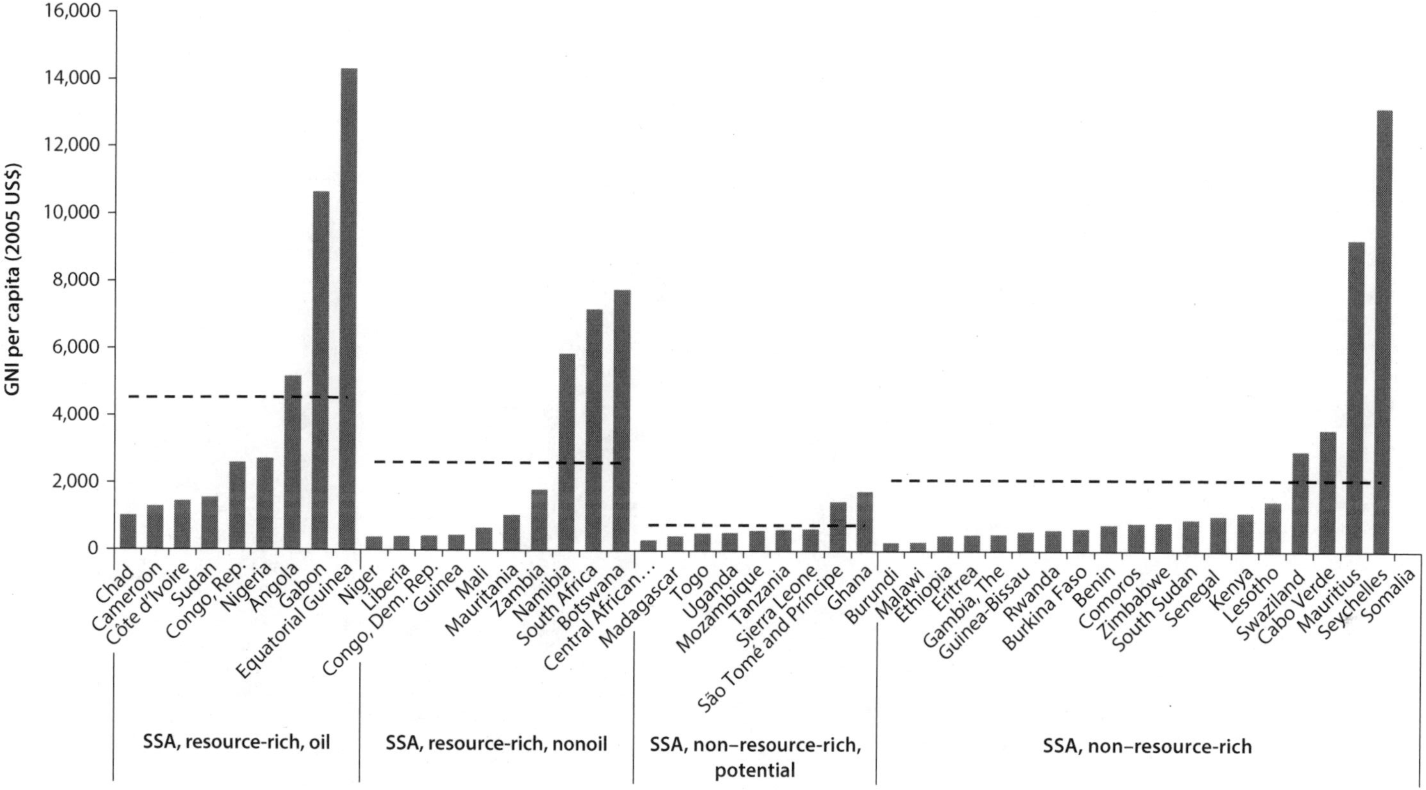

Source: World Development Indicators data.
Note: SSA = Sub-Saharan Africa; GNI = gross national income.

Figure 1.4 In SSA, Natural Resource Wealth Is Associated with Slightly Lower Poverty Rates: Share of the Population Living on Less Than US$1.25, US$2.50, and US$5 a Day, Most Recent Data Available

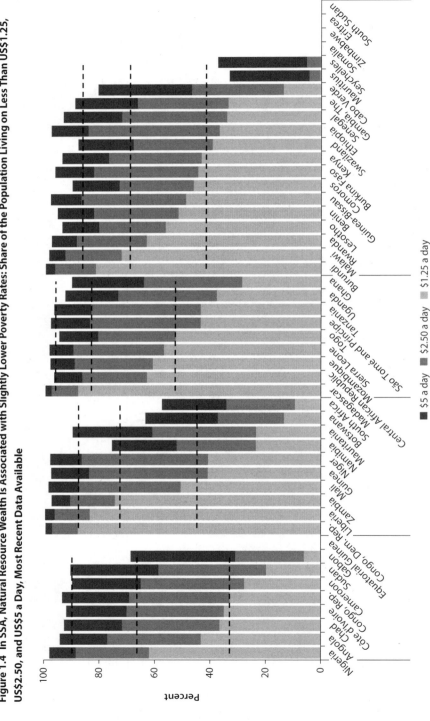

Source: PovCalNet data (extracted May 2015).

Note: SSA = Sub-Saharan Africa. Horizontal bars show mean poverty rates across countries in each grouping.

lower national income (US$776) than countries identified as not having potential resources (US$2,113). The countries that have the potential for large windfalls from natural resource extraction are starting from a substantially lower base.

Poverty rates, in contrast to national income, are only slightly lower in countries rich in natural resources (Christiaensen and Devarajan 2013). While extreme poverty in SSA, measured as the share of the population living on less than US$1.25 a day, tends to be lower in resource-rich than in non–resource-rich countries, the contrast is much smaller when the poverty threshold is set at US$2.50 a day (figure 1.4). At this threshold, average poverty is 33 percent in oil-rich SSA countries, compared with 45 percent in nonoil resource-rich countries and 46 percent in non–resource-rich countries in the region.[2]

The modest improvement in poverty is reversed after national income is taken into account; poverty reduction is worse in resource-rich countries than in other countries at the same income level. Figure 1.5 shows the differences by country classification after adjusting for GNI per capita. Poverty rates are higher in the resource-rich countries and significantly higher in oil-rich countries at the US$5-a-day poverty threshold.

Figure 1.5 Resource Wealth Is Not Associated with Substantially Lower Poverty: Headcount Poverty Rates Relative to Non–Resource-Rich SSA Countries at a Poverty Threshold of US$2.50 a Day (Poverty Rates, by Country Category, after Controlling for GNI per Capita, Most Recent Data Available)

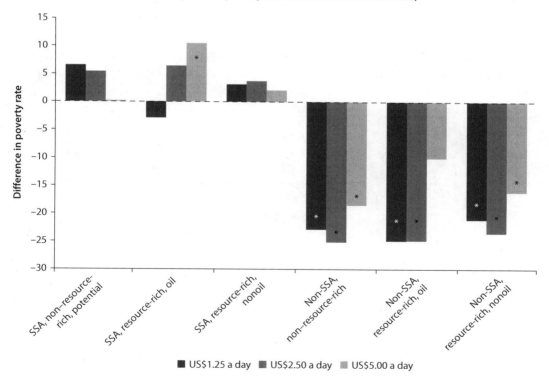

Source: Analysis of PovCalNet data (extracted May 2015).
Note: SSA = Sub-Saharan Africa; GNI = gross national income.

This is consistent with patterns of structural transformation in the region. Growth has been less poverty-reducing in SSA than in other parts of the world, and growth in resource-rich countries has reduced poverty less than growth in other countries (Chuhan-Pole 2013). Moreover, in SSA growth in agriculture and services—where the majority of poor people work—tends to result in larger reductions in poverty than growth in industry, which includes mining (figure 1.6; also see Chuhan-Pole 2014; Filmer and Fox 2014).

Whether or not a country is rich in natural resources is not systematically associated with broad measures of inequality, such as the share of income controlled by the top decile or quintile or the Gini index, which measures inequality across the entire income distribution. Inequality tends to be slightly lower in oil-rich countries and slightly higher in nonoil resource-rich countries compared with other countries in the region, but this surprising finding may have more to do with how inequality is measured than with actual inequality. Surveys used to measure household consumption often (a) fail to capture the high levels of consumption among the wealthiest and (b) exclude the wealthiest from the sample completely. Both effects would tend to underestimate inequality, especially in countries where a very few individuals control most of the wealth. This appears indeed to be the case in SSA, especially in resource-rich countries (Beegle and others 2016).

Figure 1.6 Workers in Industry Have Higher Levels of Education Than Workers in Agriculture or the Unpaid or Self-Employed Services Sector: Percentage of Workers at Each Education Level in Selected African Countries, by Type of Employment

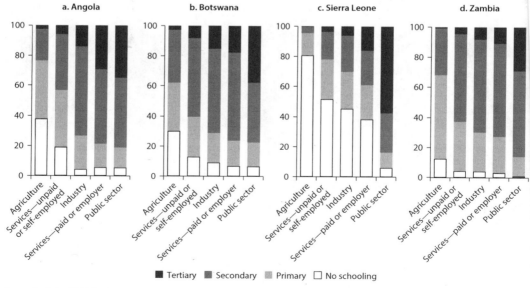

Source: Analysis of i2d2 database.

Natural Resource Wealth and Human Development

This book is concerned mainly with the link between natural resource wealth and the accumulation of human capital. The rest of this chapter first reviews evidence on levels and inequalities in human capital outcomes in SSA and then turns to indicators of government investment—and its effectiveness—in education and health.

Despite exceptions like Chile, Malaysia, and Norway, natural-resource-rich countries have often been charged with not investing enough in education and health to build a solid foundation of human capital (Birdsall, Pinckney, and Sabot 2001; Bravo-Ortega and de Gregorio 2007; Gylfason 2001; Philippot 2010).[3] This observation is consistent with the cross-country data; SSA countries that are oil-rich fare poorly on the United Nation's human development index (HDI), which integrates national income, life expectancy, educational attainment, and school participation. For each level of GNI per capita, oil-rich countries in SSA have consistently lower HDIs than other countries both inside and outside the region (figure 1.7).[4]

Figure 1.7 Resource-Rich Countries in SSA Fare Poorly on the Human Development Index: HDI and GNI per Capita, by Country Category, 2013

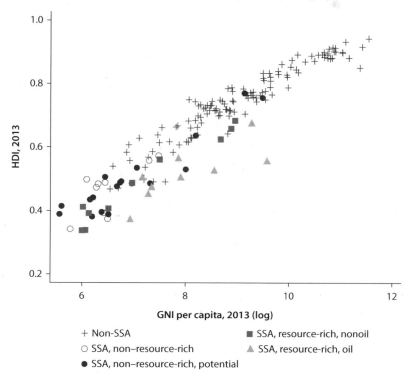

Source: Analysis of data from UNDP 2014 and World Development Indicators database.
Note: SSA = Sub-Saharan Africa; HDI = human development index; GNI = gross national income.

Education and Health Outcomes

Household surveys provide a wealth of new data that can be used to analyze both systematic patterns in education and health outcomes and within-country inequalities in outcomes (box 1.2). The data are compiled primarily from the Demographic Health Surveys (DHS) and Multiple Indicator Cluster Surveys (MICS) as well as other household surveys, such as those collected through the Living Standards Measurement Study (LSMS) program.

Box 1.2 New Data on Inequalities in Education and Health Indicators

International databases on education and health outcomes typically suffer from two problems. First, they only contain country aggregates, which precludes analysis of within-country inequalities in outcomes. Second, the data are often "smoothed" and interpolated in ways that may induce regularities that are functions of the modeling used for smoothing and interpolating rather than actual patterns (for example, if national income is used to predict a variable, subsequent associations between that variable and national income will be spurious). Both problems are overcome here by using new compilations of data based directly on household surveys.

For education outcomes, the book uses data from the Educational Attainment and Enrollment around the World database, which contains indicators from 504 surveys from 109 countries that are derived from analyses of data from the DHS, MICS, the i2d2 database, and other national household surveys.[a] This database covers 41 SSA countries (208 surveys) and 68 non-SSA countries (296 surveys). Of the 41 SSA countries, 7 are oil-rich, 10 are nonoil resource-rich, 9 are non–resource-rich with potential, and 15 are non–resource-rich. Of the 68 non-SSA countries, 13 are oil-rich, 8 are nonoil resource-rich, and 47 are non–resource-rich. Of the comparator countries, 13 are in East Asia and the Pacific, 17 are in Europe and Central Asia, 21 are in Latin America and the Caribbean, 9 are in the Middle East and North Africa, and 9 are in South Asia.

The household survey–derived indicators of education are as follows:

- The proportion of children ages 6–14 years reported to be in school, and
- The proportion of teens ages 15–19 years who have completed grade 6.

For health outcomes, the book uses the database compiled for Wagstaff, Bredenkamp, and Buisman (2014), who made it available for this analysis. It combines data from the DHS and MICS and was augmented with data from the MICS interactive website.[b] This database covers 44 SSA countries (161 surveys) and 57 non-SSA countries (175 surveys). Of the 44 SSA countries, 8 are oil-rich, 10 are nonoil resource-rich, 9 are non–resource-rich with potential, and 17 are non–resource-rich. Of the 57 non-SSA countries, 13 are oil-rich, 7 are nonoil resource-rich, and 37 are non–resource-rich. Of comparator countries, 9 are in East Asia and the Pacific, 14 are in Europe and Central Asia, 17 are in Latin America and the Caribbean, 10 are in the Middle East and North Africa, and 7 are in South Asia.

box continues next page

Box 1.2 New Data on Inequalities in Education and Health Indicators (continued)

The household survey–derived indicators of health are as follows:

- Infant mortality rate (number of deaths of children younger than age 12 months per 1,000 live births)
- Proportion of children with a full course of vaccinations (proportion ages 12–23 months who received Bacillus Calmette-Guerin (BCD), measles, and three doses of polio and diphtheria, pertussis, and tetanus (DPT), vaccines)
- Proportion of children who are stunted (children younger than 5 years old with a height-for-age z-score less than 2 standard deviations from the reference median).

a. For the Educational Attainment and Enrollment around the World database, see econ.worldbank.org/projects/edattain/.
b. For the MICS website, see http://mics.unicef.org/ and for the DHS website, see http://dhsprogram.org.

Education Indicators

Two indicators capture different aspects of education performance in these countries:

1. *School participation:* the probability that a child age 6–14 is reported as currently attending school. The measure combines both household factors that affect enrollment rates (for example, financial constraints or low demand for poor-quality schooling) as well as supply-side factors (for example, availability of schools).
2. *School attainment:* the probability that a young person age 15–19 years has completed grade 6. Among determinants of this completion rate are not only the demand and supply factors that affect enrollment but also the factors that affect school retention. Indeed, in many countries initial enrollment in school is high, but, as a result of dropouts and repetition, completion of grade 6 is much lower, especially for the poor (figure 1.8).

To assess how outcomes differ by country classification, subgroup outcomes are compared, with non–resource-rich SSA countries as the reference group and controlling for national income.[5] The analysis is carried out for each indicator first for the entire population and then by quintile.

Controlling for national income, education outcomes are systematically worse in oil-rich SSA countries than in non–resource-rich SSA countries. The percentage of children ages 6–15 years who are currently attending school and the percentage of young persons age 15–19 years who have completed grade 6 are 7–8 percentage points lower in oil-rich than in non–resource-rich countries compared with what would be expected for their level of income (figure 1.9). This pattern is more pronounced among the poor—for children and youth in the poorest quintile, the shortfall is 15–20 percentage points—although the association cuts across all household welfare levels. The pattern of results is similar, although more muted, in nonoil resource-rich countries. There, school completion is similar

Figure 1.8 Patterns of Grade Completion Vary Dramatically across Countries: Grade Completion Rate (Proportion) among Young Persons Ages 15–19 Years, by Country

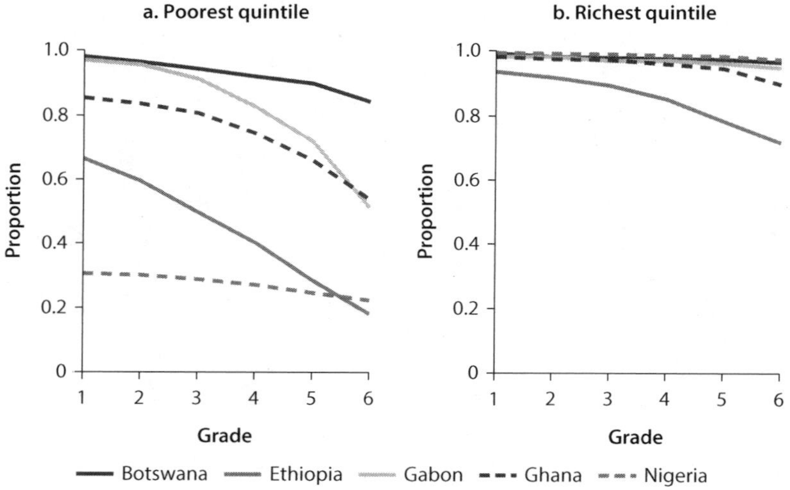

Source: Educational Attainment around the World database.

to that of non–resource-rich countries, but school participation is systematically worse, although statistically not significantly so.

The education shortfall in Africa's resource-rich countries is all the more strik-ing because there is no shortfall in resource-rich countries in other parts of the world. In countries outside SSA, grade 6 completion is systematically higher in resource-rich than in non–resource-rich countries (again, after accounting for GNI per capita). The enrollment rate is similar in oil-rich and in non–resource-rich countries, and it is significantly higher in nonoil resource-rich countries.

Health Indicators

Three measures of health and nutrition can be derived from the household survey data:

1. *Infant mortality:* This measure is typically calculated based on live births within the 10 years before the survey.
2. *Full vaccination coverage:* This indicator largely reflects the effort of the national health system because a full course of vaccinations requires sustained connec-tion to that system (for example, to complete the course of three doses for polio and DPT).
3. *Stunting:* This indicator is a chronic, cumulative measure that is higher when children face repeated periods of low early child nutrition, bouts of sickness, and subsequent low levels of nutrition. Stunting reflects issues that go beyond a country's health sector. Nevertheless, it also captures the ability of the health sector to help the country to overcome problems.

Figure 1.9 In SSA, Resource-Rich Countries Have Worse Education Outcomes after Controlling for GNI per Capita: Education Outcomes Relative to Non–Resource-Rich SSA Countries, Overall and by Quintile

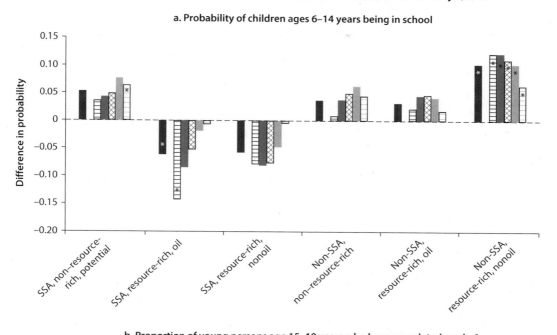

a. Probability of children ages 6–14 years being in school

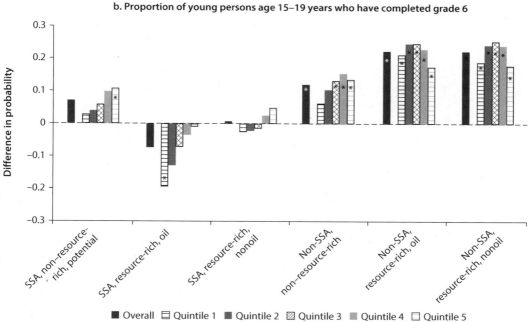

b. Proportion of young persons age 15–19 years who have completed grade 6

■ Overall ⊟ Quintile 1 ▨ Quintile 2 ⊠ Quintile 3 ▨ Quintile 4 ☐ Quintile 5

Note: SSA = Sub-Saharan Africa; GNI = gross national income. Figures report coefficients from regression models for per capita GNI and its square. Reference category is non–resource-rich SSA countries. Significance level: * = 10 percent.

Figure 1.10 Within-Country Inequalities in Health Indicators Can Be Very Large in SSA: Health Indicators in Selected Countries, by Quintile

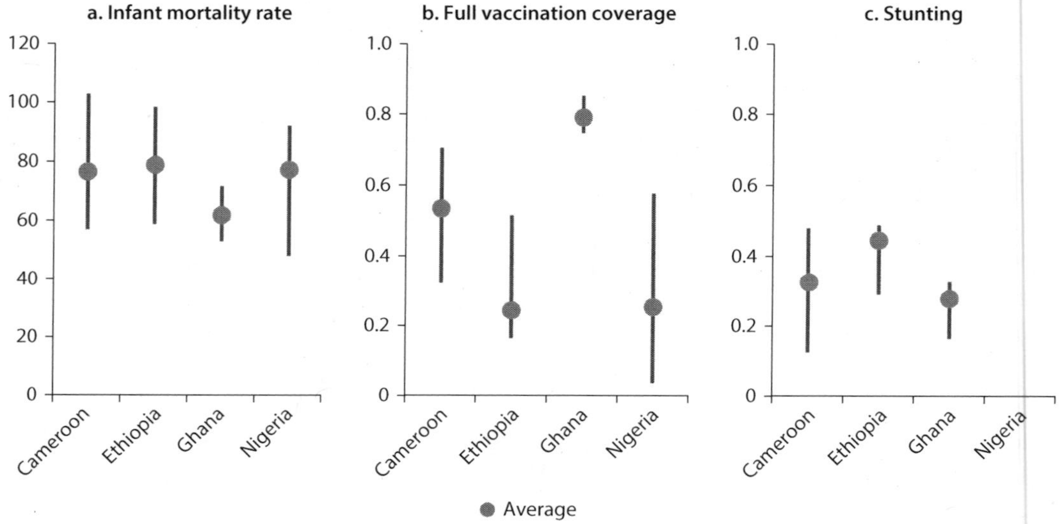

Source: Household survey data.
Note: Vertical bars show range from richest to poorest quintile.

Within-country inequalities in health indicators can be very large. For example, in Nigeria almost 60 percent of children from the richest quintile have received a full course of vaccinations, compared with almost none from the poorest quintile (figure 1.10).

Cross-country patterns for health are similar to those for education. Infant mortality rates are 30 percent higher in oil-rich SSA countries than in the non–resource-rich countries (figure 1.11), again factoring in that national income is higher in those countries and mortality would therefore be predicted to be lower; infant mortality rates in nonoil resource-rich countries are 14 percent higher. Vaccination rates are also substantially lower: the number of children ages 12–13 months who have had their full course of vaccinations is more than 30 percentage points lower in oil-rich SSA countries than in non–resource-rich countries after controlling for national income; for nonoil resource-rich countries, coverage is about 15 percentage points lower. The proportion of children who are stunted is also significantly higher in oil-rich countries. For each of these indicators, the pattern is more pronounced in the poorest quintiles.

Inequalities in Education and Health Indicators

To assess just how strong the inequality effects in education and health are, inequality is defined as the difference between the richest and poorest quintiles in each indicator (for infant mortality and stunting, the difference is reversed, since in those cases higher values indicate worse outcomes). The deficit among the poor is systematically larger in oil-rich than in nonoil resource-rich countries (table 1.1). For example, the gap in grade 6 completion is 33 percentage

Figure 1.11 In SSA, Resource-Rich Countries Have Worse Health Indicators Than Other Countries after Controlling for GNI per Capita: Health Outcomes Relative to Non–Resource-Rich SSA Countries, Overall and by Quintile

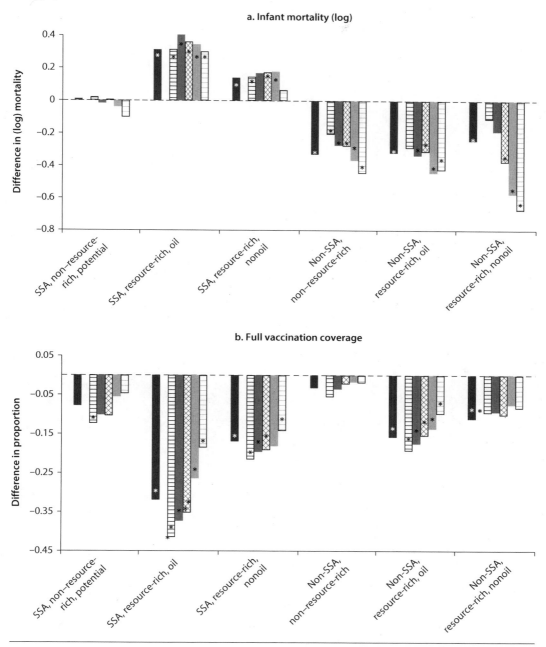

a. Infant mortality (log)

b. Full vaccination coverage

figure continues next page

Figure 1.11 In SSA, Resource-Rich Countries Have Worse Health Indicators Than Other Countries after Controlling for GNI per Capita: Health Outcomes Relative to Non–Resource-Rich SSA Countries, Overall and by Quintile (continued)

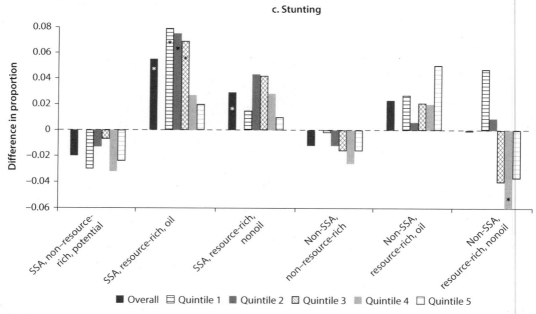

c. Stunting

Note: SSA = Sub-Saharan Africa; GNI = gross national income. Figures report coefficients from the regression model, which controls for per capita GNI and its square. Reference category is non–resource-rich SSA countries. Significance level: * = 10 percent.

Table 1.1 The Deficit among the Poor Is Systematically Larger in Oil-Rich Than in Nonoil Resource-Rich Countries: Gaps between Richest and Poorest Quintiles for Each Indicator

Indicator and region	Resource-rich, oil	Resource-rich, nonoil	Non-resource-rich, potential	Non-resource-rich	All
School enrollment[a]					
SSA	0.31	0.26	0.23	0.21	0.24
Non-SSA	0.13	0.10	—	0.17	0.15
Grade completion[b]					
SSA	0.48	0.39	0.42	0.33	0.39
Non-SSA	0.21	0.26	—	0.32	0.29
Infant mortality rate (log)					
SSA	0.48	0.50	0.49	0.41	0.46
Non-SSA	0.68	1.07	—	0.74	0.78
Full course of vaccinations					
SSA	0.36	0.23	0.26	0.17	0.24
Non-SSA	0.18	0.11	—	0.16	0.16
Stunting					
SSA	0.24	0.19	0.19	0.20	0.20
Non-SSA	0.14	0.25	—	0.20	0.21

Note: SSA = Sub-Saharan Africa; — = not available.
a. Proportion of children ages 6–14 years who are in school.
b. Proportion of young persons ages 15–19 years who have completed grade 6.

Figure 1.12 Inequalities in Education and Health Indicators Are Worse in Oil-Rich SSA Countries

a. Rich-poor gap in proportion of children ages 6–14 years who have completed grade 6

b. Rich-poor gap in proportion of children with full course of vaccination

+ Non-SSA
○ SSA, non–resource-rich
● SSA, non–resource-rich, potential
■ SSA, resource-rich, nonoil
▲ SSA, resource-rich, oil

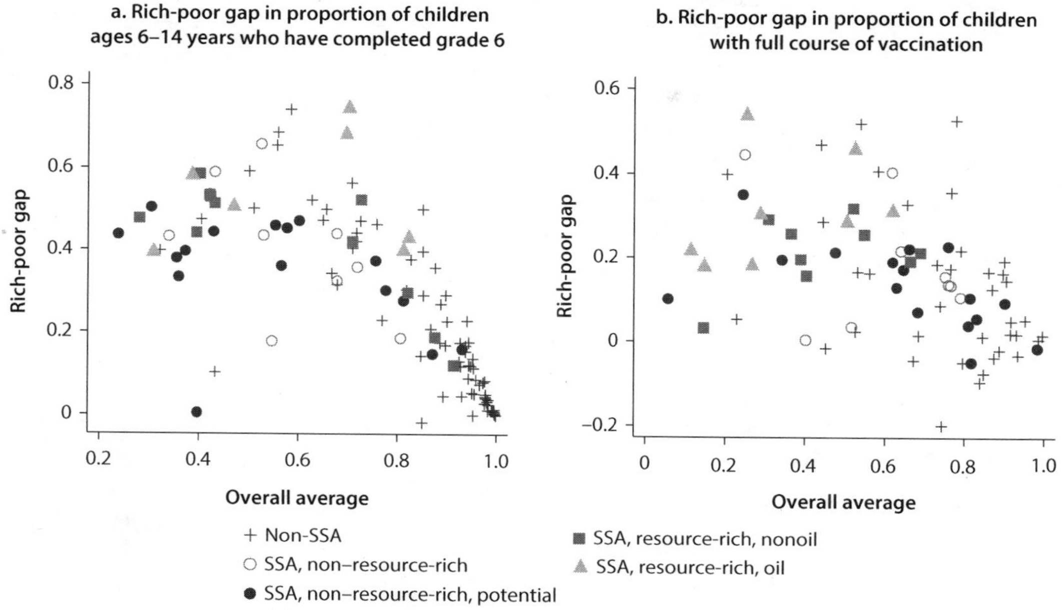

Note: SSA = Sub-Saharan Africa.

points in non–resource-rich SSA countries, compared with 48 percentage points in oil-rich countries and 39 percentage points in nonoil resource-rich countries. The gap in receiving a full course of vaccinations is 17 percentage points in non–resource-rich SSA countries, compared with 36 percentage points in oil-rich countries. This stark pattern of larger inequalities in SSA is not found in the non-SSA sample of countries.

Rich-poor gaps are remarkably large in oil-rich SSA countries for most indicator averages. Figure 1.12 plots the difference between the richest and poorest quintiles for two key indicators—grade 6 completion and full vaccination coverage—against the average value of the indicators in these countries. If at any given average inequalities are high, this will appear as a point toward the top of each chart. Clearly, oil-rich countries stand out as having particularly high inequalities. While inequalities by household welfare are large, other dimensions of inequality—such as those by gender—also tend to be larger in resource-rich countries (box 1.3).

Data Gaps and Quality of Outcomes

While the data described so far represent substantial progress in terms of ability to document patterns across countries, further analysis faces severe data limitations. Perhaps most important is the fact that crucial dimensions of human capital accumulation are not measured. In particular, there is minimal information on the quality of schooling as measured by learning assessments.

Box 1.3 Gender Gaps in Education Outcomes

The discussion in this chapter focuses on within-country inequalities related to household income. Other dimensions of inequality also appear to differ systematically between resource-rich and non–resource-rich SSA countries. Gender gaps stand out. The average difference between boys and girls in the school participation of children ages 6–14 years is 21 percentage points in non–resource-rich SSA countries, compared with 31 percentage points in oil-rich countries and 26 percentage points in nonoil resource-rich countries. The differences are starker for grade 6 completion because gender gaps tend to widen at higher levels of schooling. For example, the male-female gap is 33 percentage points in non–resource-rich SSA countries but 47 percentage points in oil-rich SSA countries.

Figure 1.13 Learning in Africa's Schools Is Lagging: Performance on the TIMSS Tests of Grade 8 Students in Selected Countries

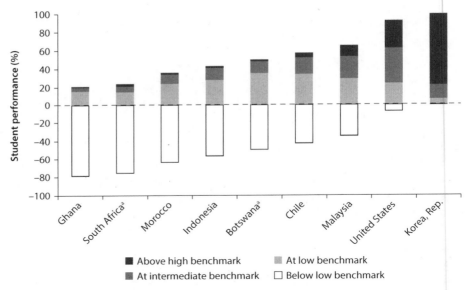

Source: Mullis and others 2012.
Note: At the TIMSS low benchmark, test takers have "some knowledge of whole numbers and decimals, operations, and basic graphs." At the intermediate benchmark, they can "apply basic knowledge in a variety of situations." At the high benchmark, they can "apply knowledge and understanding in a variety of relatively complex situations."
a. Students in grade 9.

Only three SSA countries—Botswana, Ghana, and South Africa—have participated in the Trends in International Mathematics and Science Study (TIMSS), an internationally benchmarked learning assessment; in this book, Botswana and South Africa are classified as nonoil resource-rich and Ghana is classified as non–resource-rich with potential.[6] Results from this assessment reveal substantial shortfalls in the learning outcomes that Africa's schools generate (figure 1.13). More than 50 percent of grade 9 students in Botswana and about 80 percent of grade 8 students in Ghana and grade 9 students in South Africa cannot show that they have "some knowledge of whole numbers and decimals, operations, and basic graphs." Very few students in these countries can "apply basic knowledge in a variety of situations." These learning deficits begin early, and, as discussed in chapter 4, early deficits have long-term implications—both for later education outcomes (such as the TIMSS measure in later grades) and in other realms of life.

While this chapter focuses on indicators that are measured consistently in enough countries to establish patterns for resource-rich and non–resource-rich countries, it is important to keep in mind that other, perhaps even more important, indicators cannot be integrated into the analysis. The indicators used here should be viewed as proxies for a broader concept of human capital, as they provide an incomplete picture (see Beegle and others 2016 for a fuller discussion of data needs and challenges in SSA).

Public Spending on Education and Health in Resource-Rich Countries

Relative to other types of government engagement and action, the role of public spending in determining outcomes is controversial. On average, public spending on education or health tends to be only loosely related to outcomes (Dreher, Nunnenkamp, and Thiele 2008; Filmer and Pritchett 1999; World Bank 2003). Some analysts have found positive associations between spending and child mortality and school enrollment, although others emphasize that factors like national income or general economic stability are also important (Baldacci and others 2008; Bokhari, Gai, and Gottret 2007).

The average association may be masking factors that make spending more or less effective. For instance, the impact of spending may vary across the income distribution: there is some evidence that spending matters more to improving outcomes for the poor (Bidani and Ravallion 1997). But a second factor is perhaps more pervasive: because spending can be done "well" or "poorly," there is no guarantee that it will produce better outcomes. Analysts have used direct measures of governance to show its importance in making public spending more effective in both education and health (Rajkumar and Swaroop 2008). Indirect evidence suggests that international assistance to education tends to be more effective than general public spending on education (Dreher, Nunnenkamp, and Thiele 2008); in part because aid is less prone to leakages and tends to be more pro-poor, it is typically dedicated to inputs other than teacher salaries, which form the bulk of public spending on education.

The effectiveness of government expenditures is addressed in more depth in chapter 3, which discusses the types of reforms required to make spending effective, and in chapter 4, which discusses the types of investments that have the highest payoff. The next two sections of this chapter establish patterns in spending on education and health across resource-rich and non–resource-rich countries and assess the extent to which more spending is associated with better outcomes.

Amount of Public Spending on Education and Health

Public spending on both education and health tends to be higher in resource-rich SSA countries than in other SSA countries. On average, governments in oil-rich SSA countries spend US$69 per capita on education, nonoil resource-rich countries spend US$116, non–resource-rich countries spend US$49, and countries "with potential" spend only US$19 (table 1.2).[7] The pattern for per capita public health spending is similar: on a per person basis, resource-rich SSA countries spend, on average, almost twice what non–resource-rich countries do.

The pattern is reversed, however, when public spending is considered as a share of GDP. The percentage of GDP devoted to education and health in oil-rich SSA countries is close to half the amount spent in non–resource-rich SSA countries. This is not the pattern outside SSA, where government spending on education in nonoil resource-rich countries is lower than, and that on health is similar to, government spending in non–resource-rich countries. Figure 1.14 shows spending per capita on each sector (averaged between 2000 and 2013) relative to non–resource-rich SSA countries, after controlling for national income. In both sectors, the oil-rich SSA countries spend about 60 percent less per capita.

Public Spending and Education and Health Outcomes

The relationship between spending and outcomes is typically tenuous. Money can be well-deployed, but that is not always the case. The data assembled so far can be used further to assess the extent to which the association between spending and outcomes is stronger or weaker for resource-rich countries and whether it differs for the poor. The approach used is to estimate the statistical

Table 1.2 In SSA, Resource-Rich Countries Spend Relatively Less on Education and Health Than Other Countries: Public Spending on Education and Health per Capita and as a Share of GDP, 2000–13

Indicator and country category	Education (average, 2000–13)			Health (average, 2000–13)		
	SSA	Non-SSA	All	SSA	Non-SSA	All
Spending per capita						
Resource-rich, oil	69	125	107	50	73	65
Resource-rich, nonoil	116	99	110	62	102	81
Non–resource-rich, potential	19		19	12		12
Non–resource-rich	49	170	144	29	158	134
All	62	157	124	37	137	106
Spending as a share of GDP						
Resource-rich, oil	2.9	4.7	4.1	1.7	2.4	2.2
Resource-rich, nonoil	4.3	4.5	4.4	2.9	3.0	3.0
Non–resource-rich, potential	4.1		4.1	2.7		2.7
Non–resource-rich	5.0	4.9	4.9	3.0	4.1	3.9
All	4.3	4.8	4.6	2.6	3.7	3.4

Source: World Development Indicators data.

Note: SSA = Sub-Saharan Africa. Data are calculated as an average of nonmissing values for 2000–13. Per capita amounts are expressed in constant 2005 U.S. dollars.

Figure 1.14 In SSA, Public Spending on Education and Health Is Lower in Oil-Rich Countries Than in Other Countries: Public Spending on Education and Health, Relative to Non–Resource-Rich SSA Countries, after Controlling for GNI per Capita

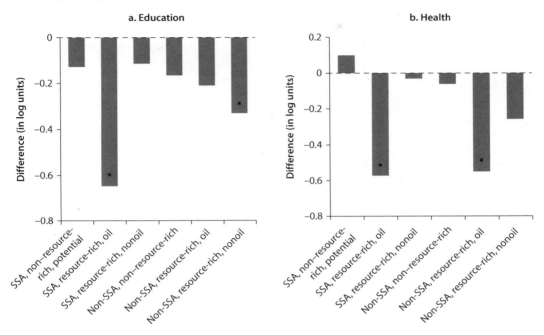

Note: SSA = Sub-Saharan Africa; GNI = gross national income. Figure reports coefficients from regression models, controlled for per capita GNI and its square. Reference category is non–resource-rich SSA countries. Significance level: * = 10 percent.

relationship between public spending in each country subgroup (for example, oil-rich SSA countries) and each outcome, in a model that controls for national per capita income, and additional variables that have been shown to be associated with outcomes and whose exclusion might lead to overinterpreting the role of public spending. The variables are income inequality (as measured by the Gini index), the extent of urbanization, ethnic and linguistic fractionalization (drawn from Alesina and others 2003), and the education of adult women in the population (drawn from Barro and Lee 2010), defined as average years of schooling of women ages 15 years and older (to guard against spurious associations, the model is estimated with and without this variable). In general, the findings are consistent with what has been documented elsewhere: there is little evidence that spending, on average, has systematic positive effects on outcomes.

Public spending per capita on education is associated with more children ages 6–14 years being in school and with more young persons ages 15–19 years having completed grade 6, but typically the magnitude of these associations is not statistically significantly different from zero (figure 1.15). For each percentage point increase in per capita education spending in a non–resource-rich SSA country, enrollment of children ages 6–14 years rises 1.2 percentage points, but more spending on education is not associated with more teenagers finishing grade 6.

The pattern for oil-rich SSA countries suggests that spending on education is significantly associated with higher enrollment, but not with grade 6 completion—a pattern that is starker for children from the poorest quintile. This is the pattern one might expect if spending increases with the number of students who attend school. But the spending is ineffective in that students fail to reach the end of the primary cycle in a timely fashion. In other (nonoil) resource-rich SSA countries, spending on education is not statistically significantly related to either school participation or grade 6 completion.

Public spending on health is likewise only weakly associated with better health outcomes (figure 1.16). In oil-rich SSA countries, a 1 percent increase in spending on health is not statistically significantly associated with lower infant mortality, better vaccination coverage, or less stunting—either overall or for children in the poorest quintile. In the nonoil resource-rich SSA countries, more spending appears to be associated with better vaccination coverage of

Figure 1.15 Public Spending on Education Is Not Associated with Statistically Significantly Higher Levels of Grade 6 Completion in Resource-Rich SSA Countries: Association between Public Spending on Education and Education Outcomes, Controlling for Other Factors

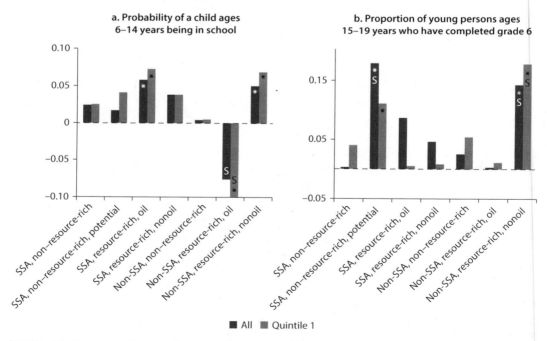

Note: SSA = Sub-Saharan Africa; GNI = gross national income. Figure reports coefficients from cross-country regression model of outcome on log of public spending on education (2000–13) in each country subgroup. Model controls for per capita GNI and its square and additional country-level variables. "S" indicates that the coefficient is significantly different from that in non–resource-rich SSA countries. Significance level: * = 10 percent.

Figure 1.16 Public Spending on Health Has Only a Weak Association with Better Health Indicators in Resource-Rich SSA Countries: Association between Public Spending on Health and Health Indicators, Controlling for Other Factors

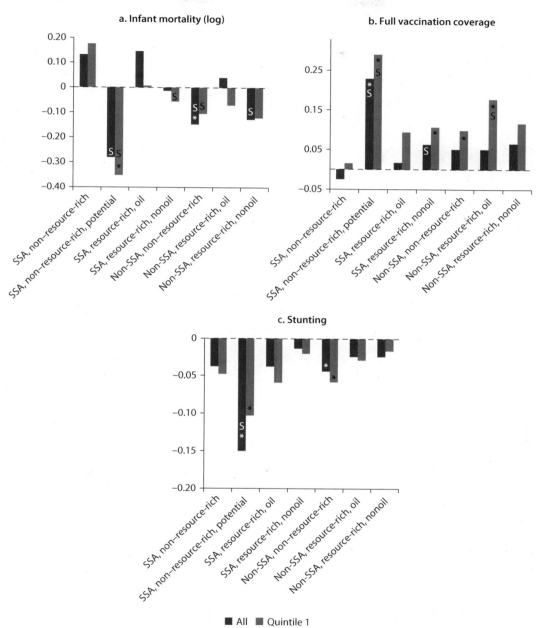

Note: SSA = Sub-Saharan Africa; GNI = gross national income. Figure reports coefficients from cross-county regression model of outcome on log of public spending on health (2000–13) in each country subgroup. Model controls for per capita GNI and its square, and additional country-level variables (see text). "S" indicates that the coefficient is significantly different from that in non–resource-rich SSA countries. Significance level: * = 10 percent.

children in the poorest quintile: a 1 percent increase in spending on health is associated with 10 percent higher vaccination coverage for these children.

Public spending on education or health in resource-rich SSA countries fails to translate systematically into sizable improvements in outcomes for either sector. While this is not inconsistent with findings from other parts of the world or with cross-country patterns documented elsewhere, it points to particular challenges for countries that have access to resources that could be invested in their people: the quality of spending is what ensures that investments translate into real improvements in human capital.

Conclusions

This chapter has shown that resource-rich countries in SSA fare poorly in terms of human capital outcomes, spend relatively little on trying to improve those outcomes, and, when they do spend, tend to get little for that investment. The next chapter makes the economic case for why countries should not give up on investing in human capital. Chapter 3 assesses the challenges confronting resource-rich countries in terms of delivering services to help to build human capital and emphasizes the vital roles of institutions, incentives, and information in overcoming those challenges. Chapter 4 then points to the types of investment that should be prioritized to get the highest returns—those that build a solid foundation of human capital that will make future investments more productive.

Notes

1. This chapter draws heavily on a more technical note prepared for this book (Filmer and Denisova 2015).

2. One of the features of resource-rich countries is that there is a gap between GNI per capita (derived from national accounts) and direct measures of per capita consumption on the basis of which poverty estimates are derived. This gap may be due to the different data sources, but household consumption is also an outcome of policies related to resource rent management. Analyses done for this book show that the share of consumption in GDP is lower in resource-rich countries. For example, in Sub-Saharan Africa in 2013, oil-rich countries had a 30 percentage point lower share of household consumption in GDP than non–resource-rich countries. Outside of Sub-Saharan Africa, this difference was 15 percentage points. This gap is a reason to assess the association between resources and national income as well as between resources and poverty.

3. Stijns (2006) argues that this finding is sensitive to the definitions used for natural resource abundance and for human capital. Nonetheless, he finds that the share of natural capital in national wealth and the share of minerals in exports tend to be negatively associated with schooling indicators.

4. Edwards (2015), using an instrumental variables strategy, shows that the negative impact of the size of the mining sector on human development outcomes is causal.

5. Specifically, each outcome (overall and for each quintile) is regressed on dummy variables for each subgroup, GNI per capita, and its square.

6. No SSA country has participated in the Programme for International Student Assessment (PISA) exercise or in the Progress in International Reading Literacy Study (PIRLS), except South Africa, which participated in PIRLS in 2006, but not in 2011.

7. These amounts are averages for 2000–13, expressed in 2005 U.S. dollars.

References

Africa Progress Panel. 2013. "Equity in Extractives: Stewarding Africa's Natural Resources for All." Africa Progress Report, Africa Progress Panel, Geneva, Switzerland.

Alesina, Alberto, Arnaud Devleeschauwer, William Easterly, Sergio Kurlat, and Romain Wacziarg. 2003. "Fractionalization." *Journal of Economic Growth* 8 (2): 155–94.

Baldacci, Emanuele, Benedict Clements, Sanjeev Gupta, and Qiang Cui. 2008. "Social Spending, Human Capital, and Growth in Developing Countries." *World Development* 36 (8): 1317–41.

Barma, Naazneen H., Kai Kaiser, Tuan Minh Le, and Lorena Viñuela. 2012. *Rents to Riches: The Political Economy of Natural Resource–Led Development.* Washington, DC: World Bank.

Barro, Robert, and Jong-Wha Lee. 2010. "A New Data Set of Educational Attainment in the World, 1950–2010." *Journal of Development Economics* 104 (C): 184–98.

Beegle, Kathleen, Luc Christiaensen, Andrew Dabalen, and Isis Gaddis. 2016. *Poverty in a Rising Africa: Africa Poverty Report.* Washington, DC: World Bank.

Bidani, Benu, and Martin Ravallion. 1997. "Decomposing Social Indicators Using Distributional Data." *Journal of Econometrics* 77 (1): 125–39.

Birdsall, Nancy, Thomas Pinckney, and Richard Sabot. 2001. "Natural Resources, Human Capital, and Growth." In *Resource Abundance and Economic Growth*, edited by R. M. Auty. Oxford University Press.

Bokhari, Farasat A. S., Yunwei Gai, and Pablo Gottret. 2007. "Government Health Expenditures and Health Outcomes." *Health Economics* 16 (3): 257–73.

Bravo-Ortega, Claudio, and José de Gregorio. 2007. "The Relative Richness of the Poor? Natural Resources, Human Capital, and Economic Growth." In *Natural Resources: Neither Curse nor Destiny*, edited by Daniel Lederman and William F. Maloney. Stanford, CA: Stanford University Press.

Christiaensen, Luc, and Shantayan Devarjan. 2013. "Making the Most of Africa's Growth." *Friends of Europe* (blog). http://www.friendsofeurope.org/Contentnavigation/Publications /Libraryoverview/tabid/1186/articleType/ArticleView/articleId/3534/Making-the-most -of-Africas-growth.aspx.

Chuhan-Pole, Punam. 2013. "Africa's Pulse (April 2013)." World Bank, Washington, DC.

———. 2014. "Africa's Pulse (April 2014)." World Bank, Washington, DC.

Dreher, Axel, Peter Nunnenkamp, and Rainer Thiele. 2008. "Does Aid for Education Educate Children? Evidence from Panel Data." *World Bank Economic Review* 22 (2): 291–314.

Edwards, Ryan B. 2015. "Mining Away the Preston Curve." *World Development* 78 (February): 22–36.

Filmer, Deon, and Anastasiya Denisova. 2015. "Human Capital in Resource-Rich Countries in Sub-Saharan Africa: Levels, Inequalities, and Spending." Background paper, World Bank, Washington, DC.

Filmer, Deon, and Louise Fox. 2014. *Youth Employment in Sub-Saharan Africa*. Africa Development Forum. Washington, DC: World Bank.

Filmer, Deon, and Lant Pritchett. 1999. "The Impact of Public Spending on Health: Does Money Matter?" *Social Science and Medicine* 49 (10): 1309–23.

Gylfason, Thorvaldur. 2001. "Natural Resources, Education, and Economic Development." *European Economic Review* 45 (4-6): 847–85.

IMF (International Monetary Fund). 2012. *Macroeconomic Policy Frameworks for Resource-Rich Developing Countries*. Washington, DC: IMF.

Lederman, Daniel, and William F. Maloney. 2007. *Natural Resources: Neither Curse Nor Destiny*. Stanford, CA: Stanford University Press.

Mullis, Ina V. S., Michael O. Martin, Pierre Foy, and Alka Arora. 2012. *TIMSS 2011 International Results in Mathematics*. Chestnut Hill, MA: TIMSS & PIRLS International Study Center; Amsterdam: International Association for the Evaluation of Educational Achievement.

Philippot, Louis-Marie. 2010. "Are Natural Resources a Curse for Human Capital Accumulation?" Centre d'Etudes et de Recherches sur le Développement International (CERDI), Izegem, Belgium.

Rajkumar, Andrew Sunil, and Vinaya Swaroop. 2008. "Public Spending and Outcomes: Does Governance Matter?" *Journal of Development Economics* 86 (1): 96–111.

Sachs, Jeffrey D., and Andrew M. Warner. 1999. "The Big Push, Natural Resource Booms and Growth." *Journal of Development Economics* 59 (1): 43–76.

———. 2001. "The Curse of Natural Resources." *European Economic Review* 45 (4-6): 827–38.

Stijns, Jean-Philippe. 2006. "Natural Resource Abundance and Human Capital Accumulation." *World Development* 34 (6): 1060–83.

UNDP (United Nations Development Programme). 2014. *Human Development Report 2014: Sustaining Human Progress—Reducing Vulnerabilities and Building Resilience*. New York: UNDP.

van der Ploeg, Frederick, and Anthony J. Venables. 2011. "Harnessing Windfall Revenues: Optimal Policies for Resource-Rich Developing Economies." *Economic Journal* 121 (551): 1–30.

Venables, Anthony J. 2016. "Using Natural Resources for Development: Why Has It Proven So Difficult?" *Journal of Economic Perspectives* 30 (1): 161–84.

Wagstaff, Adam, Caryn Bredenkamp, and Leander R. Buisman. 2014. "Progress toward the Health MDGs: Are the Poor Being Left Behind?" Policy Research Working Paper 6894, World Bank, Washington, DC.

World Bank. 2003. *World Development Report 2004: Making Services Work for Poor People*. Washington, DC: World Bank.

CHAPTER 2

An Economic Rationale for
Investing in Human Capital

Abstract

There are compelling economic arguments for governments to invest in the human capital of their people—limited access to credit narrows household choices, information failures distort investments, and spillover effects lead to suboptimal family investments. Lack of access to capital is one reason for governments to invest little in human capital—a problem that natural resource revenues can help to overcome. Investing in human capital should be an important part of the portfolio of investments using resource revenues—along with investing in infrastructure and saving through mechanisms, such as sovereign wealth funds, that allow countries to earn international rates of return on investments. A balanced portfolio is desirable, and investing in human capital has a special role to play in resource-rich settings—especially in poor countries—where the need for human capital and infrastructure investments is large. The indirect effects of enhancing human capital on reducing the incidence and cost of conflict are also a large part of the story.

Why Governments Should Invest in Human Capital

"Perfect Markets" as a Reference Point

When markets are functioning perfectly, households have a full range of choices about how to invest their disposable income. They can use their cash for consumption, savings, investing in education and training, and various other types of spending or investing. Since each type of spending has diminishing benefits, at least eventually, people would adjust their spending so that, as economists put it, the marginal returns are equalized across different types of spending. If markets were "perfect," an additional dollar spent on building human capital would yield the same return as the interest rate obtained through savings. If it were higher, households would increase their spending on skills acquisition (perhaps financed by borrowing) until the marginal return were equalized—and the ultimate household level of investment in human capital would be optimal.

In such perfect and complete markets, there would typically be no scope for the government to invest in building human capital, since households would behave optimally. However, markets are rarely perfect or complete. Indeed, the economic literature has identified several market "failures" that motivate public investments in human capital. This chapter reviews capital market failures, incomplete information, behavioral biases, and externalities.

Credit Constraints

Since private returns to human capital are high (box 2.1), it would seem inconceivable that households might choose not to send children to school. Even for very poor households, borrowing to invest in at least some years of education would be optimal. But financial markets are obviously not perfect, and studies

---

Box 2.1 Private Returns to Human Capital

While human capital is a broad concept that encompasses not only formal education but also skills, capabilities, and even health, estimating the effects of formal schooling has received the lion's share of scholarly attention. The literature on returns to education gives solid support to the notion that private returns are meaningful. A long economic tradition estimates private returns to education following a human capital approach and estimating so-called "Mincer regressions" that relate earnings to schooling and experience while controlling for a battery of factors (Becker 1975; Mincer 1958, 1974; Schultz 1960, 1961). Mincer regressions typically show large returns from education. For example, Psacharopoulos and Patrinos (2004) found that the average rate of return on an additional year of schooling is 10 percent and that the returns are especially high for primary education in low- and middle-income countries. Schultz (2004) and Filmer and Fox (2014), focusing specifically on Africa, found that returns increase at higher levels of education.

It is difficult to separate the effects of schooling on productivity from its signaling value. It could be that graduates of higher education do not earn more because of the productivity-enhancing skills they have learned but because their admission to prestigious schools acts as a signaling device for classifying whether individuals have high or low innate ability (Brown and Sessions 2004; Spence 1973). The use of "natural experiments" allows analysts to distinguish the two effects. Card (2001) surveyed the growing literature that draws on natural experiments for estimating the return to schooling and found that, in many cases, the returns are similar to those of traditional Mincer regressions. For example, the estimate of Leigh and Ryan (2008) for Australia is about 10 percent, in line with Mincer regression estimates for comparable countries. Ozier (2015) found that attaining secondary school in Kenya causally leads to a decrease in the probability of low-skill (and low-earning) self-employment and an increase in the probability of (higher-earning) formal employment.

Formal schooling is, of course, not the only way to raise human capital and earnings. A substantial literature shows that better nutrition for pregnant women and infants raises schooling

box continues next page

---

levels and economic productivity (Victora and others 2008). Strauss (1986), for example, found a very substantial positive impact of caloric intake on labor productivity in Sierra Leone. Further, comparing twins, Behrman and Rosenzweig (2004) and Black, Devereux, and Salvanes (2007) found that lower birthweight has a serious impact on future educational attainment and earnings. These findings suggest that government programs to promote sufficient and balanced nutrition during pregnancy can help to boost human capital and economic output. Weil (2007) used such microeconomic estimates from various sources to estimate aggregate returns to health. He found that eliminating health differences between countries would reduce the variance of gross domestic product (GDP) per worker by nearly a tenth.

Substantial scholarly attention has also been devoted to early childhood development. It has been found that both cognitive and noncognitive skills acquired in preschool significantly shape later education and labor market outcomes (Almond and Currie 2011). Several preschool intervention programs have had very high returns (Heckman 2006). For example, the Perry Preschool Program in the United States, which enrolled disadvantaged children starting at ages 3–4 and included both school programs and home visits, resulted in later-life higher scores on achievement tests, high school graduation, and homeownership and lower rates of receipt of welfare assistance, out-of-wedlock births, and arrests for crime. The economic return rates for the program were 15–17 percent. The Abecedarian Program, also in the United States, enrolled participants at only 4 months of age and provided intensive day-long child care. It was found to permanently raise intelligence quotient (IQ) scores and noncognitive skills. A long-run study in Jamaica showed that cognitive stimulation in early childhood resulted in substantial increases in earnings in adulthood (Gertler and others 2014), as did a nutritional intervention among severely stunted children in Guatemala (Hoddinott and others 2008).

---

show that households underinvest in education when capital markets are imperfect (Becker 1967; Cordoba and Ripoll 2013; Fiszbein and others 2009; Lochner and Monge-Naranjo 2012). Because poverty and inequality today can breed poverty and inequality tomorrow, state intervention may be desirable (Banerjee and Newman 1993; Galor and Zeira 1993).

The evidence is not only theoretical. Empirically, capital market frictions have been found to drive underinvestment in education (Lochner and Monge-Naranjo 2011). This has been shown for the United States (Carneiro and Heckman 2002) and for Mexico (Attanasio and Kaufmann 2009; Kaufmann 2014), as well as in an analysis of cross-country data (Flug, Spilimbergo, and Wachtenheim 1998). Borrowing constraints are a significant factor contributing to the large schooling-wealth gap in developing countries, with children from rich families much more likely to be enrolled at all levels of education (Filmer and Prichett 1999).

Incomplete Information

Though important, capital constraints are not likely to be the whole story. Even when returns on human capital are high, people may be reluctant to invest in it if they are poorly informed about its benefits. Indeed, inaccurate beliefs about the average returns to education seem to play a major role. For example, studies in Madagascar (Nguyen 2008) and the Dominican Republic (Jensen 2010) found that many young people drastically underestimate the returns to schooling, and this reduces school attendance. Disseminating information to correct this underestimate was effective at boosting enrollment rates in both countries.

Behavioral Biases

Even with appropriate information, people have behavioral biases that help account for underinvestment in human capital (see Fiszbein and others 2009 for a comprehensive discussion). An extreme case, "hyperbolic discounting," gives rise to a wide range of time-inconsistent behavior and self-control problems, such as procrastination. More concretely, when individuals put a much higher value on the present and a much lower value on the future, they tend to defer all actions that have high short-run costs and long-run gains, such as saving or investing in education. When tomorrow comes, the same distinction is made, and the individual continues to procrastinate (Akerlof 1991).

A related behavioral bias is "myopia," where individuals only take the next few periods into account in their decisions, ignoring implications that are far in the future. When individuals do not fully account for returns that will materialize in the future, they may opt not to invest in assets that have short-run costs and long-run gains, such as education or balanced nutrition.

While not strictly speaking a "behavioral bias," an additional factor affecting household investments in education is the distinction between the persons deciding on the investment (typically parents or guardians) and the direct beneficiaries of that investment (children themselves). To the extent that the parents' objectives are not perfectly aligned with those of their children—for example, they are not perfectly altruistic—then investment in human capital may not be optimal from the child's perspective (Becker 1991), and this perception may vary according to the sex and birth order of the child.

Externalities

Even where there are no credit constraints, incomplete information, or behavioral biases, optimizing individuals or families may underinvest in human capital if there are positive externalities to investment. Individuals balance the costs and benefits to themselves; they do not necessarily account for externalities—the benefits (or costs) to other people. If the externalities are positive, the level of investment will be socially suboptimal.

Research has documented a variety of positive externalities for education (Appiah and McMahon 2004; Lochner 2011; Moretti 2004a). Positive spillovers of being around educated people have not only been found in businesses (Moretti 2004b), but also within a local geographic area (Foster and Rosenzweig 1995; Moretti 2004a). Put differently, working next to somebody more educated not only boosts productivity within the firm but also has cross-firm spillovers arising through more efficient interactions and the spread of ideas.

In addition, some externalities are not strictly economic in nature. Four main types of externalities have been documented:

1. Higher education levels lead to better public health (Schultz 1999), lower fertility, and hence lower population growth rates (Grossman and Kaestner 1997). A substantial literature has highlighted such effects using "natural" or "quasi" experiments in developing countries. Unexpected increases in schooling age that have had different effects on different regions, age cohorts, or population groups have been used to study the effect of schooling on health and fertility outcomes in Indonesia, Malawi, Nigeria, and Uganda (Alsan and Cutler 2013; Behrman 2015; Duflo 2001; Osili and Long 2008). Clearly, rational individuals may take into account the effect of education on household fertility and health and the direct effect on them. However, having large families not only directly affects the households that make fertility decisions but also indirectly affects other households through the congestion costs of high fertility and high rates of population growth. For a recent review of fertility and its relationship to education in Sub-Saharan Africa (SSA), see Canning, Raja, and Yazbeck (2015). Similarly, if education leads to healthier people who do not transmit infectious diseases to others, ignoring this positive externality will, from a social point of view, lead to underinvestment in health-promoting assets such as education or balanced nutrition.

2. Education has also been consistently found to decrease crime rates (Currie 2001; Lochner and Moretti 2004; Schweinhart 2004). One channel driving this effect is the higher opportunity cost of forgone work income when educated individuals choose to spend time in criminal activities. When fewer people become criminals, the negative externalities of crime on the rest of the population are lower. Also, the values transmitted through socialization in school can operate to reduce crime.

3. Education promotes civic values and good citizenship (Dee 2004; Milligan, Moretti, and Oreopoulos 2004). Educated people vote more often and participate more intensively in civic associations, which may help to foster society-wide social capital. It is not just the amount of schooling that matters for building social capital; the content of education is also crucial: teaching practices have a considerable impact on social capital (Algan, Cahuc, and Shleifer 2013).

4. The likelihood of civil conflict has been found to be lower when education levels are higher (Barakat and Urdal 2009; Collier and Hoeffler 2004; Østby and Urdal 2010; Thyne 2006). As discussed later in more detail, multiple channels link education to conflict. The essential point here is that when individuals select their education levels, they do not take into account the effect their choices may have on society as a whole—in this case, through lowering the likelihood of armed fighting. There are externalities to conflict from better health as well. Indeed, worse health (proxied by high exposure to infectious diseases) has been found to increase the risk of conflict (Cervellati, Sunde, and Valmori 2014).

Why Governments Do Not Invest More in Human Capital

If public investment in human capital is indeed good policy, why is such investment insufficient? Again, in a world of perfect capital markets, the state would compute the level of human capital investment that equalizes the marginal returns to one additional dollar invested in human capital and the international interest rate. If a country had too little domestic resources to achieve this level of investment, it would borrow to finance it; if a country had excess resources, it would select the same optimal level of human capital investment and lend the surplus money on international markets. In such a frictionless world, one would expect all countries to be at their optimal level of human capital investment, and the rents made available from natural resources would not affect the observed level of human capital. Resource-poor countries would be borrowers and resource-rich countries would be lenders, but both would always reach their optimal investment in human capital.

However, the world is not frictionless. Two specific frictions lead to substantial underinvestment in human capital: credit constraints (at the national level) and poor governance.

Credit Constraints

Not all countries have equal access to international credit markets, and many—especially those with poor records of credit repayment—are severely cash-constrained. Once it reaches its borrowing limit, even a benevolent government may not be able to invest the optimal amount in human capital. When borrowing constraints are binding, a discovery of natural resources may relax budget constraints enough that a government can invest more in human capital (Van der Ploeg 2011). This implies that, in a world where credit markets are imperfect, the relationship between resource revenues and human capital investments will be positive.

Poor Governance

As discussed in chapter 1, however, resource-rich SSA countries do not invest more in human capital, even though they have the funds to do so; borrowing limits cannot be the full story. Countries with poor governance and high corruption tend to have greater discrepancies in what is earmarked for human capital investments and what is actually invested. For example, one expenditure tracking survey found that virtually no funds dedicated to health in Chad made it to the facility level (Gauthier and Wane 2005). Hence, even if there are no borrowing constraints, underinvestment in human capital can occur if governance is poor. Unfortunately, if anything, resource discoveries may exacerbate existing governance problems, as discussed in more detail in chapter 3 of this book (see also Ross 2001, 2012).

Natural Resource Revenues and Investment in Human Capital

The previous section describes why a government might want to invest in human capital and why investment might be low even when fiscal space is not an issue. This section assesses the factors that influence the trade-off between using resource revenues to invest in human capital and in other types of investment.

It starts from the perspective of a government acting as a "benevolent social planner" that maximizes social welfare and then accounts for situations where the government has other objectives.

Studies of how to invest resource revenues (surveyed by Bannon and Collier 2003 and Barma and others 2012) are still relatively rare. While some research has been done on the optimal speed of resource extraction (for example, van der Ploeg and Rohner 2012) and on investment options in resource-rich countries (van der Ploeg and Venables 2011), these studies do not take into account the option of investing in human capital. Theoretical analysts have used a so-called overlapping generations model framework (box 2.2) or dynamic stochastic general equilibrium (DSGE) modeling (box 2.3) to provide insights into these questions.

Box 2.2 Modeling Natural Resources and Human Capital across Generations

One of the key objectives for policy in countries with high levels of natural resources is to enable a finite resource to support improvements in income and welfare over a long time horizon—in particular, beyond the current generation. As described in this book, higher levels of human capital reverberate across generations: higher levels of education of parents lead to higher levels of education and health among children, and higher levels of health among parents lead to better outcomes among children.

Economists have developed theoretical models that include multiple "overlapping generations" in order to understand how natural resources might affect the incentives to accumulate human capital and how this affects growth and levels of welfare attained over the long term. Different analysts specify models differently, but the models typically break a generation's life span into two or three periods. In early periods, a generation invests in human capital, works and saves, and, in late periods, consumes its savings. The models are then used to explore and understand particular features. Different studies have emphasized alternative aspects of these relationships.

Papyrakis and Gerlagh (2006) develop a model that seeks to illustrate how natural resource wealth crowds out other forms of investment—ultimately resulting in lower long-term welfare. Their model focuses mostly on investment in physical capital, but includes the feature that human capital is more productive at higher levels of physical capital. This sets in motion a positive feedback loop, in which higher returns to human capital lead to more investment in human capital on the part of individuals (and their families). They show, however, that natural-resource-rich countries tend to have lower levels of investment, setting in motion a negative feedback loop that results in lower human capital investment and, ultimately, low levels of long-term welfare. A companion empirical study (Papyrakis and Gerlagh 2004) estimates that a 10 percent higher level of resource income decreases long-term income by 60 percent, about half of which is because of lower levels of investment. Frederiksen (2008) extends the approach and explicitly models the role of intergenerational altruism and bequests. She shows that, when bequests are low (either because of low levels of altruism or because of policy), then policies that direct transfers to the current generation lead to lower savings and investment and, ultimately, a "resource curse" (Sachs and Warner 2001).

box continues next page

Box 2.2 Modeling Natural Resources and Human Capital across Generations *(continued)*

Valente (2007) develops an overlapping generations model that incorporates two features. First, human capital is a substitute for natural resources in production; second, there are intergenerational spillovers in human capital. The key policy decisions in this model are the speed of extraction of the finite resource and the degree of public investment in human capital. According to the model, if the discount rate is relatively low (that is, the welfare of future generations matters a lot to the social planner), the optimal strategy is to invest heavily in human capital and to extract the natural resource at a slow pace. In the words of Valente (2007), "Knowledge formation and resource preservation are thus complementary targets."

Araji and Mohtadi (2014) model the situation in which natural resource rents are distributed to individuals as lump-sum transfers. Their model suggests that the transfers reduce the expected returns to human capital in the long run, thereby reducing the incentive to invest in what they term "professional" human capital (in contrast to "entrepreneurial" human capital) in the short run. According to their overlapping generations modeling, when levels of technology are low (and therefore the current return to professional human capital is low), the transfers and disincentives result in a low-level equilibrium, with low levels of income in the long run. High-technology economies avoid this trap because the return to professional human capital is sufficiently high that the incentive for investment remains. Araji and Mohtadi (2014) support their argument empirically by showing that countries with both natural resources and high levels of transfers tend to have lower public spending on tertiary education.

Box 2.3 Using Dynamic Stochastic General Equilibrium Modeling to Guide Investments

Low-income, capital-scarce economies with financial and fiscal constraints face severe challenges in managing revenues from newly found natural resources. They face demands for scaling up public investment to meet public infrastructure needs and high risks of rising public sector deficits and Dutch disease—all in an uncertain world characterized by a high occurrence of shocks and price volatility.

DSGE modeling can be used to provide insights into how to invest effectively. Specifying a small, open economy DSGE model, consistent with low-income African economies, and calibrating it with Ugandan data yield the following implications:

1. When public capital is almost unproductive, it is best to save the resource income in a sovereign wealth fund (SWF) for future generations.
2. The model considers three stylized fiscal policy approaches for managing a resource windfall: (a) investing all in public capital, (b) saving all in an SWF, and (c) taking a "sustainable-investing" approach, which proposes directing a constant share of the resource's revenues to finance public investment and saving the rest in an SWF. The gradual scaling-up of public investment (option c) yields the best outcomes, as it minimizes macroeconomic volatility.
3. When the objective is to minimize the volatility of three separate macroeconomic aggregates—private consumption, private investment, and total employment—the

box continues next page

Box 2.3 Using Dynamic Stochastic General Equilibrium Modeling to Guide Investments *(continued)*

volatility function has a convex shape. If the objective is to minimize private consumption volatility, then the model suggests that the optimal portfolio would save 30 percent of resource income in an SWF; to minimize private investment volatility, the share would be 25 percent; and to minimize total employment volatility, the share would be 15 percent.

4. The optimal oil share to be saved in an SWF decreases with the persistence of the oil shock, suggesting that the optimal share to be saved should decrease with production.

Source: Kopoin and others 2016.

Alternatives to Investing in Human Capital

Infrastructure Spending: Buying Bridges Rather Than Books

The economic logic of infrastructure spending is very similar to that of human capital investment. The direct return on infrastructure investments—such as building roads, bridges, and airports—is positive but decreasing, as is true for human capital. It starts out high when existing infrastructure is very poor and then drops until, at some point, it becomes lower than the international interest rate. From then on, investments in infrastructure yield lower marginal returns than the opportunity cost of placing funds in international capital markets.

Several recent studies have advocated that countries with poor infrastructure should invest at least part of their windfall gains in physical infrastructure (Collier and others 2010; van der Ploeg and Venables 2011).

Sovereign Wealth Funds: Saving Instead of Schooling

The idea of putting a substantial share of resource wealth into an SWF has gained support in recent years among academics and policy makers. In terms of its economic nature, an SWF boils down to investing money on international capital markets, with expected yields corresponding to the exogenously determined international interest rate. The marginal returns on SWFs are constant and equal to the international interest rate—unlike the returns to investments in physical or human capital, which decline as the level of infrastructure or human capital increases.

There are a variety of economic, fiscal, and political economy reasons to establish an SWF (Davis and others 2001; Davis, Ossowski, and Fedelino 2003; Humphreys and Sandbu 2007; Truman 2011). Putting money in an SWF enables a country to smooth resource windfalls, which can fluctuate widely over time (because of either prices or reserves). As a savings vehicle, an SWF makes it possible to spread the gains from resource revenues over several generations.

One major advantage invoked is also that an SWF is beyond the immediate reach of the government in power, which lowers the risk that resource revenues will be appropriated by the leaders. This argument, however, is controversial. One can well imagine current or future government officials abolishing the SWF and redirecting the funds for their own benefit (Rodríguez, Morales, and Monaldi 2012). That SWFs will protect windfalls from elite appropriation is thus uncertain, especially when opposition governments reaching power do not feel bound by the decisions of former rulers or in states suffering from widespread corruption.

Direct Dividends: Decentralizing Decision Making to Individuals

Chapters 3 and 4 of this report discuss the role that cash transfers—conditional or unconditional—can play in building human capital. These types of transfers have been shown to reduce poverty and to encourage families to invest more in building the human capital of their children (Fiszbein and others 2009). Cash transfers have also been discussed explicitly as a way of sharing revenues from natural resources with the population as a whole. The goal of such "direct dividends" is to distribute resource revenues to citizens, who then use the dividends as they see fit and pay taxes on them (Devarajan and Giugale 2013; Moss 2011; Sala-i-Martin and Subramanian 2013). If individuals have investment options that mirror those of an SWF (that is, fixed return given by international interest rates), one could treat investment portfolios with direct dividends as very similar to those operated by an SWF—from the standpoint of economic logic and in a frictionless world.

This does not, however, mean that direct dividends are more or less equivalent to an SWF. From an investment portfolio point of view, they may be similar if (1) all people are fully rational and knowledgeable about finance and investments and (2) the government is a benevolent social planner that makes investments in the best interests of its citizens. However, neither assumption is likely to hold. Individuals may be myopic, not feel perfectly altruistic to their offspring, or be badly informed. And governments may pursue agendas that are not necessarily those of a benevolent social planner (Ross 2012).

It has been argued that direct dividends give governments incentives to improve. According to the line of political science research that studies "rentier states" (Mahdavy 1970; Baland and François 2000), one of the main difficulties with very-resource-rich governments is that they command enough revenues to keep the state running and do not need to democratize to gain enough popular support to raise taxes. Direct dividends could break this vicious cycle because they are taxable. Hence, to get part of the money back, a state needs to trade representation for taxation. Advocates of direct dividends hope that this trade could bring a major improvement in governance.

Human Capital and the Alternatives

To be able to assess how desirable it is to channel additional funds into human capital formation, it is necessary to compare the returns to human capital formation with the returns to the main alternatives—particularly if the goal of investment is to "achieve optimal and equitable outcomes, for current and future generations."[1] This section first outlines the basic economic characteristics of the main investment options, then discusses complementarity issues, and closes with a summary of political economy concerns that affect the comparison of ways to invest resource windfalls.[2]

To summarize the points so far: human capital and infrastructure investments both start out with high marginal returns at low initial stocks; but as these marginal returns decline, the larger the stocks of human capital and infrastructure grow.[3] In contrast, the marginal returns of SWF investments (and perhaps those of invested direct dividends) are constant and driven by international capital markets. The basic logic of building a portfolio composed of different assets suggests that the marginal returns of all investment options should be equalized in equilibrium. Hence, investments in human capital should take place as long as the returns are higher than the constant returns from investments in international capital markets. Figure 2.1 illustrates this basic logic. The x-axis reflects the resource windfalls available to invest, and the vertical axis corresponds to the marginal returns of two options for capital investment; the returns from human capital investments are plotted from left to right, and those from infrastructure investments are plotted from right to left.

As illustrated in figure 2.1, in such a situation it would typically be preferable to make all three types of investments: given decreasing marginal returns, the optimal mix is achieved when the marginal returns of all three are equalized. Thus, a country with high amounts of physical capital but very little human capital would benefit from shifting some resources from physical to human capital

Figure 2.1 The Rationale for an Optimal Investment Portfolio

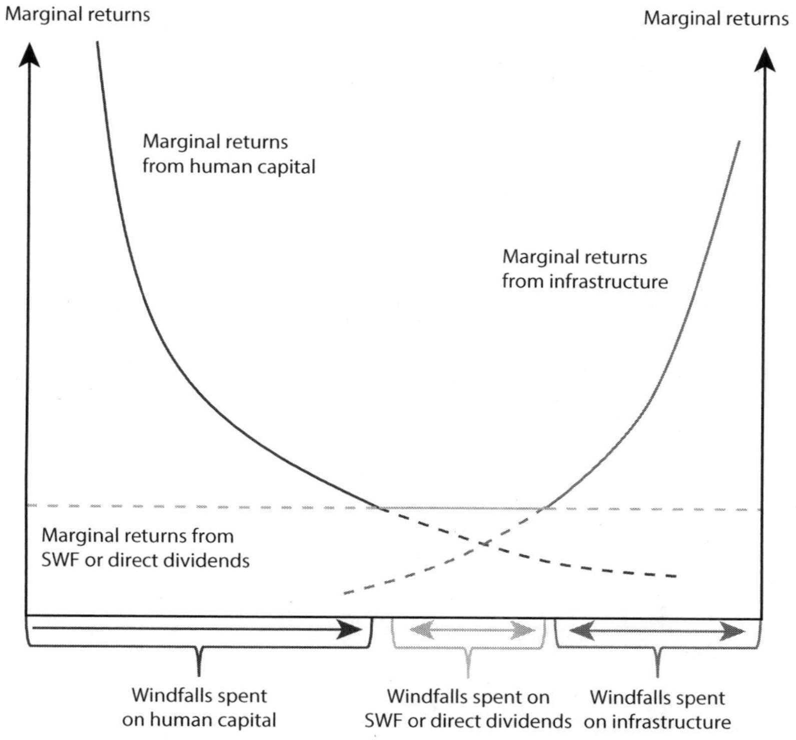

Note: SWF = sovereign wealth fund.

investments, and a country with high human capital but a complete lack of physical infrastructure would be better off doing the opposite.

The next question is what may be different in a country with initially very low levels of both human capital and physical infrastructure that has relatively small resource windfalls. This case reflects the situation of an initially poor country that suddenly discovers substantial but limited natural resource deposits.

Figure 2.2 illustrates the case: the shape of the marginal return curves for human capital, infrastructure, and the SWF is the same as in figure 2.1, but there is less resource revenue, reflected by the fact that the figure is narrower (the length of the x-axis corresponds to the resource money available). Given that investable resource cash is fairly limited in this situation, the marginal return curves of human and physical capital intersect above the international interest rate line (that is, the returns from investing in the SWF), which means that the marginal returns of human capital and physical infrastructure always lie above the opportunity cost of international capital market returns. In this case, it is best to channel all natural resource cash into human capital and physical infrastructure improvements and to defer investing in an SWF.

A central point of this analysis is that, in countries with little physical or human capital, it may be optimal to invest domestically rather than abroad

Figure 2.2 Optimal Portfolio Composition for a Less Resource-Rich Country

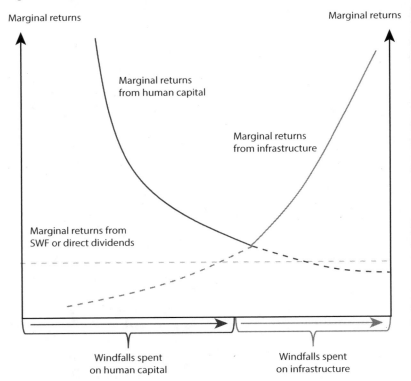

Note: SWF = sovereign wealth fund.

(see the formal models by van der Ploeg and Venables 2011 for physical infra-structure and by Rohner 2014 for human capital and physical infrastructure).

As figures 2.1 and 2.2 illustrate, the share of natural resource rents that should be invested in the various options (human capital, infrastructure, international markets) will depend on several factors. Key will be the relative shape of the marginal returns to investments in each option (which, in the case of human capital and infrastructure, will also depend on their initial levels) and, as the dif-ference between figures 2.1 and 2.2 illustrates, the size of the resource rents. Given the large number of variables, it is hard to draw implications that would be valid across all contexts. The economic modeling underpinning this discussion (described by Rohner 2014) suggests that, at lower levels of mineral wealth, countries should prioritize human capital, while, at higher levels of mineral wealth, countries should diversify, notably in infrastructure. But even this impli-cation should be taken with some caution because it relies on assumptions that may not be met in all situations.

Complementarity between Investing in Both Human Capital and Infrastructure

Figures 2.1 and 2.2 abstract from complementarities between human and physi-cal capital. This makes sense in situations where the complementarities are rela-tively small (that is, where the elasticity of substitution of the factors of production is large). In many situations, however, the complementarities between human capital and physical infrastructure may be large—higher levels of human capital boost the returns from spending on infrastructure and, similarly, infra-structure increases the returns on human capital investments.

The main logic is very similar to what is shown in figure 2.1. The marginal returns on human capital and physical infrastructure still start out very high and then decrease, and the optimal mix equalizes the marginal returns to all invest-ment options. Complementarity means that the marginal return curve for human capital investments shifts upward with more improvements in physical capital, and the marginal return curve for physical capital shifts upward when human capital is higher. Both of these forces shift the optimal portfolio mix toward human and physical capital and away from international investment schemes, such as an SWF.

This complementarity is illustrated in figure 2.3, which is structured like figures 2.1 and 2.2. The left downward-sloped curve still corresponds to the mar-ginal returns of human capital (H), and the right downward-sloped curve cap-tures the marginal returns of physical capital (K). The starting point is a situation where the resource cash has been obtained, but where there is some investment in an SWF and in physical capital, but not yet in human capital. At this point, the marginal return curves are still relatively low (represented by the dotted lines). Then, some resources are invested in human capital (1). Through the complementarity, this results in an upward shift of the marginal return curve for physical capital (2). This implies that the optimal level of physical capital invest-ments rises, which in turns leads to an upward shift of the marginal return curve

Figure 2.3 Complementarities between Human and Physical Capital

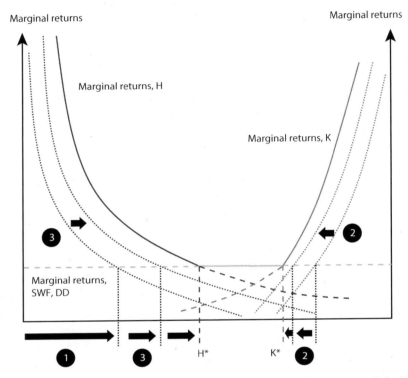

Note: DD = direct dividend; H = human capital; K = physical capital (infrastructure); and SWF = sovereign wealth fund.

for human capital (3). The country should now also increase the amount invested in human capital, which again pushes upward the marginal returns from physical capital, and so on. There are ever smaller upward shifts of both marginal return curves until equilibrium is reached, as represented by the two solid marginal return curves and the equilibrium investment amounts of human and physical capital (H* and K*, respectively).

The Role of Political Economy

For each investment option, feasibility is the main consideration. Certainly, all investment options that imply direct state intervention rise and fall with the quality and reliability of the state; the best policies can go awry when the governance environment is not conducive to effective or efficient implementation (chapter 3).

While public investment projects require management by civil servants—whose performance will be influenced by the governance environment—investing in an SWF or providing direct dividends may seem less amenable to corruption. Indeed, the experience of the República Bolivariana de Venezuela shows that governments can "raid" SWFs for their own purposes; the SWF, which was designed to guarantee majority control by the president, became a means for him to spend at his discretion and bypass normal budgetary procedures (Rodríguez, Morales, and Monaldi 2012). Media reports regarding other so-called "oil funds" suggest that these are often ripe targets for corruption.

While direct dividends money may not be subject to the same distortions as investments that have a substantial service delivery component, they may also be reoriented by rent-seeking civil servants. The political economy of how direct dividends are distributed can become an issue in itself. In Mongolia, popular pressure led politicians to offer very large transfers that resulted in half of national income being earmarked for distribution; this was more than the government had received in resource revenues (Collier 2013).

Violent Conflict: Human Capital Investment and Political Instability

Violent conflicts play a crucial role in many developing countries, and ignoring the ensuing instability could potentially lead to misguided advice (Collier and others 2003). Considering that many natural-resource-producing states suffer from political instability and violent conflict (box 2.4) and that natural resources have a substantial impact on conflict (box 2.5), it is important to take into account the risk of conflict when analyzing the relative virtues of human capital investments in resource-rich economies. Indeed, introducing the potential for armed rebellion and violent conflict into the framework outlined here suggests an additional rationale for such investments.

Violent civil conflict can be thought of as costly appropriation.[4] An opposition group forms a rebellion and tries to appropriate valuable resources. Conflict can induce inefficiencies in two main ways: (1) actors can distort their decisions to decrease the scope for appropriation, and (2) conflict has direct costs, such as the

---

Box 2.4 Natural Resources and Conflict

In recent decades, civil wars have increasingly been recognized as one of the major obstacles to development. Between 1945 and the end of the twentieth century, an estimated 16.2 million people died in 127 civil wars (Fearon and Laitin 2003). Poor countries were, and still are, hit particularly hard: 20 of the world's 34 poorest countries are affected by armed conflict (OECD 2009). According to Collier (2007, 27), "Civil war tends to reduce growth by around 2.3 percent per year, so the typical seven-year war leaves a country around 15 percent poorer than it would have been."

The theoretical literature on natural resources and conflict aims to distinguish the channels that make resource windfalls raise the risk of armed fighting. In particular, it has been argued that (1) resource revenues drive up the motivation for investing in fighting by increasing the "pie" that is up for appropriation (recent work includes Caselli and Coleman 2013; Esteban, Morelli, and Rohner 2015; Rohner, Thoenig, and Zilibotti 2013a); (2) resource abundance

box continues next page

Box 2.4 Natural Resources and Conflict *(continued)*

weakens state capacity because the state has less incentive to build legal and fiscal capacity (Besley and Persson 2011; Fearon 2005); (3) capturing resource rents relaxes rebels' borrowing constraints and makes armed rebellion financially feasible (Berman and others 2015; Collier, Hoeffler, and Rohner 2009; Fearon 2004; Guidolin and La Ferrara 2007; Nunn and Qian 2014); and (4) the unequal geographic distribution of natural resource deposits fuels the risk of secessionism and interstate wars (Caselli, Morelli, and Rohner 2015).

The empirical literature on natural resources and conflict has shown that the outbreaks and duration of conflicts are linked to the abundance of primary commodities in general (Collier and Hoeffler 2004; Collier, Hoeffler, and Rohner 2009); the presence of oil and natural gas (Dube and Vargas 2013; Fearon and Laitin 2003; Humphreys 2005; Lei and Michaels 2014; Morelli and Rohner 2015; Ross 2006), and deposits of diamonds and precious minerals (Aragon and Rud 2013; Berman and others 2015; Humphreys 2005; Lujala, Gleditsch, and Gilmore 2005; Ross 2006).

Box 2.5 Angola: Conflict, Natural Resource Wealth, and Low Human Development Outcomes

Angola is the second-largest producer of oil in Africa, and oil exports drive the country's economy (about 95 percent of total exports). Oil was first discovered in 1955, and large-scale extraction began in the 1960s. The state-owned oil company Sonangol has controlled the sector since 1976. Besides petroleum products, Angola is also the world's fifth-largest producer of diamonds (in value). More recently, large natural gas deposits have been identified, although the production of liquefied natural gas has been slow to take off.

Political stability and economic growth in Angola came only recently—in 2002. The war for independence from Portugal lasted from 1961 to 1974, and it was followed immediately by 27 years of civil war. Since 2002, Angola has achieved considerable economic growth; by 2012 gross national income (GNI) per capita was US $6,258 (in purchasing power parity terms)—almost triple what it was in 2002. Extreme dependence on oil makes the country vulnerable to volatility in commodity prices. This became evident in 2009, when a fall in real GDP—resulting from a fall in oil prices during the 2008 global financial crisis—led the country to seek assistance in a standby arrangement from the International Monetary Fund.

The civil war in Angola claimed about 1 million lives, displaced more than 4 million people, and decimated infrastructure and basic service provision. Since then, the government has made sustained efforts to rebuild its physical infrastructure. Spending on health, education, and social protection programs has accounted for more than 30 percent of the budget in recent years. But this spending has not been associated with good outcomes. The under-5 mortality rate is 164 deaths per 1,000 births, which is very high for a country at this level of income. While 85 percent of children of primary school age are enrolled in school, only 45 percent complete primary education. The secondary-level enrollment rate is currently only 32 percent. Despite the fact that 11 percent of fiscal receipts were allocated to social protection in the 2013

box continues next page

Box 2.5 Angola: Conflict, Natural Resource Wealth, and Low Human Development Outcomes
(continued)

budget, the social safety net system remains fragmented and limited in scope and suffers from inefficient targeting of beneficiaries.

The long history of armed conflict has made the country's path toward transparent and accountable governance difficult. Oil revenues were used throughout the civil war by the Popular Movement for the Liberation of Angola to fund its activities, while the rival National Union for the Total Independence of Angola used diamond sales for the same purpose. While Sonangol has remained a robust institution in Angola's economy and politics, it has frequently been used for political funding and patronage.[a]

Angola has low scores for the transparency of its budget, receiving a score of 28 out of 100 on the Open Budget Index in 2012 (classified as providing "minimal" information). The government publishes an executive budget proposal, an enacted budget, and year-end reports, but it does not produce a citizen's budget or a midyear review. While a prebudget statement, in-year reports, and audit reports are produced for internal use, they are not made public. The legislature has limited oversight powers, with no ability to hold open discussions on the budget. Corruption is frequently reported as a problem in business and politics. The country ranked very low on Transparency International's 2013 Corruption Perception Index, at 153rd out of 177 countries.

a. In 2011, the International Monetary Fund reported that Sonangol spent US$32 billion on "quasi-fiscal" activities on behalf of the government.

---

destruction costs of fighting and the opportunity costs of the rebels' forgone production. The discussion that follows starts with the distortions caused by the fact that people try to protect their income and then moves to the more direct effects and how human capital helps to avert some of these inefficiencies.

Conflict Appropriation as a Tax on Investments

Consider first the case of a fixed risk of appropriation, which, however, varies with different types of assets. The effects of such an exogenous political risk on business are similar to a tax rate that varies by type of investment. For example, presumably, it would be harder to appropriate economic production than liquid assets such as those in an SWF. While financial assets can be transferred relatively easily and hence appropriated, it is harder to hide economic output to protect it from appropriation. Also, short of slavery, it is hard to appropriate people's human capital (Acemoglu and Wolitzky 2011), and, when too large a part of earned income is confiscated, people tend to work less. Thus, the worse the political instability, the relatively more attractive it becomes to channel resource windfalls into productive investments, such as building up human or physical capital. In other words, leaving political instability and conflict appropriation out of the picture would underestimate the optimal level of human capital investment. The fact that human capital investments flow into relatively hard-to-appropriate assets such as domestic economic output makes them an even more attractive option in an investment portfolio where there is political instability and conflict risk.

Human Capital as a Conflict Deterrent

While treating political risk as fixed yields a simple intuition about some of the mechanisms at work, it is important to ask what drives rebellion. Potential rebels choose whether to spend their time working or fighting. Depending on the relative returns from productive versus appropriative activities, incentives will push rebels toward more or less fighting effort, which determines the intensity of conflict and political instability.

Appropriation is typically a negative-sum game. The "pie" to be appropriated becomes smaller when fewer people work and more engage in appropriation; moreover, combat operations may physically destroy part of the pie. Thus, economic output declines due to both (1) the opportunity cost of spending time on unproductive appropriation activities, which leads to forgone production, and (2) direct destruction in combat. If building human capital can reduce the incentives to fight, it can indirectly enhance productivity by reducing rent dissipation from conflict.

Empirical studies of conflict have indeed found that welfare expenditures are associated with a lower risk of conflict (Bodea, Higashijima, and Singh 2016); education reduces the risk of civil war (Barakat and Urdal 2009; Collier and Hoeffler 2004; Østby and Urdal 2010; Thyne 2006); and where people suffer from poor health, there is more scope for conflict (Cervellati, Sunde, and Valmori 2014). Human capital can reduce the scope for conflict and the level of political instability through three channels, which are discussed next (Rohner 2014). Human capital investment lowers the potential spoils from looting and raises the opportunity cost of fighting; education may raise the "moral costs" of fighting.

Human Capital Investment and Potential Spoils from Looting

Human capital contributes to the production of economic output, which is less appropriable than cash or financial assets. Hence, when more windfall money is transformed into human capital, the pie that successful rebels can appropriate shrinks.

Even when economic production collapses, looting potential remains. When war completely ravages some parts of a country, economic activity in the region may collapse and, whenever possible, successful rebels plunder the factors of production. When a factor of production has a high so-called "scrap value," such as infrastructure made of copper that can be sold at world market prices, potential rebels have greater looting potential and hence incentives for conflict. Given the difficulty of appropriating human capital, its scrap value is basically zero (Acemoglu and Wolitzky 2011).

Human capital investments not only lead to better outcomes for the current generation but also beget further accumulation of human capital in the generation that follows (box 2.6). This future human capital is also hard to appropriate and has a low scrap value, so human capital investments today lower looting opportunities in the long as well as the short runs.

Box 2.6 The Effect of Parents' Education on the Education of Their Children

It has long been known that a close association exists between the level of parents' education and that of their children. In recent years, a growing literature has been studying the question of whether this association is a simple correlation driven by unobservable confounding factors, such as genetically transmitted innate ability, or whether there is a causal effect. The approaches to studying this question can be classified into three groups:

1. Comparing twins who have different levels of education and who may nurture their own offspring differently (for example, Behrman and Rosenzweig 2002).
2. Estimating intergenerational education spillovers using adoptees, who do not share the same genetic pool as their families (for example, Bjorklund, Lindahl, and Plug 2006; Plug 2004; Sacerdote 2007).
3. Using educational reforms to characterize shocks to education attainment (for example, Black, Devereux, and Salvanes 2005).

The survey article by Holmlund, Lindahl, and Plug (2011) concludes that the growing body of studies aiming for a causal explanation shows a significant and robust effect of parents' education on their children's educational attainment; for the Scandinavian countries, the causal estimate is about 0.1, suggesting that an additional year of parents' schooling increases their children's schooling by one-tenth of an additional year.

Human Capital and the Opportunity Cost of Fighting

Robust public programs for human capital formation that reach all parts of society can result in a general, society-wide increase in human capital. Higher human capital boosts economic output, and thus the returns citizens receive from production. In an economy with higher human capital, working is more attractive, and the opportunity cost of giving up productive work to engage in rebellion is much higher. As stressed in the "feasibility" theory of conflict (Collier, Hoeffler, and Rohner 2009), it is much cheaper, and hence much more feasible, to put together a rebel organization in a poor country with high unemployment than in a rich country with an educated, skilled, and healthy workforce.

Empirical studies have shown that civil war participation is fueled by low opportunity costs for productive work. For example, when bad weather drives down agricultural productivity, rebel recruiting and armed combat operations surge (Hidalgo and others 2010; Jia 2014; König and others 2015; Miguel, Satyanath, and Sergenti 2004; Vanden Eynde 2011).

Education and the Moral Costs of Fighting

Schooling transmits not only knowledge but also values of cooperation and social norms (Algan, Cahuc, and Shleifer 2013); the values transmitted in the schoolroom may well foster peace. Education that emphasizes tolerance and cooperation can significantly reduce the scope for armed conflict (Davies 2003). The intellectual "enlightenment" and capacity for self-reflection transmitted through education may well sharpen the sense of moral wrongdoing and generate, at least

From Mines and Wells to Well-Built Minds • http://dx.doi.org/10.1596/978-1-4648-1005-3

in some cases, higher moral costs of engaging in violent fighting. While there is relatively little rigorous evidence at the micro level that education, on average, makes people less conflict-prone in politically unstable countries, there is indirect evidence that this conclusion is plausible. For instance, it has been found that educational attainment fosters good citizenship (see, for example, Dee 2004; Milligan, Moretti, and Oreopoulos 2004) and that educated individuals display much lower propensities for racism and much higher tolerance for people from other groups (Hainmueller and Hiscox 2007; Hodson, Sekulic, and Massey 1994).

Moreover, if education also transmits values of tolerance, intercultural exchange, and the knowledge of several national languages, it can help to raise levels of interethnic trust and social capital in a society. Several recent studies have found that interethnic trust is indeed crucial to curb the incentives for civil war; higher trust goes along with more intensive interethnic business dealings, which increase the opportunity cost of ethnic conflict (Rohner 2011; Rohner, Thoenig, and Zilibotti 2013a, 2013b).

However, schooling per se is not a panacea. In some countries and at some points in time, public schooling has been used to enforce the hegemony of a powerful group within society. The dynamics that this engenders can lead to greater tension and even contribute to conflict, as in apartheid-era South Africa.

Conflict Reduction, Human Capital, and Other Investment Options

How do these channels affect the trade-off between investing in human capital and the alternatives? First, take the case of an SWF. In terms of the three channels discussed, higher human capital stocks make a country less conflict-prone relative to investing in an SWF: (1) human capital is less easily appropriated than financial assets; (2) human capital raises the opportunity cost of productive work, while international financial investments do not; and (3) human capital formation, especially education, carries values and transmits social norms, while financial asset investments do not. In sum, for all three channels considered, fostering human capital unambiguously reduces conflict incentives, and investments in financial assets do not. Less wasteful conflict, of course, means an increase in economic output.

Next, consider the contrast with investments in physical capital. Both types of investment methods raise the opportunity cost of taking up arms. Hence, the opportunity cost channel is also present for infrastructure investments. But there are important differences between the other two channels. First, physical infrastructure has a much higher scrap value than human capital. When war ravages a region, parts of the physical infrastructure—for example, those parts made of metal—can be dismantled and sold on the black market. In contrast, because the scrap value of human capital is zero, having more human capital and less infrastructure depresses the gains that rebels expect from war.

Last, education and infrastructure affect the moral cost of fighting differently. While physical capital investments do not affect social norms and values, education has the potential to do so, and schooling that stresses the value of cooperation and tolerance may well raise the moral costs of engaging in fighting. This effect makes peace—and hence prosperity—more likely with education investments.

Conclusions

The state has a role to play in promoting human capital formation. The returns, both private and social, to enhancing human capital are in general very large, and there are reasons why families do not invest in it at the socially optimal level, including borrowing constraints, incomplete information, behavioral biases, and the presence of positive externalities. The state may, however, also be providing suboptimal levels of public human capital investments because of borrowing constraints or political economy factors.

A simple economic model suggests that investments that build human capital as well as those that build physical capital make sense, especially when both types of investment complement each other. The marginal returns from human capital start out high when stocks of human capital are low and then keep falling as stocks rise. Although investments in infrastructure also have decreasing marginal returns, financial asset investments, such as those in an SWF, yield constant marginal returns equaling the international interest rate. Countries with large natural resource rents should diversify windfalls into human capital, infrastructure, and an SWF, selecting investment levels that equalize the marginal returns from all three; small resource producers with relatively modest initial stocks of human capital and infrastructure may want to channel almost all windfall cash into investments in human and physical capital. In the poorest economies where the human capital needs are largest—and the returns to this investment are greatest—prioritizing the creation of human capital is justified.

Introducing the fact that a large share of natural-resource-rich countries suffer from conflict and political instability reinforces the possible role of human capital investments. Political instability raises the relative attractiveness of investing in human capital because it boosts economic output, which can be less easily appropriated than financial assets. In addition to directly raising productivity, investing in human capital also has an indirect positive effect on economic growth by curbing conflict. A higher opportunity cost of forgone production, relatively little potential for looting, and the possibility of raising the moral costs of fighting make fostering human capital a peace-promoting policy.

In light of this discussion, it is not surprising that several studies have found that human capital can modulate the resource curse. Behbudi, Mamipour, and Karami (2010) and Gylfason (2001) show that it is possible to break the resource curse if human capital investments are high enough. In a cross-country analysis of the impact of natural resources on growth, Bravo-Ortega and de Gregorio (2007) found that, although there is, on average, a negative effect, it masks the fact that it is only negative at low levels of human capital (measured by years of schooling) and is positive at high levels.

However, turning *investments* in human capital into *actual* human capital is difficult. The next two chapters address (a) the factors that enhance or diminish the effectiveness of those investments, especially factors that are prevalent in resource-rich countries (chapter 3); and (b) the types of investments that should be prioritized (chapter 4).

Notes

1. This is "Precept 7" of the Natural Resource Governance Institute's approach to natural resource management.

2. This part of the chapter draws extensively from a background paper by Rohner (2014).

3. Studies have shown that at the level of individuals, there may be increasing returns to schooling, at least for certain schooling levels (Belzil and Hansen 2002; Filmer and Fox 2014; Söderbom and others 2006). The model assumes that, at the macro level, further investments in human (and physical) capital come to a point of diminishing returns at some point.

4. This discussion draws heavily on the formal model developed by Rohner (2014).

References

Acemoglu, Daron, and Alexander Wolitzky. 2011. "The Economics of Labor Coercion." *Econometrica* 79 (2): 555–600.

Akerlof, George. 1991. "Procrastination and Obedience." *American Economic Review* 81 (2): 1–19.

Algan, Yann, Pierre Cahuc, and Andrei Shleifer. 2013. "Teaching Practices and Social Capital." *American Economic Journal: Applied Economics* 5 (3): 189–210.

Almond, Douglas, and Janet Currie. 2011. "Human Capital Development before Age Five." In *Handbook of Labor Economics*, edited by David Card and Orley Ashenfelter, 1315–486. Amsterdam: Elsevier.

Alsan, Marcella, and David Cutler. 2013. "Girls' Education and HIV Risk: Evidence from Uganda." *Journal of Health Economics* 32 (5): 863–72.

Appiah, Elizabeth, and Walter W. McMahon. 2002. "The Social Outcomes of Education and Feedbacks on Growth in Africa." *Journal of Development Studies* 38 (4): 27–68.

Aragon, Fernando, and Juan Pablo Rud. 2013. "Natural Resourcesand Local Communities: Evidence from a Peruvian Gold Mine." *American Economic Journal: Economic Policy* 5 (2): 1–25.

Araji, Salim M., and Hamid Mohtadi. 2014. "Natural Resources, Incentives and Human Capital: Reinterpreting the Curse." Working Paper 892, Economic Research Forum, Giza, Arab Republic of Egypt.

Attanasio, Orazio, and Katja Kaufmann. 2009. "Educational Choices, Subjective Expectations and Credit Constraints." NBER Working Paper 15087, National Bureau of Economic Research, Cambridge, MA.

Baland, Jean-Marie, and Patrick Francois. 2000. "Rent-Seeking and Resource Booms." *Journal of Development Economics* 61 (2): 527–42.

Banerjee, Abhijit, and Andrew Newman. 1993. "Occupational Choice and the Process of Development." *Journal of Political Economy* 101 (2): 274–98.

Bannon, Ian, and Paul Collier, eds. 2003. *Natural Resources and Violent Conflict: Options and Actions*. Washington, DC: World Bank.

Barakat, Bilal, and Henrik Urdal. 2009. "Breaking the Waves? Does Education Mediate the Relationship Between Youth Bulges and Political Violence?" Policy Research Working Paper 5114, World Bank, Washington, DC.

Barma, Naazneen, Kai Kaiser, Tuan Minh Le, and Lorena Vinuela. 2012. *Rents to Riches? The Political Economy of Natural Resource-Led Development*. Washington, DC: World Bank.

Becker, Gary. 1967. *Human Capital and the Personal Distribution of Income: An Analytical Approach*. Ann Arbor, MI: Institute of Public Administration.

———. 1975. *Human Capital*. Chicago: University of Chicago Press.

———. 1991. *A Treatise on the Family*. Cambridge, MA: Harvard University Press.

Behbudi, Davood, Siab Mamipour, and Azhdar Karami. 2010. "Natural Resource Abundance, Human Capital and Economic Growth in the Petroleum-Exporting Countries." *Journal of Economic Development* 35 (3): 81–102.

Behrman, Jere, and Mark Rosenzweig. 2002. "Does Increasing Women's Schooling Raise the Schooling of the Next Generation?" *American Economic Review* 92 (1): 323–34.

———. 2004. "Returns to Birthweight." *Review of Economics and Statistics* 86 (2): 586–601.

Behrman, Julia. 2015. "The Effect of Increased Primary Schooling on Adult Women's HIV Status in Malawi and Uganda: Universal Primary Education as a Natural Experiment." *Social Science and Medicine* 127 (February): 108–15.

Belzil, Christian, and Jorgen Hansen. 2002. "Unobserved Ability and the Return to Schooling." *Econometrica* 70 (5): 2075–91.

Berman, Nicolas, Mathieu Couttenier, Dominic Rohner, and Mathias Thoenig. 2015. "This Mine Is Mine! How Minerals Fuel Conflicts in Africa." Working Paper, Graduate Institute Geneva and University of Lausanne.

Besley, Timothy, and Torsten Persson. 2011. "The Logic of Political Violence." *Quarterly Journal of Economics* 126 (3): 1411–45.

Bjorklund, Anders, Mikael Lindahl, and Erik Plug. 2006. "The Origins of Intergenerational Associations: Lessons from Swedish Adoption Data." *Quarterly Journal of Economics* 121 (3): 999–1028.

Black, Sandra, Paul Devereux, and Kjell Salvanes. 2005. "Why the Apple Doesn't Fall Far: Understanding Intergenerational Transmission of Human Capital." *American Economic Review* 95 (1): 437–49.

———. 2007. "From the Cradle to the Labor Market? The Effect of Birth Weight on Adult Outcomes." *Quarterly Journal of Economics* 122 (1): 409–39.

Bodea, Cristina, Masaaki Higashijima, and Raju Jan Singh. 2016. "Oil and Civil Conflict: Can Public Spending Have a Mitigation Effect?" *World Development* 78 (February): 1–12.

Bravo-Ortega, Claudio, and José de Gregorio. 2007. "The Relative Richness of the Poor? Natural Resources, Human Capital, and Economic Growth." In *Natural Resources: Neither Curse nor Destiny*, edited by Daniel Lederman and William F. Maloney. Stanford, CA: Stanford University Press.

Brown, Sarah, and John Sessions. 2004. "Signaling and Screening." In *International Handbook on the Economics of Education*, edited by Geraint Johnes and Jill Johnes. Cheltenham, U.K.: Edward Elgar Publishing.

Canning, David, Sangeeta Raja, and Abdo Yazbeck. 2015. *Africa's Demographic Transition: Dividend or Disaster?* Africa Development Forum. Washington, DC: World Bank.

Card, David. 2001. "Estimating the Return to Schooling: Progress on Some Persistent Econometric Problems." *Econometrica* 69 (5): 1127–60.

Carneiro, Pedro, and James Heckman. 2002. "The Evidence on Credit Constraints in Post-Secondary Schooling." *Economic Journal* 112 (482): 705–34.

Caselli, Francesco, and Wilbur John Coleman II. 2013. "On the Theory of Ethnic Conflict." *Journal of the European Economic Association* 11 (Suppl. 1): 161–92.

Caselli, Francesco, Massimo Morelli, and Dominic Rohner. 2015. "The Geography of Inter State Resource Wars." *Quarterly Journal of Economics* 130 (1): 267–315.

Cervellati, Matteo, Uwe Sunde, and Simona Valmori. 2014. "Pathogens, Weather Shocks and Civil Conflicts." Working Paper, University of Bologna, Italy.

Collier, Paul. 2007. *The Bottom Billion: Why the Poorest Countries Are Failing and What Can Be Done About It.* Oxford: Oxford University Press.

———. 2013. "Under Pressure." *Finance and Development* 50 (4): 50–53.

Collier, Paul, V. L. Elliott, Håvard Hegre, Anke Hoeffler, Marta Reynal-Querol, and Nicholas Sambanis. 2003. *Breaking the Conflict Trap: Civil War and Development Policy.* Washington, DC: Oxford University Press and World Bank.

Collier, Paul, and Anke Hoeffler. 2004. "Greed and Grievance in Civil War." *Oxford Economic Papers* 56 (4): 563–95.

Collier, Paul, Anke Hoeffler, and Dominic Rohner. 2009. "Beyond Greed and Grievance: Feasibility and Civil War." *Oxford Economic Papers* 61 (1): 1–27.

Collier, Paul, Frederick van der Ploeg, Michael Spence, and Anthony J. Venables. 2010. "Managing Resource Revenues in Developing Economies." *IMF Staff Papers* 57 (1): 84–118.

Cordoba, Juan Carlos, and Marla Ripoll. 2013. "What Explains Schooling Differences across Countries." *Journal of Monetary Economics* 60 (2): 184–202.

Currie, Janet. 2001. "Early Childhood Education Programs." *Journal of Economic Perspectives* 15 (2): 213–38.

Davies, Lynn. 2003. *Education and Conflict: Complexity and Chaos.* London: Routledge.

Davis, Jeffrey, Rolando Ossowski, James Daniel, and Steven Barnett. 2001. "Stabilization and Savings Funds for Non-Renewable Resources: Experience and Fiscal Policy Implications." IMF Occasional Paper 205, International Monetary Fund, Washington, DC.

Davis, Jeffrey, Rolando Ossowski, and Annalisa Fedelino, eds. 2003. *Fiscal Policy Formulation and Implementation in Oil-Producing Countries.* Washington, DC: International Monetary Fund.

Dee, Thomas. 2004. "Are There Civic Returns to Education?" *Journal of Public Economics* 88 (9–10): 1697–720.

Devarajan, Shantayanan, and Marcelo Giugale. 2013. "The Case for Direct Transfers of Resource Revenues in Africa." Working Paper 333, Center for Global Development, Washington, DC.

Dube, Oendrila, and Juan Vargas. 2013. "Commodity Price Shocks and Civil Conflict: Evidence from Colombia." *Review of Economics Studies* 80 (4): 1384–421.

Duflo, Esther. 2001. "Schooling and Labor Market Consequences of School Construction in Indonesia: Evidence from an Unusual Policy Experiment." *American Economic Review* 91 (4): 795–813.

Esteban, Joan, Massimo Morelli, and Dominic Rohner. 2015. "Strategic Mass Killings." *Journal of Political Economy* 123 (5): 1087–132.

Fearon, James. 2004. "Why Do Some Civil Wars Last So Much Longer Than Others?" *Journal of Peace Research* 41 (3): 275–301.

———. 2005. "Primary Commodity Exports and Civil War." *Journal of Conflict Resolution* 49 (4): 483–507.

Fearon, James, and David Laitin. 2003. "Ethnicity, Insurgency, and Civil War." *American Political Science Review* 97 (1): 75–90.

Filmer, Deon, and Louise M. Fox. 2014. *Youth Employment in Sub-Saharan Africa*. Africa Development Forum. Washington, DC: World Bank.

Filmer, Deon, and Lant Pritchett. 1999. "The Effect of Household Wealth on Educational Attainment: Evidence from 35 Countries." *Population and Development Review* 25 (1): 85–120.

Fiszbein, Ariel, Norbert Schady, Francisco Ferreira, Margaret Grosh, Niall Keleher, Pedro Olinto, and Emmanuel Skoufias. 2009. *Conditional Cash Transfers: Reducing Present and Future Poverty*. Washington, DC: World Bank.

Flug, Karnit, Antonio Spilimbergo, and Erik Wachtenheim. 1998. "Investment in Education: Do Economic Volatility and Credit Constraints Matter?" *Journal of Development Economics* 55 (2): 465–81.

Foster, Andrew D., and Mark R. Rosenzweig. 1995. "Learning by Doing and Learning from Others: Human Capital and Technical Change in Agriculture." *Journal of Political Economy* 103 (6): 1176–209.

Frederiksen, Elisabeth Hermann. 2008. "Spending Natural Resource Revenues in an Altruistic Growth Model." *Environment and Development Economics* 13 (6): 747–73.

Galor, Oded, and Joseph Zeira. 1993. "Income Distribution and Macroeconomics." *Review of Economic Studies* 60 (1): 35–52.

Gauthier, Bernard, and Waly Wane. 2005. "Suivi des dépenses publiques à destination du secteur santé au Tchad: Analyse des résultats d'enquête." Development Research Group, World Bank, Washington, DC.

Gertler, Paul, James Heckman, Rodrigo Pinto, Arianna Zanolini, Christel Vermeersch, Susan Walker, Susan M. Chang, and Sally Grantham-McGregor. 2014. "Labor Market Returns to an Early Childhood Stimulation Intervention in Jamaica." *Science* 344 (6187): 998–1001.

Grossman, Michael, and Robert Kaestner. 1997. "Effects of Education on Health." In *The Social Benefits of Education*, edited by Jere Behrman and Nevzer Stacey. Ann Arbor: University of Michigan Press.

Guidolin, Massimo, and Eliana La Ferrara. 2007. "Diamonds Are Forever, Wars Are Not: Is Conflict Bad for Private Firms?" *American Economic Review* 97 (5): 1978–93.

Gylfason, Thorvaldur. 2001. "Natural Resources, Education, and Economic Development." *European Economic Review* 45 (4–6): 847–85.

Hainmueller, Jens, and Michael J. Hiscox. 2007. "Educated Preferences: Explaining Attitudes toward Immigration in Europe." *International Organization* 61 (2): 399–442.

Heckman, James. 2006. "Skill Formation and the Economics of Investing in Disadvantaged Children." *Science* 312 (June 30): 1900–02.

Hidalgo, F. Daniel, Suresh Naidu, Simeon Nichter, and Neal Richardson. 2010. "Economic Determinants of Land Invasions." *Review of Economics and Statistics* 92 (3): 505–23.

Hoddinott, John, John A. Maluccio, Jere R. Behrman, Rafael Flores, Reynaldo Martorell. 2008. "Effect of a Nutrition Intervention during Early Childhood on Economic Productivity in Guatemalan Adults." *The Lancet* 371 (9610): 411–16.

Hodson, Randy, Dusko Sekulic, and Garth Massey. 1994. "National Tolerance in the Former Yugoslavia." *American Journal of Sociology* 99 (6): 1534–58.

Holmlund, Helena, Mikael Lindahl, and Erik Plug. 2011. "The Causal Effect of Parents' Schooling on Children's Schooling: A Comparison of Estimation Methods." *Journal of Economic Literature* 49 (3): 615–51.

Humphreys, Macartan. 2005. "Natural Resources, Conflict, and Conflict Resolution: Uncovering the Mechanisms." *Journal of Conflict Resolution* 49 (4): 508–37.

Humphreys, Macartan, and Martin Sandbu. 2007. "The Political Economy of Natural Resource Funds." In *Escaping the Resource Curse*, edited by Macartan Humphreys, Jeffrey Sachs, and Joseph E. Stiglitz. New York: Columbia University Press.

Jensen, Robert. 2010. "The (Perceived) Returns to Education and the Demand for Schooling." *Quarterly Journal of Economics* 125 (2): 515–48.

Jia, Ruixue. 2014. "Weather Shocks, Sweet Potatoes and Peasant Revolts in Historical China." *Economic Journal* 124 (575): 92–118.

Kaufmann, Maria. 2014. "Understanding the Income Gradient in College Attendance in Mexico: The Role of Heterogeneity in Expected Returns." *Quantitative Economics* 5 (3): 583–630.

König, Michael, Dominic Rohner, Mathias Thoenig, and Fabrizio Zilibotti. 2015. "Networks in Conflict: Theory and Evidence from the Great War of Africa." CEPR Discussion Paper 10348, Center for Economic Policy and Research, Washington, DC.

Kopoin, Alexandre, Jean-Pascal Nganou, Fulbert T. Tchana, and Albert Zeufack. 2016. "Public Investment, Natural Resource Inflows and Optimal Fiscal Responses: A DSGE Analysis with Evidence from Uganda." Paper prepared for the CSAE Conference, Centre for the Study of African Economies Oxford University, Oxford, March 20–22.

Lei, Yu-Hsiang, and Guy Michaels. 2014. "Do Giant Oil Field Discoveries Fuel Internal Armed Conflicts?" *Journal of Development Economics* 110 (September): 139–57.

Leigh, Andrew, and Chris Ryan. 2008. "Estimating Returns to Education Using Different Natural Experiment Techniques." *Economics of Education Review* 27 (2008): 149–60.

Lochner, Lance. 2011. "Nonproduction Benefits of Education: Crime, Health, and Good Citizenship." In *Handbook of the Economics of Education*, edited by Eric Hanushek, Stephen Machin, and Ludger Woessmann. Amsterdam: Elsevier Science.

Lochner, Lance, and Alexander Monge-Naranjo. 2011. "The Nature of Credit Constraints and Human Capital." *American Economic Review* 101 (6): 2487–529.

———. 2012. "Credit Constraints in Education." *Annual Review of Economics* 4 (September): 225–56.

Lochner, Lance, and Enrico Moretti. 2004. "The Effect of Education on Crime: Evidence from Prison Inmates, Arrests, and Self-Reports." *American Economic Review* 94 (1): 155–89.

Lujala, Paivi, Nils Petter Gleditsch, and Elisabeth Gilmore. 2005. "A Diamond Curse? Civil War and a Lootable Resource." *Journal of Conflict Resolution* 49 (4): 538–62.

Mahdavy, Hossein. 1970. "The Pattern and Problems of Economic Development in Rentier States: The Case of Iran." In *Studies in the Economic History of the Middle East*, edited by Michael A. Cook. Oxford: Oxford University Press.

McMahon, Walter W. 2004. "The Social and External Benefits of Education." In *International Handbook on the Economics of Education*, edited by Geraint Johnes and Jill Johnes. Cheltenham, U.K.: Edward Elgar Publishing.

Miguel, Edward, Shanker Satyanath, and Ernest Sergenti. 2004. "Economic Shocks and Civil Conflict: An Instrumental Variables Approach." *Journal of Political Economy* 112 (4): 725–53.

Milligan, Kevin, Enrico Moretti, and Philip Oreopoulos. 2004. "Does Education Improve Citizenship? Evidence from the United States and the United Kingdom." *Journal of Public Economics* 88 (9–10): 1667–95.

Mincer, Jacob. 1958. "Investment in Human Capital and Personal Income Distribution." *Journal of Political Economy* 66 (4): 281–302.

———. 1974. *Schooling, Experience, and Earnings*. New York: National Bureau of Economic Research.

Morelli, Massimo, and Dominic Rohner. 2015. "Resource Concentration and Civil Wars." Working Paper, Columbia University, New York.

Moretti, Enrico. 2004a. "Estimating the Social Return to Higher Education: Evidence from Longitudinal and Repeated Cross-Sectional Data." *Journal of Econometrics* 121 (1): 175–212.

———. 2004b. "Workers' Education, Spillovers, and Productivity: Evidence from Plant-Level Production Functions." *American Economic Review* 94 (3): 656–90.

Moss, Todd. 2011. "Oil to Cash: Fighting the Resource Curse through Cash Transfers." Working Paper 237, Center for Global Development, Washington, DC.

Nguyen, Trang. 2008. "Information, Role Models and Perceived Returns to Education: Experimental Evidence from Madagascar." Working Paper, MIT, Cambridge, MA.

Nunn, Nathan, and Nancy Qian. 2014. "U.S. Food Aid and Civil Conflict." *American Economic Review* 104 (6): 1630–66.

OECD (Organisation for Economic Co-operation and Development). 2009. *Armed Violence Reduction: Enabling Development*. Paris: OECD.

Osili, Una Okonkwo, and Bridget Terry Long. 2008. "Does Female Schooling Reduce Fertility? Evidence from Nigeria." *Journal of Development Economics* 87 (1): 57–75.

Østby, Gudrun, and Henrik Urdal. 2010. "Education and Civil Conflict: A Review of the Quantitative, Empirical Literature." Background paper prepared for the *Education for All Global Monitoring Report 2011*.

Ozier, Owen. 2015. "The Impact of Secondary Schooling in Kenya: A Regression Discontinuity Analysis." Policy Research Working Paper 7384, World Bank, Washington, DC.

Papyrakis, Elissaios, and Reyer Gerlagh. 2004. "The Resource Curse Hypothesis and Its Transmission Channels." *Journal of Comparative Economics* 32 (1): 181–93.

———. 2006. "Resource Windfalls, Investment, and Long-Term Income." *Resources Policy* 31 (2): 117–28.

Plug, Erik. 2004. "Estimating the Effect of Mothers Schooling on Children's Schooling Using a Sample of Adoptees." *American Economic Review* 94 (1): 358–68.

Psacharopoulos, George, and Harry Patrinos. 2004. "Returns to Investment in Education: A Further Update." *Education Economics* 12 (2): 111–34.

Rodríguez, Pedro L., José R. Morales, and Francisco J. Monaldi. 2012. "Direct Distribution of Oil Revenues in Venezuela: A Viable Alternative?" Working Paper 306, Center for Global Development, Washington, DC.

Rohner, Dominic. 2011. "Reputation, Group Structure and Social Tensions." *Journal of Development Economics* 96 (2): 188–99.

———. 2014. "Barrels, Books, and Bullets: How Education Can Prevent Conflict and Promote Development in Resource-Rich Countries." Working Paper, University of Lausanne, Switzerland.

Rohner, Dominic, Mathias Thoenig, and Fabrizio Zilibotti. 2013a. "War Signals: A Theory of Trade, Trust and Conflict." *Review of Economic Studies* 80 (3): 1114–47.

———. 2013b. "Seeds of Distrust: Conflict in Uganda." *Journal of Economic Growth* 18 (3): 217–52.

Ross, Michael. 2001. "Does Oil Hinder Democracy?" *World Politics* 53 (93): 325–61.

———. 2006. "A Closer Look at Oil, Diamonds, and Civil War." *Annual Review of Political Science* 9 (June): 265–300.

———. 2012. *The Oil Curse: How Petroleum Wealth Shapes the Development of Nations.* Princeton NJ: Princeton University Press.

Sacerdote, Bruce. 2007. "How Large Are the Effects from Changes in Family Environment? A Study of Korean American Adoptees." *Quarterly Journal of Economics* 122 (1): 119–57.

Sachs, Jeffrey D., and Andrew M. Warner. 2001. "The Curse of Natural Resources." *European Economic Review* 45 (4–6): 827–38.

Sala-i-Martin, Xavier, and Arvind Subramanian. 2013. "Addressing the Natural Resource Curse: An Illustration from Nigeria." *Journal of African Economies* 22 (4): 570–615.

Schultz, Theodore. 1960. "Capital Formation by Education." *Journal of Political Economy* 68 (6): 571–83.

———. 1961. "Investment in Human Capital." *American Economic Review* 51 (1): 1–17.

———. 1999. "Health and Schooling Investments in Africa." *Journal of Economic Perspectives* 13 (3): 67–88.

———. 2004. "Evidence of Returns to Schooling in Africa from Household Surveys: Monitoring and Restructuring the Market for Education." *Journal of African Economies* 13 (Suppl 2): ii95–148.

Schweinhart, Lawrence J. 2004. *The High/Scope Perry Preschool Study through Age 40: Summary, Conclusions, and Frequently Asked Questions.* Ypsilanti, MI: High/Scope Educational Research Foundation.

Söderbom, Mans, Francis Teal, Anthony Wambugu, and Godius Kahyarara. 2006. "The Dynamics of Returns to Education in Kenyan and Tanzanian Manufacturing." *Oxford Bulletin of Economics and Statistics* 68 (3): 261–88.

Spence, Michael. 1973. "Job Market Signaling." *Quarterly Journal of Economics* 87 (3): 355–74.

Strauss, John. 1986. "Does Better Nutrition Raise Farm Productivity?" *Journal of Political Economy* 94 (2): 297–320.

Thyne, Clayton. 2006. "ABC's, 123s, and the Golden Rule: The Pacifying Effect of Education on Civil War, 1980–1999." *International Studies Quarterly* 50 (4): 733–54.

Truman, Edwin. 2011. *Sovereign Wealth Funds: Threat or Salvation?* Washington, DC: Peterson Institute for International Economics.

van der Ploeg, Frederick. 2011. "Natural Resources: Curse or Blessing?" *Journal of Economic Literature* 49 (2): 366–420.

van der Ploeg, Frederick, and Dominic Rohner. 2012. "War and Natural Resource Exploitation." *European Economic Review* 56 (8): 1714–29.

van der Ploeg, Frederick, and Anthony Venables. 2011. "Harnessing Windfall Revenues: Optimal Policies for Resource-Rich Developing Economies." *Economic Journal* 121 (551): 1–30.

Valente, Simone. 2007. "Human Capital, Resource Constraints and Intergenerational Fairness." Working Paper 07/68, Center of Economic Research at ETH (Swiss Federal Institute of Technology), Zurich.

Vanden Eynde, Oliver. 2011. "Targets of Violence: Evidence from India's Naxalite Conflict." Working Paper, Paris School of Economics, Paris.

Victora, Cesar, Linda Adair, Caroline Fall, Pedro Hallal, Reynaldo Martorell, Linda Richter, and Harshpal Singh Sachdev. 2008. "Maternal and Child Undernutrition: Consequences for Adult Health and Human Capital." *The Lancet* 371 (9609): 340–57.

Weil, David. 2007. "Accounting for the Effect of Health on Economic Growth." *Quarterly Journal of Economics* 122 (3): 1265–306.

CHAPTER 3

Delivering Human Development Services in Resource-Rich Countries

Abstract

More money is sometimes necessary to improve services, but it is never sufficient. The weakness of governance and transparency in resource-rich countries affects how well they deliver services. Systems (institutions, incentives, and information) are important for channeling the increased revenues (or parking them until capacity is available) and for transforming them into better services, especially those that help to increase human capital.

Governance Challenges and Service Delivery

While the case for investing in human capital is compelling, how to deliver the related services—health, education, and social protection—is not obvious. When resource revenues give countries more fiscal space, countries can invest more in human capital, but allocating the resources effectively and efficiently is not a given. For example, although oil-rich municipalities in Brazil have increased their spending, households have benefited less than expected (Caselli and Michaels 2013). While corruption and rent-seeking behavior by those with access to the resources are issues when making the decision on how to allocate the revenues, the lack of capacity to absorb and spend higher revenues effectively also comes into play.

This chapter argues that in many resource-rich countries in Sub-Saharan Africa (SSA), three dimensions of governance—institutions, incentives, and information—are vital for mitigating the unique challenges of rents, volume, and volatility that come with resource riches. However, these very same dimensions are among those least developed in resource-rich SSA countries. Building up institutions, incentives, and information is necessary to ensure robust governance frameworks that shape effective and efficient delivery of health, education, and social protection services.

This book considers three groups that have a stake in social service delivery: politicians and policy makers, clients and citizens, and service providers. *World Development Report 2004: Making Services Work for Poor People* articulated a framework to capture the accountability relationships between them (World Bank 2004). This chapter builds on that framework by highlighting how institutions, incentives, and information can help to strengthen both the long and short routes of accountability.[1]

The next section explains how the rest of this chapter is structured, and it is followed by sections that detail three characteristics—rents, volatility, and volume—of resource wealth and that describe possible levers associated with the governance dimensions of institutions, incentives, and information that can be used to strengthen the quality of public service delivery, especially for human development.

Accountability for Service Delivery in Resource-Rich Countries

This chapter introduces the need to build up three components of governance in resource-rich countries: institutions, incentives, and information (figure 3.1). Concentrating on these three components will enhance both the long and short routes of accountability.

Institutions are the rules that shape human interaction. Institutions can be formal rules and regulations, such as a country's constitution and laws. They can also be informal but conventional, often unwritten, codes of behavior. With respect to natural resources, formal institutions are the laws that govern natural

Figure 3.1 Accountability Framework for Service Delivery in Resource-Rich Countries

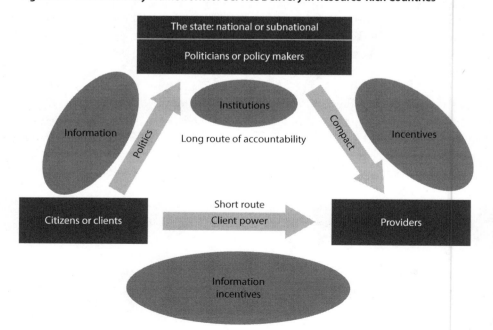

resource sectors and revenue allocation or the rules that shape the allocation of resource revenues to areas of government. They organize arrangements to deliver services at the central and local levels and through different types of providers—public, private, or not-for-profit. Informal rules, for example, may govern the relationships between competing political elites or favor relationships and kinship in the allocation of revenues.

Incentives affect the way provider organizations, their managers, and staffs are held accountable for their behavior and ability to deliver services with quality and efficiency. From this vantage point, what is of interest is how providers are selected, paid, monitored, and held accountable for their performance, notably in delivering human development services (Fiszbein, Ringold, and Rogers 2011). These relationships can be structured in a variety of ways, around the domains of human resources management, financing, procurement and management of critical inputs, information, and provider entry.

In this section, we focus on how to use revenues from natural resources to design financial incentives to strengthen either (a) performance, through results-based financing (RBF) or performance-based financing (PBF), whereby cash or nonmonetary benefits are provided in response to measurable actions or achievement; or (b) demand, through cash transfers (conditional or unconditional) to potential beneficiaries of services.

Information on inputs, outputs, and outcomes is used along the service delivery chain to shape decisions and behaviors. The rules regarding which information is collected and made available—as well as the availability, reliability, and timeliness of that information—can influence both the demand for services and their performance. The presence and pervasiveness of imperfect or minimal information in resource-rich countries have serious implications for service delivery. Citizens are often unaware of the services available to them, their rights, and the types and standards of services they should expect. This starts with scant or missing information on resource revenues and their allocation. While information is not sufficient to improve governance and accountability in service delivery, it is a necessary component. Access and rights to information are central to social accountability interventions, such as grievance redress, monitoring, and other opportunities for citizen action. Information and communication technologies (ICTs) have created opportunities for innovative approaches to accessing information, particularly in developing countries.

Diagnostics

Governance is weak in resource-rich countries, and this weakness affects service delivery. Governance is an important element of service delivery in all countries. Where governance is inadequate, public spending is not allocated effectively or efficiently to sectors where social returns are high. Instead, it is directed toward projects and sectors where rent-seeking behavior is high (Mauro 1998). Resource-rich countries are notably poor performers across governance indicators (figure 3.2).

Whereas, in a standard economic framework, natural resource deposits would always be wealth-enhancing, the large body of evidence assessing the resource

Figure 3.2 Resource-Rich Countries Are Poor Performers across Governance Indicators

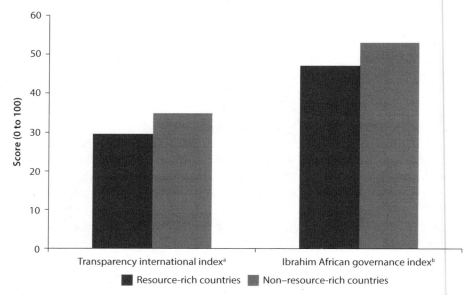

Sources: Transparency International corruption perception barometer 2013; Ibrahim African governance index 2013.
a. Measures perceived levels of public sector corruption on a scale from 0 (highly corrupt) to 100 (very clean).
b. Assesses governance progress on a scale from 0 (weak) to 100 (strong) using data from more than 30 sources.

curse suggests that the reality is not that straightforward (Ross 2012; Sachs and Warner 1999, 2001). One strand of the literature focuses on the "Dutch disease" phenomenon, in which the price increases after resource booms are so extreme that they severely harm the export industry and cause other sectors to collapse, leaving the country poorer than it was before the boom. Another strand emphasizes disincentives to invest in either human or physical capital—or both. A large and growing strand of this literature has emphasized that one main reason for the potentially destructive power of natural resources lies not in the terms of trade and relative prices but in politics and poor institutions. As described in chapter 2, bad governance, a lack of democracy (authoritarianism), and especially civil wars can make a resource windfall destroy regular economic activity (Baland and Francois 2000; Collier 2007; Dunning 2005; Ross 2001, 2012; van der Ploeg 2011). The quality of existing institutions is a key factor that mediates resource-rich countries' economic outcomes, and the political economy context shapes the management of natural resources in both the generation and distribution of revenues (Barma and others 2012). Resource-rich countries tend to be endowed with poorer institutional quality than their income levels would warrant.

Accountability relationships are especially fraught in resource-rich countries. One reason is that resource windfalls can insulate policy makers from citizens, because policy makers do not have to rely on taxes or revenues from non-extractive sectors to fund programs and projects (box 3.1; Karl 1997; Moore 2004; Ross 2001). Understanding and strengthening the link between governance

---

Box 3.1 Does Taxation Increase Transparency?

Taxation has a useful role to play in the proper functioning of a state (Brautigam, Fjeldstad, and Moore 2008; Devarajan and others 2011). Disliked as it is, taxation is fundamental to the social contract between citizens who pay taxes and state institutions that provide public goods (Brautigam, Fjeldstad, and Moore 2008). The lack—or very limited share—of tax revenue in the gross domestic product (GDP) of resource-rich countries helps to explain their poor performance (Devarajan and others 2011; Palley 2003; Sandbu 2006).

Taxation has a direct positive effect on institution building because the state has to expand and improve its revenue-generating bureaucracy (Gillies 2010). Timmons (2005) showed that a government is most likely to be sensitive to the needs of the population that carries the largest tax burden. Broad-based taxation is thus important to limit the possibility of rent seeking. While broad-based taxation and a transparent way of ensuring taxpayer rights characterize a tax system that leads to state building (Fjeldstad and Moore 2008), trust in institutions and civic engagement are prerequisites for tax compliance (Brautigam, Fjeldstad, and Moore 2008). Taxation and state building are thus mutually reinforcing: a tax system provides a mechanism through which citizens invest in the state and become interested in its development, holding it accountable for delivering results. At the same time, the state's ability to deliver to its shareholders—citizens—conditions their willingness to continue investing in the state by paying taxes. Higher tax revenues seem to be linked to more scrutiny over public spending as well as better governance and more efficient public spending (Gadenne 2011). The link seems to be particularly strong for direct forms of taxation (Devarajan and others 2011; Martin 2013). The reason is simply that individuals take much more interest in money that has passed through their pockets and tend to require higher standards when the money is spent (Sandbu 2006).

Ardanaz and Maldonado (2014) show that an increase in oil windfalls is linked to a decrease not only in fiscal transparency but also in public scrutiny of government spending. Since oil revenues are transferred directly to government coffers, citizens lack precise information on the amounts and tend to grossly underestimate them. Transfers are less visible than general taxes. Citizens tend to monitor how funds from transfers are used less closely than funds from general taxes.

Moss and Majerowicz (2013) point to subnational studies in Argentina, Nigeria, Tanzania, and Zambia, which showed that districts dependent on tax revenue tend to allocate more funds to deliver better services and are more democratic and less corrupt than districts dependent on central transfers or oil revenues. The higher a government's dependence on tax revenue, the higher its incentive to respond positively to citizens' requests because citizens control the funds. When the majority of funds come from oil transfers, the balance shifts and the allegiance of the government moves away from citizens and toward the new money provider, in this case, the oil industry. Taxation constitutes the link of accountability between the client—the tax-paying citizen—and the service provider, the government. The higher the price of the services provided—the tax—the higher the expectations of those paying, and the higher the standards to which the service provider is held. Without this link, neither party has much of a vested interest in interacting with the other one.

---

and the management of natural resource revenues are important for improving service delivery in sectors such as health, education, and social protection.

Public trust in institutions is lower in resource-rich countries than in other African countries. People also report that less budget information is available, and that there are fewer channels for public participation (figure 3.3).

Figure 3.3 Public Trust in Institutions Is Lower and Less Budget Information Is Available in Resource-Rich SSA Countries

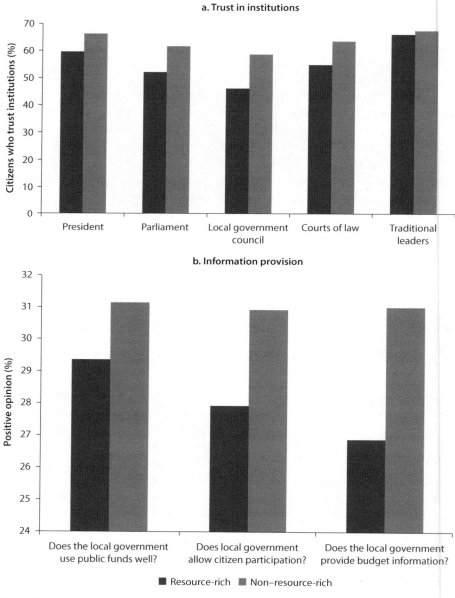

Source: AfroBarometer, round 4.

Social services, including health and education, pose particular accountability challenges. Delivery of health and education services is complex because (1) these services are *transaction-intensive and discretionary*, and monitoring and accountability mechanisms can lead to micromonitoring and overwhelm the daily interactions of teachers and health workers with students and patients; (2) there are *multiple actors and tasks*, which can "blunt the precision of incentives" (World Bank 2004a); and (3) *attribution* is not clear because outcomes result from a complex interaction between service provision and client behaviors and characteristics.

Accountability for service delivery is particularly poor in resource-rich countries. The accountability of providers is critical for the quality of services. Indicators of how providers behave, such as the absenteeism of health and education staff, provide a measure of how well service delivery is governed (Fiszbein, Ringold, and Rogers 2011). In some SSA countries, close to 40 percent of people surveyed said they occasionally or frequently encountered physician absenteeism (figure 3.4, panel a). Among the countries where absenteeism is highest are resource-rich or emerging resource-rich nations such as Zambia (40 percent), Guinea (38 percent), Mozambique (38 percent), and Sierra Leone (38 percent). A similar picture emerges in education, with more than one-third of respondents reporting that teachers are occasionally or frequently absent in Guinea, Liberia, Mozambique, and Sierra Leone (figure 3.4, panel b).

Other measures, such as the service delivery indicators (SDIs), also point to weak accountability for the delivery of public services (box 3.2).

Figure 3.4 In SSA, Accountability for Service Delivery Is Poor in Resource-Rich Countries

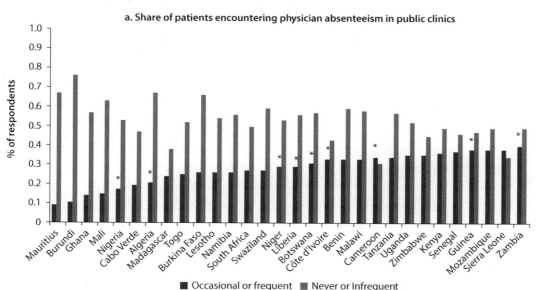

a. Share of patients encountering physician absenteeism in public clinics

■ Occasional or frequent   ■ Never or Infrequent

figure continues next page

Figure 3.4 In SSA, Accountability for Service Delivery Is Poor in Resource-Rich Countries *(continued)*

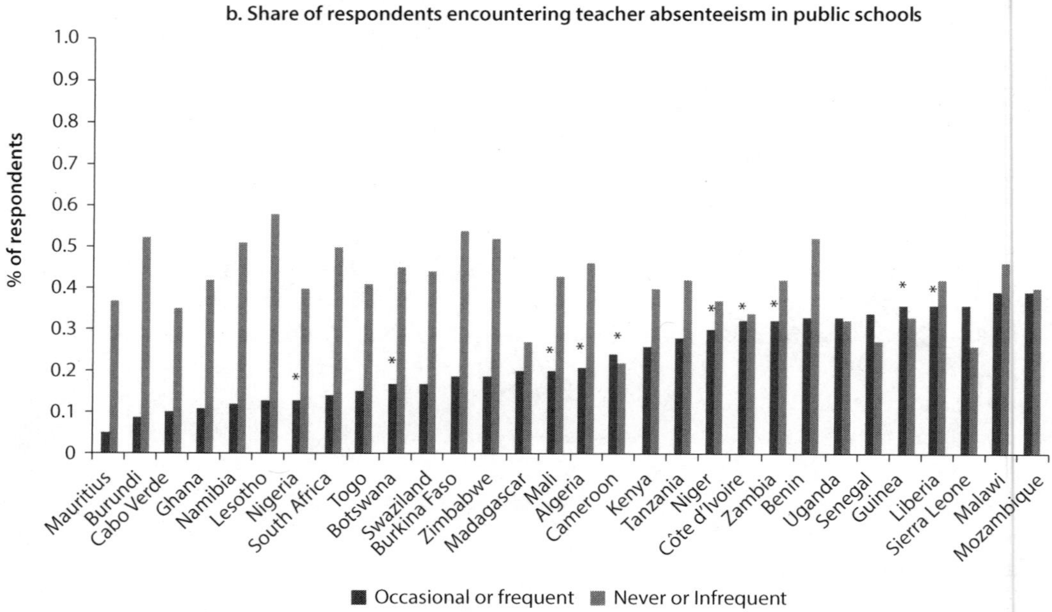

b. Share of respondents encountering teacher absenteeism in public schools

Occasional or frequent   Never or Infrequent

Source: Afrobarometer Round 5 Country Surveys, 2014.

Note: Respondents were asked to state how often they experienced doctors being absent from public clinics in during the past 12 months or teachers being absent from the local public schools during the past 12 months: "never," "once or twice," "a few times," or "often." The figure combines the "never" and "once or twice" responses as "never or infrequent" and the "a few times" and "often" responses as "occasional or frequent." Asterisks represent resource-rich countries.

Box 3.2 Service Delivery Indicators: Health and Education Services Need Improvement

Service delivery indicators track the performance and quality of service delivery in health and education through standardized facility surveys of a nationally representative sample of primary schools and frontline health facilities across African countries and over time; they cover several resource-rich countries.

SDIs for Sub-Saharan Africa[a] suggest poor service delivery, with staff in schools and health centers frequently absent, very limited time spent delivering services, and limited knowledge of the subject (among teachers) or appropriate clinical practice (among health workers).

Physician absence rates range from a low of about 30 percent in Kenya and Nigeria to almost 50 percent in Uganda. Inputs for health service delivery are not always available: only 18 percent of public facilities surveyed in Nigeria and 19 percent in Tanzania had basic equipment (weighing scale, thermometer, and stethoscope).

Teacher absenteeism ranges from 27 percent in Uganda and 23 percent in Tanzania to 15 percent in Kenya and 14 percent in Nigeria. Time spent teaching per day is well below the

box continues next page

Box 3.2 Service Delivery Indicators: Health and Education Services Need Improvement *(continued)*

official teaching hours in all countries, by as much as five hours (Uganda). The SDI education data make it clear that inputs needed for service delivery are not always the barrier. While only 19 percent of the Nigerian schools surveyed possessed the minimum infrastructure (for example, sufficient light for reading) and equipment, more than 50 percent of the Kenyan and Ugandan schools surveyed did.

SDI can help to identify different drivers of poor service delivery and allow for smarter and more targeted use of resource rents, especially in countries like Tanzania and Uganda where recent natural resource discoveries may create opportunities to address service delivery challenges.

Source: World Bank Service Delivery Indicators 2014.
a. So far, the SDI has been implemented in Kenya, Mozambique, Niger, Nigeria (in selected states: Anambra, Bauchi, and Ekiti), Senegal, Togo, Tanzania, and Uganda.

Dissatisfaction with Education and Health Services

Public dissatisfaction with services is another indicator of quality. In 16 of the 29 countries in the Afrobarometer survey (of which 7 are resource-rich countries), more than one-third of respondents expressed dissatisfaction with the way their government was handling education. If newly resource-rich countries were included, the number of resource-rich countries would increase to 10 (figure 3.5, panel a). Dissatisfaction with health services is more pronounced; in 21 of the 29 countries surveyed (of which 7 are resource-rich countries), more than one-third of respondents felt that the government was providing health services fairly badly or very badly (figure 3.5, panel b).

Resource-rich countries do not necessarily spend more on human development. As discussed in chapter 1, resource-rich SSA countries spend more per capita on education and health than other countries in the region, but spend less as a percentage of GDP (table 3.1).

These averages hide great variation; for example, Botswana spends almost 10 percent of its GDP on education, while Chad spends 2 percent. Private spending also varies from country to country.

Gaudin and Yazbeck (2012) analyzed public expenditure reviews (PERs) of health in 70 countries, 24 of them in Africa. On average, in 2008 public spending on health reached 2.4 percent of GDP and private spending was an additional 2.6 percent, but again this hides huge variations: in 2004 Guinea had total health expenditures of 13 percent of GDP, but 11.8 percent was private, leaving just 1.2 percent public; in the Democratic Republic of Congo, public spending was 0.6 percent. Corruption and bad governance, inadequate data collection and reporting, and issues of spending and equity in targeting arise in more than 90 percent of African PERs, pointing to generalized government failures, lack of funding, and lack of organization.

Figure 3.5 Citizens' Dissatisfaction with the Provision of Public Health and Education Is High in SSA

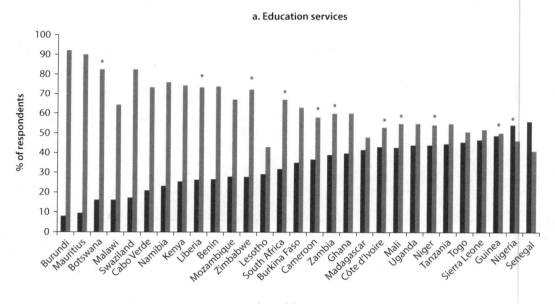

a. Education services

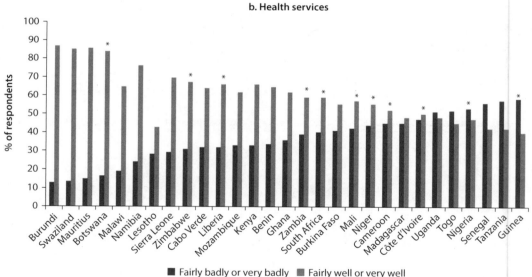

b. Health services

■ Fairly badly or very badly   ■ Fairly well or very well

Source: Afrobarometer Round 5 Country Surveys 2014.

Note: Respondents were asked to state how well or badly the current government is improving basic health and education services: "very badly," "fairly badly," "fairly well," "very well," "don't know" or "haven't heard enough." The figure aggregates the responses in two categories Asterisks represent resource-rich countries.

Table 3.1 Resource-Rich SSA Countries Spend More per Capita but Less as a Share of GDP on Health and Education

Indicator and country category	Health (average, 2000–13)			Education (average, 2000–13)		
	SSA	Non-SSA	All	SSA	Non-SSA	All
Spending per capita						
Resource-rich, oil	50	73	65	69	125	107
Resource-rich, nonoil	62	102	81	116	99	110
Non–resource-rich, potential	12		12	19		19
Non–resource-rich	29	158	134	49	170	144
All	37	137	106	62	157	124
Spending as a share of GDP						
Resource-rich, oil	1.7	2.4	2.2	2.9	4.7	4.1
Resource-rich, nonoil	2.9	3.0	3.0	4.3	4.5	4.4
Non–resource-rich, potential	2.7		2.7	4.1		4.1
Non–resource-rich	3.0	4.1	3.9	5.0	4.9	4.9
All	2.6	3.7	3.4	4.3	4.8	4.6

Source: World Development Indicators data.

Note: SSA = Sub-Saharan Africa. Data are calculated as an average of nonmissing values for 2000–13. Per capita amounts are expressed in constant 2005 U.S. dollars.

Moreover, few recent PERs are available for resource-rich countries—they are available only for Equatorial Guinea (World Bank 2010a); Gabon (World Bank 2012a), Liberia (World Bank 2012b), Niger (World Bank 2013a), Uganda (World Bank 2013b), Republic of Congo (World Bank 2014b), Mozambique (World Bank 2014c) and Madagascar (World Bank 2015c).

Money is not enough; the quality of public spending on education also matters. As described in chapter 1, the quality and allocation of spending matter, in particular for equity and efficiency. For example, disproportionate public spending at the tertiary level can be regressive, if the poor are not likely to go beyond secondary school. Both resource-rich and non–resource-rich countries are spending, on average, about 45 percent of their total education budget on primary schools and about 18 percent on tertiary education. Resource-rich countries spend about 35 percent on secondary schooling, and non–resource-rich countries spend about 28 percent. However, in resource-rich Niger, about 60 percent goes to primary education, while in resource-rich Cameroon and the Republic of Congo, 53 percent goes to secondary schooling (figure 3.6). As described in figure 1.15 in chapter 1, public spending is only weakly correlated with the probability that school-age children (ages 6–14 years) attend school and with the proportion of young persons ages 15–19 years who have completed grade 6.

In health, while spending levels are still an issue for some countries, issues regarding the quality of spending, allocation of resources, procurement of essential drugs, and management of human resources are pervasive (box 3.3).

Figure 3.6 Public Spending on Education Is Only Weakly Correlated with Outcomes, 2010

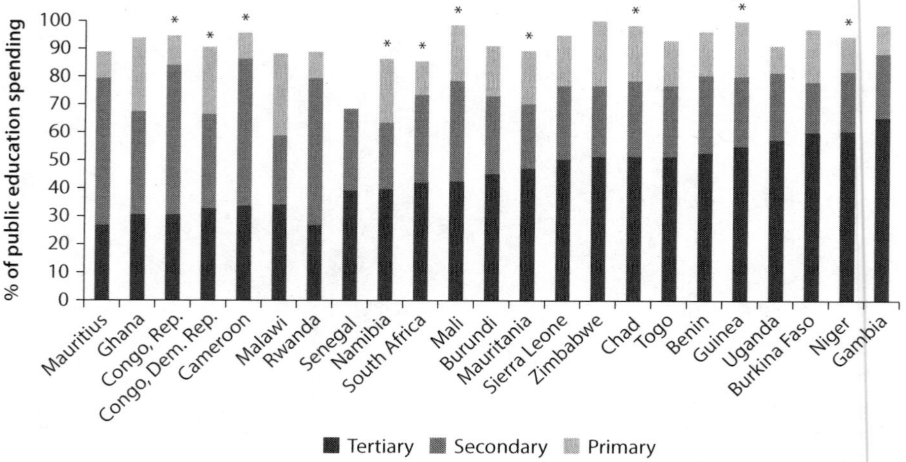

Source: UNESCO, Institute for Statistics 2012.
Note: Asterisks represent resource-rich countries.

Box 3.3 Public Expenditures on Health Services in Ethiopia, Guinea, Malawi, Madagascar, Senegal, and Sierra Leone

The 2006 and 2013 Malawi PERs (World Bank 2007, 2013b) highlighted serious quality problems, arising mainly from the lack of skilled health workers and frequent "downloading" of clinical tasks to staff with poor or no supervision. This lack of quality is evident in a high—and rising—maternal mortality rate (from an estimated 613 deaths per 100,000 live births in 2007 to 638 in 2014). Malawi had the lowest density of physicians (0.05) and nurses (0.26) per capita, lower on both counts than Angola, Sudan, and the Democratic Republic of Congo. Because satisfaction was low, few used the services.

The 2010 Sierra Leone PER (World Bank 2010b) emphasized the declining share of spending on health relative to other sectors, large differences between actual and planned spending, and low spending by international standards. Additional donor disbursements substituted for national funding rather than increasing total resources for the health sector and for primary care in particular, especially preventive programs. Yet in six of the eight years between 2001 and 2008, the Ministry of Health and Sanitation substantially underspent its allocations. Major deviations from the budget were found in spending on drugs and medical supplies. Poor governance was blamed for significant waste. Official cost recovery through the sale of publicly supplied drugs and other medical supplies broke down, mostly because of drug shortages; health facilities bought drugs from private vendors and operated informal versions of cost recovery systems. Informal fees were levied because of low or unpaid salaries.

The PER stressed the lack of transparency and accountability—even of basic accounting in facilities. Misclassified expenditures and coding mistakes were common, and data on

box continues next page

Box 3.3 Public Expenditures on Health Services in Ethiopia, Guinea, Malawi, Madagascar, Senegal, and Sierra Leone *(continued)*

revenues and expenditures were absent. The PER found that the Anticorruption Commission had achieved some progress in curbing corruption; notably, in 2009 the minister of health and sanitation was indicted for alleged corrupt practices.

The 2007 and 2015 Madagascar PERs (World Bank 2007a, 2015c) raised the problem of unpredictable external financing. The country remains heavily dependent on external funds, which are volatile, making it difficult for the government to program health activities. In particular, external donors and the government have different budget cycles. Dispersion is also pervasive; rules, actors, and calendars for budget preparation and execution are different for wages and salaries, other operational expenditures, and investment. Delays in procurement are blamed on the lack of procedures for external projects. The low percentage of the state budget that goes to the sector supports mostly salaries. Public spending is not distributed equitably—in particular, between the capital and rural areas.

In Ethiopia, Guinea, and Senegal (World Bank 2004b, 2004c, 2004d), obstacles to better health service delivery included underdeveloped human resources, inadequate management, and the lack of monitoring of staff training and performance. Funds and personnel were inadequately distributed between the center and the regions. The PERs emphasized the need to extend the network of qualified physicians, midwives, and nurses into rural and very poor regions. To sustain staff morale and improve retention, "soft" investments (such as assigned housing, technical support, and recognition or performance rewards) would be key to maintaining good working conditions.

Sources: Gaudin and Yazbeck 2012; World Bank 2015b.

Public Expenditures and Safety Nets

Safety nets can help to reduce chronic poverty and vulnerability and act as springboards to promote productive inclusion. Safety nets are noncontributory transfer programs targeted to the poor or vulnerable (Grosh and others 2008). They include instruments such as general subsidies, fee waivers to access basic social services, and in-kind and cash transfers, and they can be universal or targeted. Revenues from resources could be channeled to finance such safety net investments—in particular, those with direct effects on access to and the use of human development services and on poverty alleviation.

However, resource-rich countries tend not to use the most effective interventions. Resource-rich countries rely heavily on expensive general subsidy programs to redistribute income. Most developing countries spend about 1–2 percent of GDP on safety nets; in most African countries, spending averages about 1.7 percent of GDP and 4.4 percent of total government spending (Grosh and others 2008; Monchuk 2013):

- In Zambia, total spending on transfers of all kinds amounted to about US$540 million in 2010. However, the amount spent on programs that explicitly provide transfers to the poor was only about US$50 million, and much of this was

donor spending on discrete programs. Spending on genuine safety nets represented only about 0.2 percent of GDP in 2010—even lower than in other
low-income countries, where the range was from about 0.5 to 3.5 percent. If
the total US$540 million were targeted to the poorest 39 percent of the popu-
lation, it would be enough to transfer about K 36,000 per capita per month,
which would almost entirely eradicate the food gap (Tesliuc, James, and
Rosemary 2013).

- In Mali, few resources are allocated to social safety nets—about 0.5 percent of
GDP in 2008, excluding general food subsidies—and most of those are from
external sources (Cherrier, del Ninno, and Razmara 2011).

Many countries use expensive and regressive general subsidies—mostly
untargeted—to redistribute income. Of the 17 countries in a 22-country analysis of SSA countries with some form of general subsidies, 10 are resource-rich
or newly so. In 2011, fuel subsidies in the region accounted for 1.5 percent of
GDP, and 5.5 percent of total government revenues (IMF 2013). The economic
rationale for energy subsidies lies in reducing energy costs for firms and potentially increasing their profits and stimulating productive investments, which
would create jobs. However, energy subsidies tend to be foremost political
economy instruments that create economic distortions, catering to specific
constituencies and crowding out social investments. General food subsidies also
distort consumption patterns, and most are regressive. They also create distortions in food production and value chains, often to the detriment of the poorest
farmers.

In Cameroon, between 2008 and 2010, all subsidy programs averaged 6.28
percent of the government budget and 1.39 percent of GDP. But this spending
was mostly regressive; most of the subsidized items were not in the consumption
basket of the bottom quintile of the income distribution. Only subsidies on kero-
sene were pro-poor (del Ninno and Tamiru 2012).

Contributors to Weak Governance in Resource-Rich Countries

Three characteristics of resource-rich environments—rents, volume, and
volatility—exacerbate the governance problems of service delivery.

Rents

Resource rents create a sense of "free money" that can distort spending decisions.
Rents are the difference between the revenues from and the extraction costs of
natural resources and are different from other forms of revenue. Resource rents
can induce rent-seeking behavior with perverse effects: unequal fiscal distribution, inefficient and unproductive ventures, poor governance, and corruption
(Arezki and Gylfason 2013; Barma and others 2012; Karl 2004; Robinson and
Torvik 2005). Resource rents, estimated at about US$4 trillion annually, provide
a larger margin of fiscal space for resource-rich than for non–resource-rich countries to invest in sustainable development and better outcomes for their populations. However, the creation of assets, whether infrastructure or human capital,

requires deferring benefits, because the return will likely be realized several years in the future rather than in the present budget or electoral cycle (Barma and others 2012). The benefits are broad and nonrival, so politicians cannot take credit for them. Instead, they tend to use the rents as political currency and channel them to certain constituencies, creating and sustaining vested interest groups. The rentier state lives off unearned income, and the rents induce patronage behaviors. In particular, a class of "rent-seeking pseudo-entrepreneurs" enjoys an umbilical relationship with the state (Pritchett and Werker 2012). These business elites are intertwined in the state's capturing of resource rents and become entrenched obstacles to transformative measures. The disproportionate influence of quasi-autonomous, state-owned oil or mining companies affects public investment (Kaiser 2012; Rajaram and others 2014). In addition, the exact amount of the rents can easily be concealed from public scrutiny, fostering a culture of secrecy.

The government's dependence on resource rents tends to weaken its bargaining power with developers. Because the extraction and collection of natural resource revenues is often extremely centralized, the state is itself an enormous prize: in thinly institutionalized environments, the victor can claim all the spoils (see the discussion on conflict in chapter 2; Barma and others 2012). Building in mechanisms to ensure that rents are shared broadly—for example, distributing rents through public goods rather than hoarding them as private goods—is crucial to breaking this dynamic.

By limiting the need to generate other forms of government revenue, such as tax collection, natural resources can lead to an attenuation of state administrative and institutional capacity building. Indeed, the quality of public institutions in resource-rich countries is often lower than it should be for their level of GDP.

Volume

Large inflows of capital can overwhelm public sector capacity and temporarily inflate the prices of inputs. In many developing countries, poor management of public investment undermines the ability to allocate resources effectively and efficiently for human development. In resource-rich developing countries, the sheer volume of resources available for public investment strains absorption capacity when project management capabilities are minimal. Resource-rich countries face the risk that resource windfalls will crowd out factors of production in nonresource sectors, overwhelming the capacity of the target sector or temporarily inflating prices—the phenomenon known as Dutch disease (Dobronogov and Keutiben 2014).

Volatility

Resource-rich countries are vulnerable to revenue volatility because of fluctuations in commodity prices. Resource price volatility can impede economic growth by creating uncertainty (Ross 2012). Volatility puts pressure on public investment decisions; because public investment is discretionary, capital spending, which is typically used for investment projects, is more vulnerable to cuts than recurrent expenditures like public sector wages and transfer programs (Bacon and Kojima 2008; Barma and others 2012).

Natural resource price volatility has a highly negative effect on growth (van der Ploeg and Poelhekke 2009). Resource-rich countries face two distinct political economy trajectories. One is during the boom years, when priority is given to rent seeking; the political economy challenges then are to create and apply medium-term planning strategies and adhere to fiscal rules. The second trajectory is during the bust years, when commodity prices fall and the political economy challenges shift to sustaining spending on various public programs and preserving human capital gains (Barma and others 2012). The macro effects of volatility, such as a fall in the real wages of service providers in education and health, compounds the political economy challenge. This is happening now in many countries with the plunge in the prices of oil, iron ore, and other minerals since June 2014.

The volume of capital inflows is also related to the volatility of booms and busts. Volatility has a negative impact on the financing of the public investment portfolio. The boom-and-bust cycles typical of resource prices are mirrored in the rapid scaling up and down of capital spending in resource-rich countries. Arezki and Ismail (2013) noted that the response of current and capital expenditures to changes in oil prices is asymmetric; current spending shoots up rapidly during booms, and capital spending drops even faster during busts. When inflation shoots up, construction of facilities may halt and never resume or the supply of crucial imported inputs may dry up, with increased stockouts.

The volatility of natural resource prices affects public investment decision making. Price volatility is a problem because (1) it can jeopardize economic growth due to the uncertainty it creates about the future, which discourages investment, particularly by the private sector; and (2) it interferes with the government's ability to "productively invest [its] resource revenues by shortening the government's planning horizon" (Ross 2012). Although the current soft oil prices are contributing to the reduced fiscal space of resource-rich countries, particularly oil exporters, they also present an opportunity for those countries to tackle subsidy reforms that would ultimately enlarge the fiscal resources for pro-poor spending and investment (Fabrizio and others 2014; World Bank 2015b).

Devarajan and others (2014) have analyzed the economic implications of various budget rules for managing natural resource revenues. They employed a dynamic stochastic general equilibrium analysis to identify spending rules of thumb for managing and allocating resource revenues over time in low-income countries like Niger.[2] They concluded that what is preferable is a fiscal regime that takes a balanced approach to addressing price volatility, investing a predetermined share of the windfall in a sovereign wealth fund (SWF) and the rest in public infrastructure.

Price volatility entails risk and transaction costs. For example, shifts in the factors of production (labor, capital, and land) across sectors (agriculture, minerals, and others) face transaction costs (Frankel 2012). Resource-rich countries should consider policy options to mitigate price volatility and other potentially negative aspects of resource dependence: (1) setting and adhering to fiscal rules that are immune to political manipulation—Chile's fiscal institutions are a well-known model; (2) creating commodity funds with rules about the payout rate; and (3) distributing resource wealth equally per capita (Gelb and Majerowicz 2011; Ross 2007; Sala-i-Martin and Subramanian 2003).

Public investment management (PIM) in resource-rich countries is thus subject to two challenges: technical or capacity, and political economy (Arezki, Dupay, and Gelb 2012). Robust PIM requires technical expertise. Sound PIM requires experts to undertake project appraisals, supervise construction, and manage all aspects of the investment; design and maintain the necessary accountability checks and balances; and, particularly in resource-rich countries, integrate resource rents into the budgeting cycle for public investments. Arezki, Dupay, and Gelb (2012) showed that, on average, the quality of public investment is lower in resource-rich, low-income countries than in non–resource-rich ones. Investing in the technical capabilities needed for sound management of public investment is central to the "investing in investing" approach recommended for developing countries, especially those that are resource-rich (Collier 2010, Kyobe et al. 2011). Box 3.4 describes eight features for achieving PIM efficiency identified by Rajaram and others (2014), based on a review of country experiences.

To strengthen the management of its public investments, Chile spent an extended period building project appraisal capacity across various levels and agencies of government and made the public investment program available to the public online. Other countries have set up a project monitoring function that reports directly to government leaders, such as the Strategic Policy Unit in the Office of the President in Sierra Leone (Rajaram and others 2014).

The political economy of public investment in resource-rich countries, particularly during resource booms, is often distorted by highly visible rents and pressures on public officials to allocate them to groups that are of strategic interest. One outcome can be to concentrate decision making about resource rent allocation at the highest levels of government, "to bypass the regular budget cycle and procedural rules" (Kaiser 2012, 167; Rajaram and others 2014). This cycle undermines the very institutions needed to maximize resource wealth investments. Timor-Leste, a resource-rich developing country, has invested heavily in reforming its PIM to take better advantage of its resource windfall. For instance, it has reinforced the transparency mechanisms for the annual budget and the Petroleum Fund, and no public investments are made off-budget, even those of the national oil company (Rajaram and others 2014). Another challenging outcome is the short-term horizon of public officials, who tend to be biased toward present consumption needs at the expense of future returns on investments in health, education, and investment systems such as PIM.

Box 3.4 Eight "Must-Have" Features for an Efficient Public Investment Management System

An investment choice is justified as a welfare-improving public policy when:

- The actual investment project management is effective and leads to the completion of the project on schedule.
- There is efficient and sustainable operation of the asset created by public investment.
- There is a process of learning to improve future project selection, implementation, and operation.
- Investment is undertaken through an allocation of risk that is more likely to ensure efficient and effective implementation of the project. Risk management is one of the key challenges when it comes to coordinating public and private investment modalities.

As illustrated in figure B3.4.1, effective PIM systems require not only the alignment of capacities and incentives to improve project design and selection (the first four features) but also credible commitments and long-term investments in technical and administrative capacity to improve project implementation (the last four features). Building such systems is not trivial, since it tries to address problems of transparency and accountability, which are especially acute in resource-rich countries.

Figure B3.4.1 Features of an Efficient Public Investment Management System

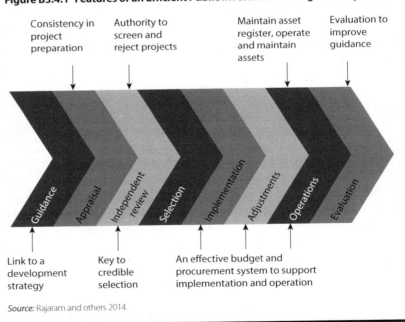

Source: Rajaram and others 2014.

Levers for Improving the Governance of Service Delivery

The first main section of chapter spelled out the governance challenges confronting resource-rich countries—rents, volume, and volatility—and their effects on public investment choices and systems. This section sets out three entry points for mitigating these challenges: institutions, incentives, and information.

Institutions

Institutions shape human interaction. They can be formal, through rules such as a country's constitution and laws, or informal, with conventional, but often unwritten, codes of behavior. In resource-rich countries, a robust institutional environment is needed for the effective management of natural resource wealth. Formal institutions might include legislation on natural resource sectors and revenue allocation, rules that shape the allocation of resource rents to various levels of government, or the responsibility of legislative bodies to create rules that strengthen accountability and transparency (box 3.5).

Box 3.5 The Role of Parliaments in Managing Resource Wealth

Parliaments can do a great deal to foster domestic accountability. Their mandate is to manage the policy making and implementation processes through legislation and regulation, to scrutinize public spending, and to represent citizen needs and demands in decision making. Four of their functions can strengthen governance in resource-rich countries:

1. *Legislative.* The legislative function covers drafting, reviewing, and passing bills. This function enables parliament to create a legal framework for effective and efficient management of resource wealth. For example, parliament can introduce laws to establish decentralized systems of service delivery and provide earmarks for social sector spending (table 3.1).

2. *Regulatory.* Parliament can use its oversight responsibility to hold the executive accountable for the execution of laws and policies. Parliamentary committees can use hearings and investigations to press government officials on resource wealth allocation and service delivery.

3. *Representative.* As a representative of the public, parliament ensures that the voices and preferences of the public are heard; one method is to pass access-to-information laws.

4. *Budgetary.* Parliament's "power of the purse" gives it the opportunity to ensure that the annual budget process is used to promote an efficient and effective allocation of resource revenues.

Parliaments are not monoliths: they comprise various committees, different political parties, various coalitions, and so forth. Typically, specialized committees such as budget, oil or mining, and public accounts are prominent players in resource wealth management. Committees on social sectors—such as health, education, and social protection—and other

box continues next page

Box 3.5 The Role of Parliaments in Managing Resource Wealth *(continued)*

outside players can also exert influence. Members of parliament need the capacity to organize internally and to manage potential conflicts of interest in order to oversee effectively how resource wealth is managed. Ghana's Petroleum Revenue Management Act (2011) authorized the creation of a public interest and accountability committee composed of members of civil society to complement the oversight role of parliament. The law also stated that, in the absence of a national development plan, the budget should give priority to sectors like health and education.

Parliaments may encourage a long-term view of resource wealth management and develop policies and mechanisms to mitigate the tension between long- and short-term pressures. Botswana is often cited as taking a long-term view of resource wealth investment. Its budget allocation process favors investments in human development, and the Ministry of Education and Skills Development has consistently been a top recipient of budget allocations.

Sources: Alesina and Perotti 1996; Natural Resource Governance Institute 2013; Ministry of Finance, Republic of Ghana 2011.

Institutions constitute the framework for the long route of accountability (leading from citizens to the state and from the state to providers). However, reinforcing institutions often means tackling rules and norms that challenge entrenched interests or have long existed. A relatively sound institutional environment can help to mitigate the risks associated with the particular characteristics of resource-rich countries. Institutional structures (1) set the rules for allocation and spending of rents; (2) allow for systems to deal with the inherent volatility of prices and volumes associated with resource rents; and (3) enable citizens to hold policy makers accountable for allocating resources and regulating public service delivery.

This section focuses on *decentralization* and *private sector provision* of services as two possible ways (1) to build up the institutional environment at various levels of government (for example, central and subnational) and for various types of providers (private, both for-profit and not-for-profit; and public) and (2) to shape the allocation of rents to provide services related to human development. In resource-rich countries, there is a risk that mineral rents will be captured partly by civil servants through higher wages, as is the case in Ghana and Tanzania. This is a challenge not only for the efficiency of service delivery but also for the strengthening of PIM, and it creates liabilities in downtimes. In that perspective, unions of teachers and health providers are key actors to engage early on, as they can influence both the legislative and the executive branches.

Decentralization and Intergovernmental Relations
Issue
Decentralizing service delivery to the local level could improve services through better information about local needs, greater accountability and responsiveness

of local agents, and more citizen participation. One way to promote the efficient delivery of human development services is to examine the relationship between central and subnational government agencies and shift responsibilities and resources, if feasible. The rationale for decentralization is that localizing service delivery can make the state more responsive and accountable, increase the voice and participation of citizens, encourage cost-effectiveness, and reduce bureaucracy (Bardhan 2002; Faguet 2004). However, minimizing spatial inequities in human development outcomes and reducing disparities in per capita spending on social services is an especially important policy goal in resource-rich countries. Two opposing factors play a role in the financing equation. On the one hand, the resources tend to be located in poorer and more remote areas, which tend to bear most of the direct social and environmental costs of extractions and where service provision is more challenging. On the other hand, the royalties from the resources may potentially create large differentials in own-source revenues between the local jurisdictions where the natural resources are located and most others. Decentralized provision may best be combined with centralized financing. The distribution rules need to be negotiated clearly and transparently between the center and local governments to avoid creating political tensions and conflict.

Pros and Cons

Although decentralizing service delivery can alleviate information asymmetries, other trade-offs may arise. Local governments are said to have certain advantages over central governments, such as (1) better information about local needs and conditions; (2) responsibility for smaller, more homogeneous jurisdictions; and (3) public officials who are more accountable to voters (Galiani, Gertler, and Schargrodsky 2008). In other words, decentralization can alleviate information asymmetries, agency costs, and collective action problems in service delivery. However, decentralization can also be less efficient in delivering services if central agencies are better able to achieve economies of scale and better equipped to deliver the services technically and organizationally—or if local elites have captured subnational institutions. The theoretical literature highlights these trade-offs, which require context- and service-specific resolution (for an extensive review of decentralization and governance, see Bardhan 2002; and Faguet 2014).

Empirical Evidence

Empirical studies provide a mixed view of how decentralization affects the delivery of health and education services. A review of studies from the last 20 years that have tried to assess the causal impact of decentralization on health and education found a variety of effects (Channa and Faguet 2012). In general, decentralization pushes up spending, but more for education than for health. However, its relationship with health or education outcomes is less clear.

Evidence from Bolivia and Indonesia showed increased local investment in education. After Bolivia underwent devolution reform in 1994, studies found a statistically significant increase in investment in education (Channa and Faguet 2012;

Faguet 2004). Similarly, political decentralization to Indonesian districts was associated with more public spending overall; when aggregated, overall spending on education increased, but not spending on health (Skoufias and others 2011). In China, a significant relationship was found between county-level fiscal decentralization and infant mortality rates (Uchimura and Jütting 2009).

In education, cross-country analyses of international student assessments—such as the Programme for International Student Assessment and the Trends in International Mathematics and Science Study—found that countries with more local decision-making authority and greater accountability have better learning outcomes (Fuchs and Woessmann 2007). In Kenya, test scores were significantly higher for pupils taught by contract teachers hired by the parent-teacher association than for pupils taught by government teachers (Duflo, Dupas, and Kremer 2012). This was attributed to the fact that the association had the power to hire and fire contract teachers, but no control over government teachers.

A review of Uganda's public spending on education paints a pessimistic picture of resource allocation between the central and local authorities. Uganda's local governments rely on transfers from the central government for more than 90 percent of their revenue, yet transfers have fallen from about 5 to about 3.5 percent of GDP, which has led to a steep decline in local government spending on social services. Education budgets have been especially hard hit; between 2001/02 and 2011/12 real per capita transfers were reduced nearly 20 percent (World Bank 2013d). Public spending per capita also varies greatly across districts, by a factor of 6.3 in 2010. The number of students per primary school teacher varies from 32 to 100. Heightening value-for-money in education in the districts that are lagging behind could help the country to achieve better outcomes without raising costs.

Summary on Decentralization

The evidence for decentralization as a potential mechanism for improving governance of service delivery is mixed.[3] On the one hand, it seems to be associated with an increase in public spending on health and education. This association is promising for resource-rich countries because it provides a means of transferring rents to subnational levels. On the other hand, the evidence on actual human development outcomes is sparse and mixed:

1. Decentralization efforts are most effective when the responsibilities of different levels of government are clearly defined. The Ugandan case highlights how a shift in central government priorities can affect local government budgets and priorities. There needs to be a clear understanding of what roles are most suitable for the central and local levels and what capacity is available at both.
2. Local actors are likely to be more effective if they have the appropriate authority and capacity to undertake their responsibilities.
3. Closely related to clearly defining the responsibilities of central and local governments is the need to put in place complementary fiscal rules that (1) take into account the size of the rents from natural resources and the associated

price volatility and that (2) ensure equitable and efficient local distribution based both on needs and own-resource capacities (some of which are associated with the geographic location of the rents). For example, in Brazil, the fiscal decentralization of health care allocated the majority of funding to hospitals, which are mainly in richer localities (World Bank 2003), and discussion about changing the allocation rules for revenues from the new oil fields have generated many discussions.

Private Provision of Services
Issue
Private providers already play a significant role in the delivery of services related to human development, across the income distribution. Private providers are responsible for delivering at least half the health services in SSA (IFC 2011). For example, in Chad, Niger, and Uganda, more than 40 percent of people in the lowest economic quintile who seek health care for children with symptoms of acute respiratory infection go to private, self-financing providers. In Côte d'Ivoire, the government addressed the lack of spaces in government-run secondary schools by sponsoring students to attend private (religious and secular) secondary schools and training institutions (LaRocque 2008). Resource-rich countries can use their resource rents and formulate institutional rules and mechanisms to enhance partnerships with the private sector for service delivery, particularly in education and health.

Pros and Cons
Private providers, it is argued, can have a positive impact on human development outcomes. They can (1) create competition in a particular market; (2) offer more flexible service delivery arrangements (for example, contract teachers and health care workers); (3) improve efficiency and service delivery outcomes by increasing risk sharing between government and private partners; and (4) increase choices for users of services. However, such partnerships may also exacerbate unequal access to high-performing schools or hospitals and reduce the government's control over public services (for a review of public-private partnerships in education, see Brugha and Zwi 1998; IFC 2011; and Patrinos, Barrera-Osorio, and Guáqueta 2009).

Public-private partnerships (PPPs) use a variety of arrangements, ranging from government funding of existing private schools and hospitals to expanding access to contracts to deliver a range of inputs and introduce management efficiencies that the public sector lacks (Patrinos, Barrera-Osorio, and Guáqueta 2009).[4] For example, The Gambia and Mauritius subsidize private schools, mostly faith-based nonprofits, either with school inputs, such as teacher salaries and textbooks, or through grants to students.

At the other end of the spectrum, in some countries, the framework for the relationships between public and private sectors is still incipient. In the Republic of Congo, official relationships between the public and private sectors are limited, apart from tax and regulation issues, so a dialogue mechanism has been proposed to increase their interaction in the health sector (Makinen, Deville, and Folsom 2012). In Mali, there is no formal dialogue between the public and private health sectors, but private community health facilities are more closely integrated into the policy environment than the traditional for-profit private operators (Lamiaux, Rouzaud, and Woods 2011).[5]

Empirical Literature

The evidence suggests that in those education systems that have PPPs, students perform better on a variety of indicators (Angrist, Bettinger, and Kremer 2006; Barrera-Osorio and others 2011; Bettinger, Kremer, and Saavedra 2010). Other studies, such as that by Uribe and others (2005), have not found any difference in student performance between public and private schools.

In the health sector, there is a continuing, robust debate about the relationship of private providers to health systems and health outcomes (see Basu and others 2012; Brugha and Zwi 1998). In their review of related research studies, Basu and others (2012) concluded that the private sector is not necessarily more efficient, accountable, or medically effective than the public sector; however, the public sector appears to lack timeliness and hospitality toward patients and has a more limited availability of equipment, medications, and trained medical health providers.

It is important to acknowledge the heterogeneity of the private actors that deliver services. For example, agencies providing health and education services may be nonprofit or for-profit, faith-based or secular, or affiliated with a variety of other groups. Their motivations vary; some are driven by a profit motive, others by religious views, and others by another moral or social imperative. Do these varying motivations affect service delivery? Reinikka and Svensson (2010) found religious nonprofit health care providers to be intrinsically more motivated to serve poor people in Uganda. There is some evidence that faith-based private schools do not reach the poor more than public schools, but they do reach the poor substantially more than private secular schools (Wodon 2013).

Summary on the Private Provision of Human Development Services

Building the governance environment is important for strengthening the private provision of services. The emerging, and mixed, evidence of the impact of PPPs highlights the need for government policies to create a policy and regulatory environment that is relevant to all actors in a sector. Of the 45 African countries covered in a study by the International Finance Corporation (IFC 2011), 38 have an official policy of working with the private sector, although limited capacity is a major impediment to doing so.

Better regulation is one way of building up private provision and thus improving service delivery outcomes. In many countries, significant amounts of public resources have been used to regulate the private sector and improve service delivery, with limited success (Basu and others 2012). Private actors in Ghana's health sector identified as problems inadequate information on regulations, complex and nontransparent regulations, and the limited capacity of the responsible public agencies to monitor and evaluate private providers. The public agency responsible for regulation could not identify a significant number of private providers to assess accreditation and quality (Ojo 2013).

The Côte d'Ivoire government pays private secondary schools a contractual fixed amount to educate a student. The private schools must be certified and meet several criteria to receive subsidies, including meeting input specifications and quality indicators and having prior education experience (Sakellariou and Patrinos 2009). In Uganda, as part of the Universal Secondary Education Policy of 2007, the government contracts out the education of students not served by public and government-aided schools. A memorandum of understanding with the Ministry of Education sets requirements for private schools to submit performance data on a range of indicators, make periodic progress reports, and be subject to periodic reviews and assessments of academic performance. The ministry pays a fixed fee per student (LaRocque 2008).

Patrinos, Barrera-Osorio, and Guáqueta (2009) outlined recommendations for strengthening PPPs, particularly in education, among them (1) clearly defining operating requirements and performance standards for private schools; (2) setting output measures, including quality indicators, in contracts for education services; and (3) establishing special agencies to manage private school operations and the flow of funds from government to private schools in order to consolidate expertise on education PPPs.

Incentives

Incentives affect the way provider organizations, their managers, and their staff are held accountable for their behavior and ability to deliver services with quality and efficiency. From this vantage point, what is of interest is how providers are selected, paid, monitored, and held accountable for their performance, notably in delivering human development services (Fiszbein, Ringold, and Rogers 2011). These complex relationships are often characterized by both information asymmetries and varying motivations and objectives. A principal-agent problem arises, in that a principal who desires certain results needs to ensure that the agent responsible for doing the requisite tasks actually does so. If agents shirk their responsibilities (due to information asymmetries and different motivations), the principal must then put in place a mechanism—a contract or compact—to align the incentives.

There are different ways to structure these relationships, among them performance incentives—result- or performance-based financing (RBF or PBF)—which may be cash or nonmonetary benefits provided against measurable actions or achievement and cash transfers (conditional or unconditional) that seek to heighten demand. During booms, resource-rich countries have the fiscal space to employ incentive structures that can affect service delivery. During busts, well-targeted transfer programs can prove to be a more efficient means of spending public resources than general subsidies (for example, fuel subsidies).

From Mines and Wells to Well-Built Minds • http://dx.doi.org/10.1596/978-1-4648-1005-3

Supply Side: Results-Based Financing

Issue

RBF refers to the "transfer of money or material goods conditional on taking a measurable action or achieving a predetermined performance target" (Musgrove 2011; Oxman and Fretheim 2009).[6] In health care, for example, financing mechanisms traditionally focused on inputs—such as infrastructure, medical supplies, and equipment—on the implicit assumption that quality would follow (Morgan and Eichler 2011; HRITF and World Bank 2014). RBF interventions can target various stakeholders; for example, consumers, when they undertake health-related behaviors, such as having a child immunized, or providers, when they achieve performance targets, such as a percentage of children immunized.[7]

Pros and Cons

RBF has the potential to address problems such as the underuse of services, low quality of care, and inefficient delivery of services. RBF shifts some of the risk borne by the principal under traditional financing arrangements where payment does not depend on results (Pearson, Johnson, and Ellison 2010). That is, RBF is expected to improve the quality and availability of services due to increased motivation derived from incentives—financial or otherwise. Different aspects of quality can be assessed in an RBF scheme—(1) inputs: linking performance incentives to inputs needed for care, such as the availability of essential drugs or accreditation; (2) process: linking performance incentives to compliance with evidence-based guided care (following treatment protocols) or patient satisfaction; and (3) outcomes: linking performance incentives to mortality and morbidity indicators (Ergo and others 2012).

Critiques of RBF schemes for health and education question whether material rewards replace or conflict with intrinsic motivation. If educators or health care providers are already strongly motivated, skeptics argue, incentives that provide rewards convey a lack of trust in the providers, which has a negative impact on quality (see, for example, Benabou and Tirole 2006; Eichler, Levine, and Performance-Based Incentives Working Group 2009; Ellingsen and Johannesson 2008). Participants in the incentives intervention may also learn to game the system; for example, teachers may only work the exact times needed to meet target income (Fehr and Goette 2007), or health care providers may only offer services to the group targeted by the incentive, reducing overall provision (Eichler, Levine, and Performance-Based Incentives Working Group 2009).

Empirical Evidence

Impact evaluations paint a mixed picture of how RBF affects human development outcomes. Careful attention to program design and implementation is critical to RBF success. In health, RBF is said to increase autonomy, strengthen autonomy, and empower frontline workers and facility managers. New evidence

---

Box 3.6 Results-Based Financing: A Tale of Two Sub-Saharan African Countries

Rwanda. Rwanda was the first African country to implement RBF (*l'approche contractuelle*) in its health sector. The program was adopted as national policy in the 2005–09 Health Strategic Plan and was later incorporated into the National Finance Law (Morgan and Eichler 2011). The quality of service being delivered in hospitals was assessed in two ways: a team of central-level evaluations made random visits, and a team of medical professionals from peer hospitals performed reviews. The quality of primary care services was assessed through frequent monitoring and supervision by district hospitals. Impact evaluations conducted in 2009 found significant improvements. There was a 21 percent increase from the baseline in the probability of deliveries in a health care facility. There was little impact on child vaccinations, although immunization rates in Rwanda were already high when the program began (Basinga and others 2011).

The Democratic Republic of Congo. Between 2009 and 2013, the effect of various health financing mechanisms, including RBF, was evaluated in the Haut-Katanga District as part of the World Bank–supported Projet d'Appui à la Réhabilitation du Secteur de la Santé. The evaluation analyzed the effect of the financing mechanism on service provision in terms of (1) availability of services; (2) price of health services and the cost to patients; (3) health worker satisfaction, work-related stress, and motivation; (4) service use; (5) patient satisfaction; and (6) health status of the population. The results found no significant increases in service use and coverage. However, the incentives did lead to a reduction in absenteeism in facilities receiving results-based incentives compared with facilities in the control group (Health Results Innovation Trust Fund and World Bank 2014).

---

on RBF in health service delivery suggests both significant and insignificant results (box 3.6).

In education, a combination of financial incentives and monitoring can make a difference. In India, teacher pay incentives and monitoring to discourage teacher absenteeism yielded a decrease in teacher absenteeism of 21 percentage points and an increase in student test scores of 0.17 standard deviation compared with the control group (Duflo, Hanna, and Ryan 2012). In Chile, incentives had a positive short-term impact on student performance, but did not improve learning in the long term (Contreras and Rau 2009).

Summary on RBF

Supply-side RBF interventions highlight the role of incentives in improving governance for the delivery of human development services. For resource-rich countries, where service delivery challenges like worker absenteeism are especially high, RBF offers a promising approach. RBF interventions also provide a credible alternative to the common practice of simply increasing supply-side resources in order to improve outcomes.

Demand Side: Conditional and Unconditional Cash Transfers and Direct Dividend Payments

Issue

Distributing resource wealth through cash transfers is one mechanism for facilitating redistribution and poverty reduction, increasing the transparency of resource use, and supporting citizen engagement. Cash transfer programs provide noncontributory cash grants to beneficiaries to satisfy minimum consumption needs (Garcia and Moore 2012). Such programs can be conditional or unconditional, with the former providing benefits only to program participants who have adhered to prescribed conditions (for example, children must regularly attend school; or a household adult must attend seminars covering such topics as health and nutrition). Unconditional cash transfer programs provide cash grants to all eligible and registered participants.[8] Cash transfers, which can distribute resource rents directly to citizens (box 3.7), have been demonstrated to be effective in tackling poverty and vulnerability.

Box 3.7   Direct Dividend Payments

Direct dividend payments (DDPs) consist of the direct distribution to citizens of all or part of the resource revenues. While the idea of DDPs is not new, it has recently gained international recognition (Devarajan and Giugale 2013; Devarajan, Minh Le, and Raballand 2010; Gillies 2010; McGuirk, Rajaram, and Giugale 2016; Moss and Majerowicz 2013; Moss and Young 2009). In 1976, the State of Alaska established one of the earliest DDP systems, the Alaska Permanent Fund, which receives at least 25 percent of oil revenues. The fund invests the revenues, and every Alaska resident gets a share of the dividends. In countries like Bolivia and Mongolia, resource payments are more targeted: in Mongolia, the Child Money Fund uses mining revenues to pay poor families with children; in Bolivia, Renta Dignidad spends oil and natural gas proceeds on pensions for everyone older than 65 years of age, differentially by income.

DDP proponents focus on the potential and theoretical governance gains that the approach delivers. By giving citizens a direct payment out of resource revenues, the program would create a nationwide constituency a more responsible management of these resources (Devarajan, Minh Le, and Raballand 2010; Palley 2003; Sandbu 2006). The DDP literature also points to the empowering effects the program could have by eliminating the state's monopoly on resource revenue and transferring the cash to citizens. By diminishing the total funds available to the state, the policy forces the government to be more cautious about spending and increases the opportunity cost of misspending (Shaxson 2008). DDPs could also mitigate the principal-agent problems that affect the allocation of public funds where institutions are weak—that is, they circumvent the problem by eliminating the intermediary maker of decisions about spending public resources (the state) and give decision-making power to the individuals (Devarajan, Minh Le, and Raballand 2010; Moss and Young 2009; Sandbu 2006).

Direct payments could create an environment conducive to good governance. But they could just as easily create an environment of entitlements, where the citizens' lobby focuses only on the size of the cash transfers (Collier 2013; Sandbu 2006). Another risk of circumventing

box continues next page

Box 3.7 Direct Dividend Payments *(continued)*

the state system is of undermining the public sector's institutional capacity or absolving it of any responsibility toward its citizens (Gillies 2010). If state institutions are completely bypassed, the likely result is that the government will never become more efficient and the system will never have to reform, as there will be no pressure to do so. The literature showcases the example of Alaska, where studies have found citizens disengaged from public life, growing disinterest in scrutinizing public spending, a perception of the government as a distributor of funds, and a powerful lobby against redirecting cash transfers to public investment (Cowper 2007; Devarajan, Minh Le, and Raballand 2010; Goldsmith 2002).

McGuirk, Rajaram, and Giugale (2016) analyzed the theoretical conditions under which DDPs are rational for political candidates. They found, first, that propitious political conditions—including competitive elections, undeveloped patronage networks, and a high degree of budgetary accountability—increase the share of resource revenues to be spent on citizens' welfare. They then showed that a high poverty headcount and inefficient public institutions will each strengthen the political incentive to provide direct dividend transfers relative to public goods. This combination of conditions is rare, which may explain why relatively few countries have implemented or plan to implement direct dividend transfers. Leaders who are not constrained by electoral incentives—for example, those facing term limits and no internal party discipline—are more likely to renege on policy proposals and extract more rents for personal benefit.

DDP proponents point to one essential adjustment that could help to mitigate some of the potential downfalls: taxing the payments (Devarajan, Minh Le, and Raballand 2010). Taxes would create incentives for optimized behavior. On the one hand, political as well practical costs to the state are associated with taxation, so there is an incentive to spend more carefully. On the other hand, in giving tax money back to the state, citizens have an incentive to scrutinize the use of these funds and to keep institutions accountable for the delivery of public services. However, taxation would work only if a substantial enough percentage of revenues is distributed via DDPs; otherwise, there is little incentive to tax (Gillies 2010).

Some mainstream critiques of DDPs point out that because resource-rich countries in Africa have a severe infrastructure gap and poor levels of human development, investment in such public goods should have priority. Proponents, however, point to the high levels of leakage and very low levels of service delivery in these countries to justify allocating public funds to DDPs (Moss and Majerowicz 2013). Arezki, Dupay, and Gelb (2012) showed that the higher the resource revenue, the higher the "adjustment costs" governments incur and concluded that the optimal public spending policy should focus on direct payments rather than public investment. Devarajan and others (2011) and Devarajan and Giugale (2013) have pointed out that DDPs could even increase spending on public goods due to the additional scrutiny of public spending.

Pros and Cons

Demand-side programs like cash transfers are thought to be more efficient in using resources and more effective at improving outcomes than supply-side-only interventions (Patrinos 2007). Also, cash transfers may potentially transform the social and economic relationships within households and communities by "providing opportunities for social groups who are often denied access to decision-making structures to build 'bridges' and social connections both horizontally, with other community members, and vertically, with state actors" (Samuels, Jones, and Malachowska 2013). Cash transfers, particularly those with conditions, are expected to increase citizens' demand for services and thus strengthen their stake in how services are delivered.

Among the challenges facing cash transfer programs are (1) the large number of beneficiaries; (2) the sharing of program responsibilities across many government agencies (social welfare, education, and health) and levels (central, municipal, and local); (3) high visibility; and (4) the need for well-functioning payment and accounting systems.

Empirical Evidence

Cash transfer programs improve outcomes such as consumption, nutrition, education, and health (a more detailed discussion is available in chapter 4). In analyzing the pilot conditional cash transfer program in three districts in Tanzania, Evans and others (2014) noted positive effects on the health and education outcomes for households that received the transfers. For example, those households were 5 percentage points less likely to be sick (average across all ages). Soares and Teixeira (2010) found that Mozambique's Food Subsidy Program raised the proportion of household expenditures on food by 22 percent, with even larger increases for female-headed households. Household adults were more likely to be working (increased probability of 17 percent for male adults and the elderly and 24 percent for female adults, although the increase was only marginally significant), and boys ages 5–9 years were less likely to work (decreased probability of 29 percent). An evaluation of Zambia's program in three districts found positive effects on consumption, particularly nonfood consumption (RHVP 2009). Levine, van der Berg, and Yu (2009), who analyzed Namibia's grant system, concluded that the transfers significantly decreased the number of poor people, with an even more notable decrease in the number of those who were extremely poor.

Better accountability mechanisms matter for improving the governance of both cash transfers and service delivery. Social protection programs like cash transfers can affect social relationships by allowing social groups, particularly the vulnerable, to participate in decision-making processes and interact with other stakeholders. In their qualitative and participatory assessment of cash transfer programs in Kenya, Mozambique, Uganda, the West Bank and Gaza, and the Republic of Yemen, Samuels, Jones, and Malachowska (2013) identified three ways to enhance accountability in cash transfer programs:

1. *Grievance mechanisms to provide formal channels for citizens to express dissatisfaction and demand redress.* The three categories of grievance redress mechanisms are (a) mechanisms within government agencies—such as hotlines, complaints offices, and websites—that field complaints about government programs and services; (b) independent institutions—such as ombudsmen, tribunals, and civil society organizations—that operate outside the formal government bureaucracy and may have little to no public authority to enforce their findings; and (c) the courts. Most cash transfer programs have a grievance and complaints procedure, but their record is mixed.

2. *Program feedback loops to provide continuing information about program experiences through suggestion boxes or meetings with direct beneficiaries.* Limited interactions between program officials and beneficiaries undermined the effectiveness of feedback loops in Mozambique and the Republic of Yemen (Samuels, Jones, and Malachowska 2013).
3. *Monitoring and evaluation to assess whether program objectives are being met and how the program is being implemented and delivered and to identify lessons learned.*

Access to information and audits should also be considered a key mechanism for improving the accountability and governance of cash transfer programs. The rationale is that having access to budget information, operations manuals, and rigorous independent evaluations will give citizens incentives to use the information to address program strengths and weaknesses (for example, to perform social audits on program and provider performance). However, the assumption obscures the reality that access to information and audits without active campaigns to inform citizens of their rights and the standards and program performance they should expect are unlikely to make service delivery more accountable (Ringold and others 2012). In resource-rich developing countries, where access to information on resource wealth is severely limited, promoting the accountability of cash transfer programs for service delivery through access to information and audits will have to confront this challenge.

Summary on Cash Transfers

Cash transfers as a demand-side program to encourage citizens' participation in service delivery have proved promising for promoting human capital accumulation. In SSA, cash transfers are becoming increasingly common, and as they spread, it is important to identify accountability mechanisms that not only enhance human capital but also change the social relations that inhibit the formation of human capital. For resource-rich countries, cash transfers are one way to distribute resource wealth and stimulate citizens' demand for better services.

Information

Citizens want information about natural resources and how they are used. Access to information can enable social accountability, through redress, monitoring, and other opportunities for citizen action. In resource-rich countries, where public institutions and civil society may be weak and information scarce or opaque, giving citizens access to information may be particularly powerful. Box 3.8 summarizes the policy recommendations of a recent research report on transparency and political engagement (Khemani 2016).

Citizens are often unaware both of the amount of resource revenues and their use. They generally lack information about the services available to them, their rights, and the quality and standard of services they should expect. In Tanzania, two-thirds of the population reported that they would like more information about natural gas discoveries (Gaddis and others 2014). They expect the

---

Box 3.8 Transparency to Improve the Quality of Political Engagement

Sustainable improvements in governance can happen when two forces—transparency and political engagement—interact and work together to strengthen institutions (Khemani 2016). Targeted information that interacts with political engagement, enabling citizens to select and sanction leaders on the basis of performance in delivering public goods, can strengthen institutions by shaping how leaders behave in office, disciplined by the threat of challengers. The study concludes with four key policy recommendations:

1. Policies should support the generation of reliable and impartial evidence on the performance of leaders tasked with the delivery of public policies. This should include information on the consequences of policy actions for public good outcomes.

2. Policies should promote healthy competition in media markets, complemented by regulations to support public interest programming. Sponsorship of appealing programs, or so-called "infotainment," to communicate the findings of technical evidence, holds potential to change norms and persuade citizens to shift political beliefs in ways that strengthen the demand for good policies.

3. Information on the provision of public goods at the local level is more relevant to voters' decisions in local elections than is information at the national level. Performance assessments of both current incumbents and challengers, delivered regularly during a term in office but also at the time of elections, can make it easier for citizens to use information to hold leaders accountable.

4. Governments should experiment with the design of public sector institutions to take advantage of the interaction between growing political engagement and transparency, and they should do so in crosscutting ways. Models of individual citizen engagement should not rest on organized groups within each school or health clinic—rather, it should target individual domains of citizen action, such as a local administrative level with a range of service delivery responsibilities.

Source: Adapted from Khemani 2016.

---

government to provide information and think that education and health should be priority sectors for investment.

The gap between laws mandating transparency and accountability and their actual influence on service delivery is large. Few countries, including those that are resource-rich, have access-to-information laws or mandate that information be provided about the human development sectors. Yet in resource-rich countries where information asymmetries are particularly skewed, the lack of legal requirements for access to information undermines opportunities for governance and efforts at accountability for the allocation of resource rents. Even in countries that do have access-to-information laws, their application may be minimal and channels for grievance redress may be absent or difficult to access. Generally, resource-rich countries fail to provide basic information about the extractive sector; where they do, those transparency initiatives tend to be externally driven, such as the Extractive Industries Transparency Initiative, with little local ownership (Revenue Watch Institute 2010). According to the 2013 resource governance index, which analyzes the governance environment of resource-rich countries and assigns a composite score of 0–100, 11 of the 15 Sub-Saharan resource-rich countries analyzed had weak or failing scores.[9]

Social Accountability

Issue

Social accountability, also known as "bottom-up" accountability, refers to tools citizens can use to influence the quality of service delivery by holding providers accountable. It covers interventions to provide citizens with information and channels to use it, such as citizen monitoring, oversight, and feedback on public sector performance; user-centered access to and dissemination of public information; public complaints and grievance redress mechanisms; and citizens' participation in resource allocation decisions, such as participatory budgeting. Social accountability interventions aim "to improve institutional performance by bolstering both citizen engagement and the public responsiveness of states and corporations" (Fox 2014).

While the emphasis is on citizen action, policy makers and service providers are central to making these types of interventions more effective. Social accountability initiatives give resource-rich countries another possible means of enhancing the governance environment regarding resource wealth management and service delivery.

Pros and Cons

From a theoretical perspective, there is no clear prediction of the impact of social accountability interventions. On the one hand, citizens' participation in and monitoring of policy making and program planning can help to ensure that service and program objectives reflect citizens' needs and priorities. Citizens' monitoring and evaluation can also help to ensure the proper use of resources and provide feedback on problems and successes in service delivery. Participatory budgeting in Porto Alegre, Brazil, is a well-known citizen participation program that has increased school enrollment and improved water and sanitation services (Shah 2007). Factors that contributed to the success of this initiative include access to information, inclusion and participation, and local organizational capacity.

As noted, citizens often lack trust in government institutions and their ability to deliver services. Social accountability can help to enhance government legitimacy by allowing citizens to have a say in government services. Social accountability can also increase revenues. In Porto Alegre, municipal revenues increased almost 50 percent in four years (De Sousa Santos 1998; Schneider and Baquero 2006). More transparency in the use of funds and inclusion of citizens in making decisions about resource allocation have motivated citizens to pay taxes.

While giving citizens information about service delivery and channels to use it has potential, there are major caveats and bottlenecks to making social accountability work on the side of citizens and policy makers (Molina 2014; Ringold and others 2012):

1. Citizens may not have access to information, be able to absorb or use information, or feel empowered to engage with service providers. They also face other constraints, such as limited time and attention spans, poor literacy, and collective action problems. Efforts that task citizens with tracking budget allocations for local services (schools or health centers) or engaging in community targeting for cash transfer programs may not be effective if time commitments are prohibitive; they may not include the poor or vulnerable because other priorities are more pressing (Alatas and others 2010; Banerjee and Mullainathan 2008).
2. Even if citizens use social accountability interventions to highlight service delivery challenges, providers may not respond. Some experimental evidence suggests that increasing citizens' information can be effective in making providers accountable to their clients (see Andrabi, Das, and Khwaja 2009; Currie, Lin, and Zhang 2011). Other studies found no change in the relationship between providers and clients (Keefer and Khemani 2011). This raises the issue of other factors—such as the political, historical, and cultural dynamics and the role of incentives for service providers—that shape the interactions between citizens and providers.

Empirical Evidence

The literature does not provide a clear picture of how social accountability interventions affect service delivery and is particularly sparse for resource-rich countries. Reinikka and Svensson (2004, 2005, 2011) analyzed the impact of user-centered public information access and dissemination on improving education outcomes in Uganda. They found a significant reduction in the capturing of funds, especially in areas with higher newspaper penetration. They also found that, in such areas, both enrollment rates and test scores experienced a significant jump. Lieberman, Posner, and Tsai (2014) analyzed the impact of an information campaign on educational outcomes in rural Kenya. They found that the intervention, which was designed to reduce the information gap of parents about their children's outcomes and ways to improve them, had no discernible impact on education outcomes. They concluded that providing information about the quality of services in developing countries is in itself not enough to generate a change in behavior.

Tanzania's health sector was decentralized in the mid-1990s to ensure better service and greater community participation by creating council health service boards to design service delivery improvement plans and participatory health care budgeting. However, although the formal structures were generally set up properly, the actual influence of citizens on the process was limited, and participatory planning at the community level was not reflected in the priorities set (Friis-Hansen and Cold-Ravnkilde 2013; Maluka and others 2010 and 2011;

Tidemand, Olsen, and Sola 2008). These results are in sharp contrast to the findings from Porto Alegre's participatory budgeting and underscore the limitations of such interventions in environments with feeble formal processes of decision making and accountability. Bjorkman and Svensson (2009) estimated the impact of a Citizen Report Card intervention—a pilot community involvement and monitoring of primary health service delivery—on health clinic performance in Uganda. A year after the intervention, treatment communities saw increased use and improved health outcomes. The most significant results were reduced child mortality and higher child weight in communities that were more involved in monitoring and where the provider exerted more effort in delivering health services.

Summary on Social Accountability

While social accountability interventions are increasingly used to bring citizens into the policy-making and program implementation processes of public service delivery and seem promising avenues for citizens' participation and monitoring of service delivery, it is crucial to understand the context in which they take place. This bottom-up or demand-side approach is said to improve service delivery outcomes, enhance government legitimacy, and assert citizens' voices. However, both theoretical and empirical research studies have found mixed expected and actual outcomes from such interventions:

1. Accountability interactions take place in unique social, political, historical, and cultural contexts, which may not change easily and quickly. Relationships between citizens and providers or policy makers may be such that citizens are reluctant to challenge their authority (Ringold and others 2012).
2. Social accountability may not improve the quality of service delivery on its own, unless supported by fairly well-functioning formal institutions (for example, access-to-information laws, transparent budget-making processes, and audit and other formal monitoring institutions). Fox (2014) distinguished between "tactical" and "strategic" accountability programs. Tactical programs focus too heavily on applying specific tools such as citizen scorecards, are too short term in planning and objectives, and are often implemented as isolated projects. Strategic programs are more long term, are integrated with other transparency and accountability initiatives, and have several entry points. This strategic approach to social accountability is promising.

Accountability relationships in resource-rich countries may be especially high-stakes, given the rents, volume, and volatility of natural resource wealth and the inadequacy of their institutions. However, there are encouraging examples of citizens' groups organizing themselves to demand better services through monitoring and participation (box 3.9).

Box 3.9 Social Accountability in Resource-Rich Countries

The Democratic Republic of Congo. In the Katanga Province of the Democratic Republic of Congo, the civil society organization Commission Diocésaine de Justice et Paix (CDJP) led an initiative to engage with a local mining company and others (government officials, other civil society organizations) to promote transparency and accountability in the extractives sector. The mining company and government officials were initially reluctant to disclose information, but, through a series of workshops that reinforced relationships among the actors, "champions" within the government, and an extended civil society network, the CDJP was able to audit the allocation of resource rents to local communities (Integrity Action 2014a).

Côte d'Ivoire. In the rural community of Jacqueville, residents and a mining company disagreed about the company's allocation of resources to rehabilitate teachers' quarters and construct an additional building for its own purposes. The community contended that the rehabilitation was not done properly. The civil society organization, Initiative pour la Justice Sociale, la Bonne Gouvernance, et la Transparence en Côte d'Ivoire (Social Justice), sought constructive engagement between the community and the mining company. Social Justice organized a series of trainings to sensitize the community on its rights, facilitated a meeting between the mining company and the community, and engaged the media to shed light on the project and its problems. These strategies were effective components of a social accountability campaign (Integrity Action 2014b).

Information and Communication Technology
Issue

The rapid rate of change has created opportunities for innovative approaches to access to information, particularly in developing countries. The emergence of new ICTs has created numerous ways to make data transparent and information accessible and to conduct monitoring and reporting activities. Among these technologies are community radio, mobile phone apps, short message service (SMS), social media, wikis, interactive mapping, and websites (Avila and others 2010; Bertot, Jaeger, and Grimes 2010; Wittemyer and others 2014; for a more encompassing treatment of digital dividends, see World Bank 2016).

Developing countries have seen an unprecedented diffusion of ICTs. The number of smartphone owners in developing countries now exceeds that in the developed world (World Bank 2016). Since 2005 mobile phone subscription rates in both resource-rich and non–resource-rich SSA countries have been rising, increasing at a higher rate in the former than in the latter (figure 3.7). ICTs can help citizens to expand their resources and knowledge, demand public services, and have a voice in the governance processes shaping service delivery.

Figure 3.7 Mobile Phone Subscriptions Are Rising More Quickly in Resource-Rich Than in Non–Resource-Rich SSA: Mobile Phone Subscription Rate, 2000–13

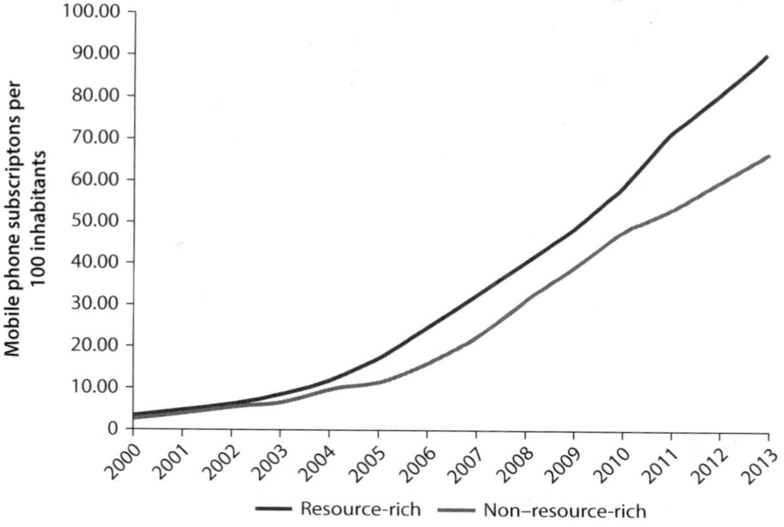

Source: ITU 2013.
Note: SSA = Sub-Saharan Africa.

Pros and Cons

ICTs can be used to relieve information asymmetries, reduce some time constraints for participation, and expand platforms and means of communication. They can enhance both the demand for and supply of governance. New technologies give citizens the means to demand better service by broadening the distribution of information and facilitating networking among geographically dispersed people. ICTs can allow policy makers and service providers to engage citizens in policy- and decision-making processes, expand stakeholder participation, offer greater access to public information, and deliver services to targeted groups (UNDP 2014). They allow information to both flow downward (government-to-citizens) and upward (citizens-to-government) (Wittemyer and others 2014).

ICTs cannot operate in a vacuum, as mentioned in World Bank (2016). The benefits of using ICTs to expand access to information, broaden participation, and improve service delivery are realized when the state fosters an environment that allows citizens to access public information easily. Citizens also need to be informed that the information is available and how to access and use it. Without access-to-information laws and other regulations that deal with the use of ICTs, their benefits will be minimal. Analyses of open government initiatives and right-to-information laws and policies highlight the importance of having a capable civil service and bureaucracy and buy-in by users, civil servants, policy makers, politicians, and other stakeholders (McGee and Gaventa 2010).

Citizens who cannot afford access to certain ICT-driven platforms are also excluded. This undermines one of the advantages of ICTs as an inclusive means for participation.

Empirical Evidence

There are numerous examples of ICT-enabled programs that stimulate access to information and service delivery, and the empirical evidence on impact is emerging.

In 2009, the ICT4GOV Program was introduced in South Kivu in the Democratic Republic of Congo to facilitate decentralization of governance and service delivery. ICT4GOV uses mobile technology to enhance the participatory budgeting approach to service delivery in a variety of ways: (1) SMS texts are used to alert households about participatory budgeting assembly meetings; (2) citizens use their mobile phones (via SMS texting) to vote on issues to include in the agenda; (3) voting outcomes are shared via SMS texting; and (4) mobile phones are used to monitor and evaluate programs as citizens provide feedback via SMS. Preliminary findings from an external evaluation found a positive impact on tax revenues; citizens are more likely to pay their taxes because they are now more likely to associate tax payment with improvements in services. In some jurisdictions, tax collection has risen 20-fold since the project began. Communities now have investment budgets and are devoting up to 40 percent to investments. In Luhinja, 54 classrooms were constructed; in Bagira, a new health center was built and the sewage system is being repaired; and in Ibanda, water fountains and public toilets were installed at local markets (Gigler and Bailur 2014).

As part of a school grant program in Indonesia, SMS text messages to parents proved to be an effective way to convey program details as well as to trigger parental participation in school activities (Cerdan-Infantes and Filmer 2015).

The Check My School Program in the Philippines uses open data to promote citizens' monitoring of public school performance. The program combines on-the-ground community monitoring with ICT-enabled mechanisms, such as an online platform to access information on the provision of education services. Data from the Department of Education are presented in a user-friendly format on a website, and the data are validated (or not) from visits to schools by "infomediaries" (community leaders and other socially active individuals). An analysis of the pilot phase noted that motivated, well-organized civil society groups; "champions" within government agencies; endorsement by the Department of Education; and access to information proved to be the conditions that enabled the launch of the program (Shkabatur 2014).

Stop Stockouts is a regional campaign in some African countries (Kenya, Madagascar, Malawi, South Africa, Uganda, Zambia, and Zimbabwe) to ensure that all public health facilities are stocked with essential medicines. Stop Stockouts uses SMS from visiting researchers to monitor medicines' availability in public health facilities—"pill checks." Impact evaluation is under way for this campaign.

Summary on ICTs

ICTs are potential governance game changers, but context and offline institutional settings matter. ICTs allow policy makers and service providers to offer services on a variety of platforms and citizens to be active in making decisions and monitoring service delivery. ICTs offer both top-down and bottom-up approaches, but efforts to use ICTs as governance mechanisms in service delivery will have to contend with issues such as the general policy environment for ICT-enabled approaches, the selection of participants, and how broad-based participation is.

Improving the Governance of Human Development Services in Resource-Rich Countries

Recent windfall natural resource rents have created a significant window of opportunity for many SSA countries to put in place policies and programs that transform the rents into sustained growth. Investing in human capital is vital. However, just as the availability of resource rents presents opportunities, it also presents challenges for delivering services that contribute to developing human capital. Table 3.2 summarizes the discussion of the role of institutions, incentives, and information in overcoming challenges particular to resource-rich countries.

Table 3.2 Guiding Principles for Improving the Governance of Service Delivery in Resource-Rich Countries

Indicator	Institutions	Incentives	Information
Rents	Draft and reinforce the formal rules and structures that shape allocation of rents. For example, • A fiscal regime that maximizes broad-based allocation of rents • Decentralized arrangements to allow for subnational transfer of rents • Rules to guide private provision of services	Consider incentive-based interventions that link allocation of rents to service delivery outcomes and use	Reduce information asymmetries to stimulate citizens' monitoring of government spending and service provision: • Disclose contract terms and support third-party monitoring of bundled contracts • Improve the flow of information about resource rents • Use analytical and diagnostic tools such as public expenditure tracking to determine allocation of resources
Volume	Strengthen public investment management to make PIM more efficient	Establish clear PIM rules to guide capital versus recurrent spending	Provide quality-of-service information to assess the efficiency and effectiveness of sectors that maximize social welfare
Volatility	Establish and adhere to fiscal rules that help to smooth spending-related decisions during booms and busts; promote countercyclical spending; separate regulatory from service provision agencies	Consider earmarks to protect social spending; provide matching grants and performance-based transfers	Disseminate information on countercyclical mechanisms to protect social spending; provide clarity on budget assumptions related to resource rents and allocation

Note: PIM = public investment management.

From Mines and Wells to Well-Built Minds • http://dx.doi.org/10.1596/978-1-4648-1005-3

Institutional design that shapes rent allocation, incentives that address asymmetries, and information interventions that stimulate transparency can maximize spending of resource rents on human capital. The fiscal regime and decentralized arrangements between central and local authorities can help governments to spend resource wealth and allocate rents to sectors that contribute to human capital. It is important for resource-rich countries to have the capacity to collect resource revenues, prioritize their allocation and spending, and minimize capturing. Decentralized service delivery with a centralized funding formula allows for the subnational distribution of rents to health, education, and social protection. It has the potential to encourage responsiveness and participation by local authorities, local service providers, and citizens. However, decentralized services are likely to be most effective when the rules and responsibilities of all stakeholders are clear.

Both supply and demand incentives for service delivery can mitigate information and motivation asymmetries for all concerned. RBF as a supply-side-incentive intervention makes financing contingent on results. Where service delivery is low or quality is poor, RBF has promise for tackling these challenges. Cash transfers are demand-side incentive programs to stimulate citizens' use of services that help to form human capital, but also to create spaces where participation and accountability are possible for a wide cross section of social groups. Well-designed cash transfers also provide an effective and efficient means of public spending.

The lack or inadequate availability of information on mining contracts, resource revenues, and public spending of resource revenues make it harder to establish a governance environment that enables service delivery. Access-to-information laws can help to relieve information asymmetries and stimulate citizens' and third-party monitoring of government spending and service provision. Better tracking of public expenditures through diagnostic tools also has potential for improving the flow of information about the allocation and spending of resource rents.

Building the capacity of PIM systems is vital for managing resource rents that are subject to price and volume volatility. Public investment strategies in resource-rich countries have to contend with boom-and-bust cycles that are peculiar to natural resources. During boom periods, high public investment in certain sectors can strain their absorptive capacity, particularly where project management capabilities are weak. Price volatility also affects the financing of the public investment portfolio. During bust cycles, capital spending is among the first to be cut or eliminated. Building up PIM requires strong and sustained political commitment and significant "investment in investing"; it potentially allows for clear rules to smooth expenditure-related decisions.

Boxes 3.10 and 3.11 summarize the experience of Botswana and Chile in investing natural resource wealth and harnessing investment returns to foster broad-based development, highlighting the key features of their governance environment.

Box 3.10 Botswana: A Diversified Portfolio of Investing Natural Resource Wealth

Botswana is the world's top producer of diamonds by volume and widely considered as a success story in administering its diamond wealth. The first large diamond mine was discovered in 1967, a year after independence from Britain. Since then, diamonds have been a major source of government revenue and have driven GDP growth. The Mines and Minerals Act of 1967 vested all mining revenues in the national government, thus reducing the potential for regional conflicts over ownership rights. Botswana is also rich in other minerals, such as copper, nickel, gold, and coal; total mining exports accounted for 79 percent of export earnings in 2011. Diamond exports drove impressive growth from the early 1970s through the late 1990s—GDP per capita, which was less than US$1,000 at independence (in 2011 purchasing power parity dollars), currently exceeds US$15,000. Diamond deposits are due to peak around 2016, and their value is expected to drop sharply after 2020—with depletion expected around 2030.

Government has invested the vast majority of mineral revenues in human and physical capital development—one estimate puts the value at close to 90 percent over the 1983–2014 period, with roughly half of that going to infrastructure and half to human capital investments (African Development Bank 2016). In the 2014 budget, education was allotted 28 percent of government finances, which amounts to about 8 percent of GDP. More than 90 percent of children age 7–13 were in school in 2011, and the country boasted a primary completion rate of 95 percent. Access to secondary school is nearly universal. The Ministry of Health was the second-biggest recipient of allocations from the 2014 budget, with 15.7 percent of funding, and the government consistently spends more than 5 percent of GDP on health care. Botswana spent about 4.4 percent of GDP in 2013 on social protection programs (including safety nets, pensions, and active labor market programs). However, social protection programs are not as efficient as they could be because many of them suffer from limited coverage, fragmentation, poor targeting, and suboptimal monitoring: only 20 percent of poor households are covered by social safety nets (or one-third of eligible individuals, according to International Monetary Fund assessments).

In addition to investing, Botswana has saved a sizable—albeit smaller—share of its natural resource revenues in a sovereign wealth fund. The Pula Fund, a long-term investment portfolio established in 1994, receives some of the income from diamond exports and is managed by the Bank of Botswana. Government deposits are included in the bank's financial statements. The fund was worth about US$6.9 billion in 2013 and has as a dual purpose: to preserve some of the wealth for future generations and to be used as a stabilization measure—for example, to ensure liquidity in the post-2008 global financial crisis. Some media reports have pointed to unexplained drawdowns (Konopo and others 2016).

Botswana has held democratic elections, deemed free by international observers, since independence, although the Botswana Democratic Party has been continuously elected and in power since 1966. Despite criticism of its domination of the political scene, the one-party rule may have contributed to the continuity of successful national-level policies. It has pushed a legal framework promoting strong governance.

box continues next page

Box 3.10 Botswana: A Diversified Portfolio of Investing Natural Resource Wealth *(continued)*

Botswana does not have a freedom-of-information law (efforts to introduce a bill to that effect in 2012 were unsuccessful), but the government publishes almost all budget documents recommended by the Open Budget Initiative, including a citizens' budget. The country has a budget process that includes a participatory dimension—the "budget *pitso*," or consultation forum, which allows the community to be involved. This practice has its roots in the traditional tribal system of consultation in Botswana, the *kgotla*, distinguished by the fact that anyone can express opinions, and decisions are made by consensus. Also significant is that the annual budget process is coordinated with the six-year national development plans that are developed in consultation with civil society members and senior political offices. Botswana has consistently had a low prevalence of corruption, and in 2016 it ranked 35 out of 176 countries in Transparency International's corruption perceptions index.

Box 3.11 Chile: Managing Natural Resource Wealth for Stability

Chile has been resource dependent for more than a century. In the late nineteenth and early twentieth centuries, the country relied heavily on exports of nitrate (of which it was the world's largest producer), but with the discovery of synthetic nitrate, copper became its main export. By the mid-1970s copper represented around 80 percent of Chilean exports—although this fell to close to 40–50 percent in 2000–10, in part due to a major drive for diversification. The national copper corporation—Corporación Nacional del Cobre de Chile—was founded in 1976 after copper mines and fields were nationalized in 1971 and today produces more copper than any other company in the world. Between 1980 and 2014, GDP per capita almost tripled—from under US$7,500 (in 2011 purchasing price parity dollars) to close to US$22,000. GDP per capita grew 2.8 percent per year, on average, in the 1980s, 4.8 percent in the 1990s, 2.5 percent in the 2000s, and 3.5 percent between 2010 and 2014; growth rates closely tracked copper prices year-to-year.

A key part of Chile's approach to managing resource revenue has been its use of savings funds to channel budget surpluses. In 1985 the government created the Copper Stabilization Fund, which was split into two sovereign wealth funds in 2007 (under the Fiscal Responsibility Law):

- The Pension Reserves Fund, which aims to mitigate expected future pension liability shortfalls.
- The Economic and Social Stabilization Fund, which serves macroeconomic stabilization purposes.

The Pension Reserves Fund is a savings fund with no withdrawals allowed for 10 years that receives around 0.2–0.5 percent of GDP, depending on the overall budget surplus (the initial installment was US$600 million). The Economic and Social Stabilization Fund is a stabilization fund (similar to the original fund) that receives fiscal surpluses, which are above 1 percent of

box continues next page

Box 3.11 Chile: Managing Natural Resource Wealth for Stability *(continued)*

GDP (the initial installment was US$5 billion). Since the 1990s, government expenditures have been largely independent of copper price fluctuations—budget surpluses were saved instead of being used to offset taxes, and the savings could be used subsequently in times of budget deficits. The funds have served as a major instrument for fiscal discipline. According to Arellano (2011): "Fiscal discipline contributed to good macroeconomic performance, which created favorable conditions for economic growth. This then translated into the main source of resources to fund social policy. This is the social dividend of fiscal discipline."

Indeed, having a stable program of government expenditures has enabled Chile to maintain a robust, consistent, and balanced investment program for human development. Overall social spending (which includes education, health, and social protection) increased by a factor of 2.5 between 1990 and 2006, with a particularly strong increase in the areas of education and health, which increased by a factor close to 4. Education spending has emphasized preprimary education and service delivery in primary education (primary education was universalized in the 1980s). Public spending on health has emphasized infrastructure, although salaries for health personnel have grown significantly as well. Most of the population receives health insurance through public health insurance or via the private health insurance system with compulsory contributions. A large part of social spending has gone to old-age pensions. A substantial effort also went into implementing targeted programs for the poor. In particular, the program Chile Solidario has taken a comprehensive approach to tackling extreme poverty by assisting families through a range of social services, including access to education, health, training, and employment in addition to cash transfers.

Chile's emergence from military rule in the early 1990s was marked by a desire for consensus in order to sustain a successful transition to democracy. This consensus resulted in the introduction of relatively stable policies and reforms during this period. Describing the process, Arellano (2011) identifies constitutional and fiscal institutions as key. Also important was "managing people's expectations." Resource revenue windfalls associated with price increases put pressure on politicians to increase public spending rapidly in unsustainable ways. Arellano concludes, "The rejection of populism and the promotion of gradualism in satisfying social needs and fulfilling goals has been a crucial, constant factor."

Notes

1. The "short" route of accountability is the ability of citizens as clients to hold service providers directly accountable. When this direct path is not available, citizens can use voice and politics to influence policy makers and politicians and to hold them accountable; policy makers, in turn, can use the compact with providers to hold them accountable. This is the "long" route of accountability (World Bank 2004).

2. They use a 1-2-3-4 model: for one country, two types of capital (private and public), three sectors (tradable, nontradable, and resources), and four goods (domestic goods, traditional exports, natural resource exports, and import goods).

3. For an analysis of fiscal and administrative decentralization, see World Bank 2015a.

4. For a review of options to structure PPPs, see http://globalpractices.worldbank.org /ppp/pages/en/kblanding.aspx.

5. Mali's community health centers are run by community health associations that are constituted under private law as distinct from public health entities (Lamiaux, Rouzaud, and Woods 2011).

6. This includes a gamut of schemes such as pay-for-performance, performance-based incentives, or output-based aid.

7. For more information on RBF in health, see https://www.rbfhealth.org/mission; in particular, see the webinar series at https://www.rbfhealth.org/resource/webinar -results-based-financing-health.

8. The term *cash transfers* generally covers both unconditional and conditional transfers. Any separate discussion of one type of program is identified as such.

9. The composite score comprises (1) institutional and legal setting, (2) reporting practices, (3) safeguards and quality control, and (4) enabling environment (Natural Resource Governance Institute 2013).

References

African Development Bank. 2016. *Economic Outlook: Botswana.* Abidjan: African Development Bank.

Alesina, Alberto, and Roberto Perotti. 1996. "Budget Institutions and Budget Deficits." NBER Working Paper 5556, National Bureau of Economic Research, Cambridge, MA.

Alatas, Vivi, Abhijit Banerjee, Rema Hanna, Benjamin A. Olken, and Julia Tobias. 2010. "Targeting the Poor: Evidence from a Field Experiment in Indonesia." NBER Working Paper w15980, National Bureau of Economic Research, Cambridge, MA.

Andrabi, Tahir, Jishnu Das, and Asim Ijaz Khwaja. 2009. "Report Cards: The Impact of Providing School and Child Test Scores on Educational Markets." Department of Economics, Harvard University, Cambridge, MA.

Angrist, Joshua, Eric Bettinger, and Michael Kremer. 2006. "Long-Term Educational Consequences of Secondary School Vouchers: Evidence from Administrative Records in Colombia." *American Economic Review* 96 (3): 847–62.

Ardanaz, Martin, and Stanislao Maldonado. 2014. "Natural Resource Windfalls and Efficiency of Local Government Expenditures: Evidence from Peru." Working Paper 014578, Universidad de Rosario, Bogotá.

Arellano, José Pablo. 2011. "El cobre comopalanca del desarrollo para Chile." Mimeo, CIEPLAN.

Arezki, Rabah, Arnaud Dupay, and Alan Gelb. 2012. "Resource Windfalls, Optimal Public Investment, and Redistribution: The Role of Total Factor Productivity and Administrative Capacity." IMF Working Paper 12/200, International Monetary Fund, Washington, DC. https://www.imf.org/external/pubs/ft/wp/2012/wp12200.pdf.

Arezki, Rabah, and Thorvaldur Gylfason. 2013. "Resource Rents, Democracy, Corruption and Conflict: Evidence from Sub-Saharan Africa." *Journal of African Economies* 22 (4): 552–69.

Arezki, Rabah, and Kareem Ismail. 2013. "Boom-Bust Cycle, Asymmetrical Fiscal Response and the Dutch Disease." *Journal of Development Economics* 101 (March): 256–67.

Avila, Renata, Hazel Feigenblatt, Rebekah Heacock, and Nathaniel Heller. 2010. *Global Mapping of Technology for Transparency and Accountability: New Technologies.* London: Transparency and Accountability Initiative, Open Society Foundation.

Bacon Robert, and Masami Kojima. 2008. "Coping with Oil Price Volatility." Energy Sector Management Assistance Program Report, World Bank, Washington, DC.

Baland, Jean-Marie, and Patrick Francois. 2000. "Rent-Seeking and Resource Booms." *Journal of Development Economics* 61 (2): 527–42.

Banerjee, Abhijit V., and Sendhil Mullainathan. 2008. "Limited Attention and Income Distribution." *American Economic Review* 98 (2): 489–93.

Bardhan, Pranab. 2002. "Decentralization of Governance and Development." *Journal of Economic Perspectives* 16 (4): 185–205.

Barma, Naazneen, Kai Kaiser, Tuan Minh Le, and Lorena Viñuela. 2012. *Rents to Riches: The Political Economy of Natural Resource-Led Development*. Washington, DC: World Bank.

Barrera-Osorio, Felipe, David S. Blakeslee, Matthew Hoover, Leigh L. Linden, and Dhushyanth Raju. 2011. "Expanding Educational Opportunities in Remote Parts of the World: Evidence from an RCT of a Public-Private Partnership in Pakistan." eEngender Impact: the World Bank's Gender Impact Evaluation Database, World Bank, Washington, DC.

Basinga, Paulin, Paul J. Gertler, Agnes Binagwaho, Agnes L. Soucat, Jennifer Sturdy, and Christel M. Vermeersch. 2011. "Effect on Maternal and Child Health Services in Rwanda of Payment to Primary Health-Care Providers for Performance: An Impact Evaluation." *The Lancet* 377 (9775): 1421–28.

Basu, Sanjay, Jason Andrews, Sandeep Kishore, Rajesh Panjabi, and David Stuckler. 2012. "Comparative Performance of Private and Public Healthcare Systems in Low-and Middle-Income Countries: A Systematic Review." *PLoS Medicine* 9 (6): e1001244.

Benabou, Roland, and Jean Tirole. 2006. "Incentives and Prosocial Behavior." *American Economic Review* 96 (5): 1652–78.

Bertot, John C., Paul T. Jaeger, and Justin M. Grimes. 2010. "Using ICTs to Create a Culture of Transparency? E-Government and Social Media as Openness and Anti-Corruption Tools for Societies." *Government Information Quarterly* 27 (3): 264–71.

Bettinger, Eric, Michael Kremer, and Juan E. Saavedra. 2010. "Are Educational Vouchers Only Redistributive?" *Economic Journal* 120 (546): F204–28.

Björkman, Martina and Jakob Svensson. 2009. "Power to the People: Evidence from a Randomized Field Experiment on Community-Based Monitoring in Uganda." *Quarterly Journal of Economics* 124 (2): 735–69.

Brautigam, Deborah, Odd- Helge Fjeldstad, and Mick Moore, eds. 2008. *Taxation and State-Building in Developing Countries: Capacity and Consent*. Cambridge: Cambridge University Press.

Brugha, Ruairí, and Anthony Zwi. 1998. "Improving the Quality of Private Sector Delivery of Public Health Services; Challenges and Strategies." *Health Policy and Planning* 13 (2): 107–20.

Caselli, Francesco, and Guy Michaels. 2013. "Do Oil Windfalls Improve Living Standards? Evidence from Brazil." *American Economic Journal: Applied Economics* 5 (1): 208–38.

Cerdan-Infantes, Pedro, and Deon Filmer. 2015. "Information, Knowledge and Behavior: Evaluating Alternative Methods of Delivering School Information to Parents." Policy Research Working Paper 7233, World Bank, Washington, DC.

Channa, Anila, and Jean-Paul Faguet. 2012. "Decentralization of Health and Education in Developing Countries: A Quality-Adjusted Review of the Empirical Literature." Economic Organization and Public Policy Discussion Paper 38, Suntory and Toyota

International Centres for Economics and Related Disciplines, London School of Economics and Political Science.

Cherrier, Cecile, Carlo del Ninno, and Setareh Razmara. 2011. "Mali Social Safety Nets." Social Protection and Labor Discussion Paper 1412, World Bank, Washington, DC. http://documents.worldbank.org/curated/en/2011/01/19759986/mali-social-safety -nets.

Collier, Paul. 2007. *The Bottom Billion: Why the Poorest Countries Are Failing and What Can Be Done About It*. Oxford: Oxford University Press.

———. 2010. *The Plundered Planet: Why We Must—and How We Can—Manage Nature for Global Prosperity*. Oxford: Oxford University Press.

———. 2013. "Under Pressure." *Finance and Development* 50 (4): 50–53.

Contreras, Dante, and Tomás Rau. 2009. "Tournaments, Gift Exchanges, and the Effect of Monetary Incentives for Teachers: The Case of Chile." Departamento de Economía and Centro de Microdatos, Universidad de Chile, Santiago.

Cowper, Steve. 2007. "A Word to the Wise: Managing Alaska's Oil Wealth." In *Sovereign Wealth Management*, edited by Jennifer Johnson-Calari and Malan Rietveld. London: Central Banking Publications.

Currie, Janet, Wanchuan Lin, and Wei Zhang. 2011. "Patient Knowledge and Antibiotic Abuse: Evidence from an Audit Study in China." *Journal of Health Economics* 30 (5): 933–49.

del Ninno, Carlo, and Kaleb Tamiru. 2012. "Cameroon Social Safety Nets: Africa Social Safety Net and Social Protection Assessment Series." Social Protection and Labor Discussion Paper 1404, World Bank, Washington, DC. http://documents.worldbank .org/curated/en/2012/06/19746812/cameroon-socail-safety-nets.

De Sousa Santos, Boaventura. 1998. "Participatory Budgeting in Porto Alegre: Towards a Redistributive Democracy." *Politics and Society* 26 (4): 461–510.

Devarajan, Shantayanan, Yazid Dissou, Delfin S. Go, and Sherman Robinson. 2014. "Budget rules and resource booms : a dynamic stochastic general equilibrium analysis". Policy Research Working Paper 6984, World Bank, Washington, DC.

Devarajan, Shantayanan, Helene Ehrhart, Tuan Minh Le, and Gael Raballand. 2011. "Direct Distribution, Taxation, and Accountability in Oil-Rich Economies: A Proposal." CGD Working Paper 281, Center for Global Development, Washington, DC.

Devarajan, Shantayanan, and Marcelo Giugale. 2013. "The Case for Direct Transfers of Resource Revenues in Africa." Working Paper 333, Center for Global Development, Washington, DC.

Devarajan, Shantayanan, Tuan Minh Le, and Gaël Raballand. 2010. "Increasing Public Expenditure Efficiency in Oil-Rich Economies: A Proposal." Policy Research Working Paper 5287, World Bank, Washington, DC.

Dobronogov, Anton, and Octave Keutiben. 2014. "Containing Volatility: Windfall Revenues for Resource-Rich Low-Income Countries." Policy Research Working Paper 6956, World Bank, Washington, DC.

Duflo, Esther, Pascaline Dupas, and Michael Kremer. 2012. "School Governance, Teacher Incentives, and Pupil-Teacher Ratios: Experimental Evidence from Kenyan Primary Schools." WBER Working Paper w17939, National Bureau of Economic Research, Cambridge, MA.

Duflo, Esther, Rema Hanna, and Stephen P. Ryan. 2012. "Incentives Work: Getting Teachers to Come to School." *American Economic Review* 102 (4): 1241–78.

Dunning, Thad. 2005. "Resource Dependence, Economic Performance, and Political Stability." *Journal of Conflict Resolution* 49 (4): 451–82.

Eichler, Rena, Ruth Levine, and the Performance-Based Incentives Working Group. 2009. *Performance Incentives for Global Health*. Performance-Based Incentives Working Group Report. Washington, DC: Center for Global Development.

Ellingsen, Tore, and Magnus Johannesson. 2008. "Pride and Prejudice: The Human Side of Incentive Theory." *American Economic Review* 98 (3): 990–1008.

Ergo, Alex, Ligia Paina, Lindsay Morgan, and Rena Eichler. 2012. "Creating Stronger Incentives for High-Quality Health Care in Low- and Middle-Income Countries." Maternal and Child Health Integrated Program (MCHIP), Washington, DC.

Evans, David, Stephanie Hausladen, Katrina Kosec, and Natasha Reese. 2014. *Community-Based Conditional Cash Transfers in Tanzania: Results from a Randomized Trial*. Washington, DC: World Bank.

Fabrizio, Stefania, Kamil Dybczak, Valentina Flamini, and Javier Kapsoli. 2014. "Angola: Fuel Price Subsidy Reform the Way Forward." IMF Country Report 15/28, Fiscal Affairs Department, International Monetary Fund, Washington DC. http://www.imf.org/external/pubs/ft/scr/2015/cr1528.pdf.

Faguet, Jean-Paul. 2004. "Does Decentralization Increase Responsiveness to Local Needs?" *Journal of Public Economies* 88 (4): 1294–316.

———. 2012. *Decentralization and Popular Democracy: Governance from Below in Bolivia*. Ann Arbor: University of Michigan Press.

———. 2014. "Decentralization and Governance." *World Development* 53 (January): 2–13.

Fehr, Ernst, and Lorenz Goette. 2007. "Do Workers Work More If Wages Are High? Evidence from a Randomized Field Experiment." *American Economic Review* 97 (1): 298–317.

Fiszbein, Ariel, Dena Ringold, and F. Halsey Rogers. 2011. "Making Services Work: Indicators, Assessments, and Benchmarking of the Quality and Governance of Public Service Delivery in the Human Development Sectors." Policy Research Working Paper 5690, World Bank, Washington, DC.

Fjeldstad, Odd-Helge, and Mick Moore. 2008. "Tax-Reform and State-Building in a Globalised World." In *Taxation and State-Building in Developing Countries: Capacity and Consent*, edited by Deborah Brautigam, Odd- Helge Fjeldstad, and Mick Moore, 235–60. Cambridge: Cambridge University Press.

Fox, Jonathan. 2014. "Social Accountability: What Does the Evidence Really Say?" Global Partnership for Social Accountability Working Paper 1, World Bank, Washington, DC.

Frankel, Jeffrey A. 2012. "The Natural Resource Curse: A Survey of Diagnoses and Some Prescriptions." In *Commodity Prices and Inclusive Growth in Low-Income Countries*, edited by Rabah Arezki, Catherine Pattillo, Marc Quintyn, and Min Zhu. Washington, DC: International Monetary Fund.

Friis-Hansen, Esbern, and Signe Marie Cold-Ravnkilde. 2013. *Social Accountability Mechanisms and Access to Public Service Delivery in Rural Africa*. DIIS Report 2013:31. Copenhagen: Danish Institute for International Studies.

Fuchs, Thomas, and Ludger Woessmann. 2007. "What Accounts for International Differences in Student Performance? A Re-Examination Using PISA Data." *Empirical Economics* 32 (2–3): 433–64.

Gaddis, Isis, Jacques Morisset, Youdi Schipper, and Elvis Mushi. 2014. "Managing Natural Resources: What Do Citizens Say?" Brief 11, Twaweza, Dar es Salaam. http://www.twaweza.org/uploads/files/NaturalResources-EN-FINAL.pdf.

Gadenne, Lucie. 2011. "Tax Me, but Spend Wisely: The Political Economy of Taxes, Theory and Evidence from Brazilian Local Governments." Paris School of Economics, Paris.

Galiani, Sebastian, Paul Gertler, and Ernesto Schargrodsky. 2008. "School Decentralization: Helping the Good Get Better, but Leaving the Poor Behind." *Journal of Public Economics* 92 (10): 2106–20.

Garcia, Marito, and Charity M. T. Moore. 2012. *The Cash Dividend: The Rise of Cash Transfer Programs in Sub-Saharan Africa*. Washington, DC: World Bank.

Gaudin, S., and A. S. Yazbeck. 2012. "Health Sector Policy Challenges in Low- and Middle-Income Countries: Learning from Public Expenditure Reviews." World Bank, Washington, DC.

Gelb, Alan, and Stephanie Majerowicz. 2011. "Oil for Uganda—or Ugandans? Can Cash Transfers Prevent the Resource Curse?" CGD Working Paper 261, Center for Global Development, Washington, DC.

Gigler, Björn-Sören, and Savita Bailur, eds. 2014. *Closing the Feedback Loop: Can Technology Bridge the Accountability Gap?* Washington, DC: World Bank.

Gillies, Alexandra. 2010. "Giving Money Away? The Politics of Direct Distribution in Resource-Rich States." CGD Policy Paper 231, Center for Global Development, Washington, DC.

Goldsmith, Scott. 2002. *The Alaska Permanent Fund Dividend: An Experiment in Wealth Distribution*. Geneva, Switzerland: Basic Income European Network.

Grosh, Margaret E., Carlo del Ninno, Emil Tesliuc, and Azedine Ouerghi. 2008. *For Protection and Promotion: The Design and Implementation of Effective Safety Nets*. Washington, DC: World Bank.

Health Results Innovation Trust Fund and World Bank. 2014. *A Smarter Approach to Delivering More and Better Reproductive, Maternal, Newborn, and Child Health Services*. RBF Progress Report, Washington, DC: World Bank. http://www.hritfreport.org/.

IFC (International Finance Corporation). 2011. *Healthy Partnerships: How Governments Can Engage the Private Sector to Improve Health in Africa*. Washington, DC: World Bank.

IMF (International Monetary Fund). 2013. *Case Studies on Energy Subsidy Reform: Lessons and Implications*. Washington, DC: IMF.

Integrity Action. 2014a. "Championing Integrity in the Democratic Republic of Congo's Extractive Industries. An Experience from Katanga Province." *The Cases in Integrity Series*. http://integrityaction.org/case-study/championing-integrity-democratic-republic-of-congo%E2%80%99s-extractives-industries-an.

Integrity Action. 2014b. "Promoting Integrity through Constructive Engagement." Cases in Integrity Series. http://integrityaction.org/index.php/case-study/promoting-integrity-through-constructive-engagement-ivory-coast.

ITU(International Telecommunications Union). 2013. "Measuring the Information Society." https://www.itu.int/en/ITU-D/Statistics/Documents/publications/mis2013/MIS2013_without_Annex_4.pdf.

Kaiser, Kai. 2012. "Investing Resource Wealth: The Political Economy of Public Infrastructure Provision." In *Rents to Riches? The Political Economy of Natural*

Resource–Led Development, edited by Naazneen Barmam, Kai Kaiser, Tuan Minh Le, and Lorena Viñuela, 165–216. Washington, DC: World Bank.

Karl, Terry. 1997. *The Paradox of Plenty: Oil Booms and Petro-States.* Berkeley: University of California Press.

———. 2004. "The Social and Political Consequences of Oil." In *Encyclopedia of Energy*, edited by Cutler Cleveland, 661–72. San Diego: Elsevier.

Keefer, Philip, and Stuti Khemani. 2011. "Mass Media and Public Services: The Effects of Radio Access on Public Education in Benin." Policy Research Working Paper 5559, World Bank, Washington, DC.

Khemani, Stuti. 2016. *Making Politics Work for Development.* Policy Research Report, Washington, DC: World Bank.

Konopo, Joel, Keabetswe Newel, Ntibinyane Ntibinyane, and Olebile Letlole. 2016. "Botswana Repeatedly Raids Preservation Fund." *Mail and Guardian*, February 5. http://mg.co.za/article/2016-02-04-botswana-repeatedly-raids-preservation-fund.

Kyobe, Annette, Jim Brumby, Chris Papageorgiou, Zac Mills, and Era Dabla-Norris. 2011. "Investing in Public Investment: An Index of Public Investment Efficiency." IMF Working Paper 11/37, International Monetary Fund, Washington, DC.

LaRocque, Norman. 2008. "The Practice of Public-Private Partnerships," In *School Choice International: Exploring Public-Private Partnerships*, edited by Rajashari Chakrabarti and Paul E. Peterson, 71–90. Cambridge, MA: MIT Press.

Lamiaux, Matthieu, François Rouzaud, and Wendy Woods. 2011. *Private Health Sector Assessment in Mali.* Washington, DC: World Bank.

Levine, Sebastian, Servaas van der Berg, and Derek Yu. 2009. "Measuring the Impact of Social Cash Transfers on Poverty and Inequality in Namibia." Stellenbosch Economic Working Paper 25/09, Department of Economics and Bureau for Economic Research, University of Stellenbosch, Stellenbosch, South Africa.

Lieberman, Evan, Daniel Posner, and Lily Tsai. 2014. "Does Information Lead to More Active Citizenship? Evidence from an Education Intervention in Rural Kenya." *World Development* 60 (August): 69–83.

Makinen, Marty, Leo Deville, and Amanda Folsom. 2012. *Assessment of the Private Health Sector in the Republic of Congo.* Washington, DC: World Bank.

Maluka, Stephen, Anna-Karin Hurtig, Miguel San Sebastiån, ElizabethShayo, Jens Byskov and Peter Kamuzora. 2011. "Decentralization and Health Care Prioritization Process in Tanzania: From National Rhetoric to Local Reality." *International Journal of Health Planning and Management* 26 (2): 102–20.

Maluka, Stephen, Peter Kamuzora, Miguel San Sebastiån, Jens Byskov, Øystein E. Olsen, Elizabeth Shayo, Benedict Ndawi, and Anna-Karin Hurtig. 2010. "Decentralized Health Care Priority-Setting in Tanzania: Evaluating against the Accountability for Reasonableness Framework." *Social Science and Medicine* 71 (4): 751–59.

Martin, Lucy. 2013. "Taxation and Accountability: Experimental Evidence for Taxation's Effect on Citizen Behavior." Paper presented at the Working Group in African Political Economy Workshop, Washington, DC, May 20.

Mauro, Paolo. 1998. "Corruption and the Composition of Government Expenditure." *Journal of Public Economics* 69 (2): 263–79.

McGee, Rosemary, and John Gaventa. 2010. *Synthesis Report: Review of Impact and Effectiveness of Transparency and Accountability Initiatives.* London: Transparency and Accountability Initiative, Open Society Foundation.

McGuirk, Eoin, Anand Rajaram, and Marcelo Giugale. 2016. "The Political Economy of Direct Dividend Transfers in Resource Rich Countries. A Theoretical Consideration." Policy Research Working Paper 7575, World Bank, Washington, DC.

Ministry of Finance, Republic of Ghana. 2011. "Petroleum Revenue Management Act" (Act 815) accessed at http://www.mofep.gov.gh/sites/default/files/reports/Petroleum _Revenue_Management_Act_%202011.PDF.

Molina, Ezequiel. 2014. *Can Bottom-Up Institutional Reform Improve Service Delivery?* Washington, DC: Inter-American Development Bank.

Monchuk, Victoria. 2013. *Reducing Poverty and Investing in People: The New Role of Safety Nets in Africa.* Washington, DC: World Bank.

Moore, Mick. 2004. "Revenues, State Formation, and the Quality of Governance in Developing Countries." *International Political Science Review* 25 (3): 297–319.

Morgan, Lindsay, and Rena Eichler. 2011. *Performance-Based Incentives in Sub-Saharan Africa: Experiences, Challenges, Lessons.* Bethesda, MD: Health Systems 20/20, Abt Associates.

Moss, Todd, and Stephanie Majerowicz. 2013. "Oil-to-Cash Won't Work Here! Ten Common Objections." CGD Policy Paper 024, Center for Global Development, Washington, DC.

Moss, Todd, and Lauren Young. 2009. "Saving Ghana from Its Oil: the Case for Direct Cash Distribution." CGD Working Paper 186, Center for Global Development, Washington, DC.

Musgrove, Philip. 2011. *Financial and Other Rewards for Good Performance or Results: A Guided Tour of Concepts and Terms and a Short Glossary.* Washington, DC: World Bank.

National Resource Governance Institute. 2013. Natural Resource Funds Briefs. Botswana Pula Fund. http://www.resourcegovernance.org/sites/default/files/NRF_Botswana _July2013.pdf.

Ojo, Ifelayo. 2013. "Governance Indicators for Health Provider Entry: Results of Field Research in Ghana and Kenya," mimeo, 26 pp. Office of the World Bank, Washington, DC.

Oxman, Andrew D., and Atle Fretheim. 2009. "Can Paying for Results Help to Achieve the Millennium Development Goals? Overview of the Effectiveness of Results-Based Financing." *Journal of Evidence-Based Medicine* 2 (2): 70–83.

Palley, Thomas. 2003. *Combating the Natural Resource Curse with Citizen Revenue Distribution Funds: Oil and the Case of Iraq.* Washington, DC: Foreign Policy in Focus.

Patrinos, Harry A. 2007. *Demand-Side Financing in Education.* Education Policy Series. Paris: UNESCO.

Patrinos, Harry A., Felipe Barrera-Osorio, and Juliana Guáqueta, 2009. *The Role and Impact of Public-Private Partnerships in Education.* Washington, DC: World Bank.

Pearson, Mark, Martin Johnson, and Robin Ellison. 2010. *Review of Major Results-Based Aid (RBA) and Results-Based Financing (RBF) Schemes.* London: DFID, Human Development Resource Center.

Pritchett, Lant, and Eric Werker. 2012. "Developing the Guts of a GUT (Grand Unified Theory): Elite Commitment and Inclusive Growth." ESID Working Paper 16/12, Effective States and Inclusive Development Centre, Manchester.

Rajaram, Anand, Tuan Minh Le, Kai Kaiser, Jay-Hung Kim, and Jonas Frank. 2014. *The Power of Public Investment Management: Transforming Resources into Assets for Growth*. Washington, DC: World Bank.

Reinikka, Ritva, and Jakob Svensson. 2004. "Local Capture: Evidence from a Central Government Transfer Program in Uganda." *Quarterly Journal of Economics* 119 (2): 679–705.

———. 2005. "Fighting Corruption to Improve Schooling: Evidence from a Newspaper Campaign in Uganda." *Journal of the European Economic Association* 3 (2–3): 259–67.

———. 2010. "Working for God? Evidence from a Change in Financing of Nonprofit Health Care Providers in Uganda." *Journal of the European Economic Association* 8 (6): 1159–78.

———. 2011. "The Power of Information in Public Services: Evidence from Education in Uganda." *Journal of Public Economics* 95 (7): 956–66.

Natural Resource Governance Institute. 2013. Resource Governance Index, accessed at http://www.resourcegovernance.org/resource-governance-index.

Revenue Watch Institute. 2010. Revenue Watch Index. http://www.revenuewatch.org/rwindex2010/pdf/RevenueWatchIndex_2010.pdf.

RHVP(Regional Hunger and Vulnerability Program). 2009. "Impact of Social Cash Transfers on Household Welfare, Investment, and Education in Zambia." Wahenga Brief 17, RHVP, Johannnesburg. http://www.wahenga.net/node/223.

Ringold, Dena, Alaka Holla, Margaret Koziol, and Santhosh Srinivasan. 2012. *Citizens and Service Delivery: Assessing the Use of Social Accountability Approaches in Human Development*. Washington, DC: World Bank.

Robinson, James A., and Ragnar Torvik. 2005. "White Elephants." *Journal of Public Economics* 89 (2): 197–210.

Ross, Michael. 1999. "The Political Economy of the Resource Curse." *World Politics* 51 (2): 297–322.

———. 2001. "Does Oil Hinder Democracy?" *World Politics* 53 (3): 325–61.

———. 2007. "How Mineral-Rich States Can Reduce Inequality," In *Escaping the Resource Curse*, edited by Macartan Humphreys, Jeffrey D. Sachs, and Joseph E. Stiglitz. New York: Columbia University Press.

———. 2012. *The Oil Curse: How Petroleum Wealth Shapes the Development of Nations*. Princeton, NJ: Princeton University Press.

Sachs, Jeffrey D., and Andrew M. Warner. 1999. "The Big Push, Natural Resource Booms, and Growth." *Journal of Development Economics* 59 (1): 43–76.

———. 2001. "The Curse of Natural Resources." *European Economic Review* 45 (4–6): 827–38.

Sakellariou, Christos, and Harry A. Patrinos. 2009. "The Equity Impact of Public Finance of Private Education Provision in Côte d'Ivoire." *International Journal of Educational Development* 29 (4): 350–6.

Sala-i-Martin, Xavier, and Arvind Subramanian. 2003. "Addressing the Natural Resource Curse: An Illustration from Nigeria." NBER Working Paper 9804, National Bureau of Economic Research, Cambridge, MA.

Samuels, Fiona, and Nicola Jones with Agnieszka Malachowska. 2013. *Holding Cash Transfer to Account: Beneficiary and Community Perspectives*. London: ODI.

Sandbu, Martin E. 2006. "Natural Wealth Accounts: A Proposal for Alleviating the Natural Resource Curse." *World Development* 34 (7): 1153–70.

Schneider, Aaron, and Marcelo Baquero. 2006. "Get What You Want, Give What You Can: Embedded Public Finance in Porto Alegre." IDS Working Paper 266, Institute of Development Studies, University of Sussex, Brighton, U.K.

Shah, Anwar, ed. 2007. *Participatory Budgeting*. Washington, DC: World Bank.

Shaxson, Nicholas. 2008. "Oil for the People: A Solution to the Resource Curse." Paper presented at the conference "Tax Justice, Transparency, and Accountability," Essex University, Colchester, U.K., July 3–4.

Shkabatur, Jennifer. 2014. "Check My School: A Case Study on Citizens' Monitoring of the Education Sector in the Philippines." In *Closing the Feedback Loop: Can Technology Bridge the Accountability Gap?* edited by Björn-Sören Gigler and Savita Bailur, 149–88. Washington, DC: World Bank.

Skoufias, Emmanuel, Ambar Narayan, Basab Dasgupta, and Kai Kaiser. 2011. "Electoral Accountability, Fiscal Decentralization, and Service Delivery in Indonesia." Policy Research Working Paper Series 5614, World Bank, Washington, DC.

Soeters, Robert, Peter B. Peerenboom, Pacifique Mushagalusa, and Célestin Kimanuka. 2011. "Performance-Based Financing Experiment Improved Health Care in the Democratic Republic of Congo." *Health Affairs* 30 (8): 1518–27.

Tesliuc, Cornelia, Smith W. James, and Sunkutu Musonda Rosemary. 2013. "Zambia: Using Social Safety Nets to Accelerate Poverty Reduction and Share Prosperity." Social Protection and Labor Discussion Paper 1413, World Bank, Washington, DC. http://documents.worldbank.org/curated/en/2013/03/19893339/zambia-using -social-safety-nets-accelerate-poverty-reduction-share-prosperity.

Tidemand, P., Hans Bjorn Olsen, and Nazar Sola. 2008. *Local Level Service Delivery, Decentralisation and Governance: A Comparative Study of Uganda, Kenya, and Tanzania Education, Health and Agriculture Sectors*. Tanzania Case Report. Tokyo: Japan International Cooperation Agency.

Timmons, Jeffrey. 2005. "The Fiscal Contract: States, Taxes, and Public Services." *World Politics* 15 (4): 530–67.

Uchimura, Hiroko, and Johannes Jütting. 2009. "Fiscal Decentralization, Chinese Style: Good for Health Outcomes?" *World Development* 37 (12): 1926–34.

UNDP (United Nations Development Programme). 2014. *Human Development Report 2014: Sustaining Human Progress—Reducing Vulnerabilities and Building Resilience*. New York: UNDP.

UNESCO, Institute for Statistics. 2012. Global Education Digest 2012. http://www.uis .unesco.org/Education/Documents/ged-2012-en.pdf.

Uribe, Claudia, Richard J. Murnane, John B. Willett, and Marie Andrée Somers. 2005. "Expanding School Enrollment by Subsidizing Private Schools: Lessons from Bogota." NBER Working Paper w11670, National Bureau of Economic Research, Cambridge, MA.

van der Ploeg, Frederick. 2011. "Natural Resources: Curse or Blessing?" *Journal of Economic Literature* 49 (2): 366–420.

van der Ploeg, Frederick, and Steven Poelhekke. 2009. "Volatility and the Natural Resource Curse." *Oxford Economic Papers* 61 (4): 727–60.

Wittemyer, Renee, Savita Bailur, Nicole Anand, Kyung- Ryul Park, and Björn-Sören Gigler. 2014. "New Routes to Governance: A Review of Cases in Participation, Transparency, and Accountability." In *Closing the Feedback Loop: Can Technology Bridge the Accountability Gap?* edited by Björn-Sören Gigler and Savita Bailur, 43–70. Washington, DC: World Bank.

Wodon, Quentin. 2013. *Education in Sub-Saharan Africa: Comparing Faith-Inspired, Private Secular, and Public Schools.* Washington, DC: World Bank. http://imagebank. worldbank.org/servlet/WDSContentServer/IW3P/IB/2013/12/19/000442464_2013 1219122103/Rendered/PDF/834990PUB0Educ00Box382092B00PUBLIC0.pdf.

World Bank. 2003. "Decentralization of Health Care in Brazil: A Case Study of Bahia." Report 24417, World Bank, Washington, DC.

———. 2004a. *World Development Report 2004: Making Services Work for Poor People.* Washington, DC: World Bank.

———. 2004b. *Ethiopia. Public Spending in the Social Sectors.* Public expenditure review (PER). Washington, DC: World Bank. http://documents.worldbank.org/curated /en/455401468255860888/Public-spending-in-the-social-sectors.

———. 2004c. *Guinea: Strengthening Public Expenditure Management for Poverty Reduction and Growth.* Public expenditure review (PER). Washington, DC: World Bank. http:// documents.worldbank.org/curated/en/257621468771290480/Guinea-Strengthening -public-expenditure-management-for-poverty-reduction-and-growth-public -expenditure-review.

———. 2004d. *Senegal: Public Expenditure Review.* Public expenditure review (PER). Washington, DC: World Bank. http://documents.worldbank.org/curated/en /617291468169156225/Senegal-Public-expenditure-review.

———. 2007a. *Madagascar: Executive Summary.* Public expenditure review (PER). Washington, DC: World Bank. http://documents.worldbank.org/curated/en /232861468271517888/Executive-summary.

———. 2007b. *Malawi: Public Expenditure Review 2006.* Public expenditure review (PER). Washington, DC: World Bank. http://documents.worldbank.org/curated/en /778841468053059535/Malawi-Public-expenditure-review-2006.

———. 2010a. *Equatorial Guinea: Public Expenditure Review.* Washington, DC: World Bank. http://documents.worldbank.org/curated/en/2010/01/15553341/equatorial -guinea-public-expenditure-review.

———. 2010b. *Sierra Leone: Public Expenditure Review.* Public expenditure review (PER). Washington, DC: World Bank. http://documents.worldbank.org/curated/en /794401468300853207/Sierra-Leone-Public-expenditure-review.

———. 2012a. *Gabon—Public Expenditure Review: Better Management of Public Finance to Achieve Millennium Development Goals.* Washington, DC: World Bank. http:// documents.worldbank.org/curated/en/2012/03/16630495/gabon-public-expenditure -review-better-management-public-finance-achieve-millennium-development-goals.

———. 2012b. *Liberia—Public Expenditure Review: Human Development. Public expenditure review (PER). Washington, DC. © World Bank. https://openknowledge.worldbank .org/handle/10986/12313License: CC BY 3.0 Unported."*

———. 2013a. *Niger—Public Expenditure Review (PER) 2012.* Washington DC: World Bank. http://documents.worldbank.org/curated/en/2013/12/18836366/niger-public -expenditure-review-2012.

———. 2013b. *Service Delivery with More Districts in Uganda: Fiscal Challenges and Opportunities for Reforms—Public Expenditure Review.* Washington, DC: World Bank. http://documents.worldbank.org/curated/en/2013/06/18018983/service

-delivery-more-districts-uganda-fiscal-challenges-opportunities-reforms-public
-expenditure-review.

———. 2014a. "Prosperity for All: Ending Extreme Poverty." Note for the World Bank Group 2014 Spring Meetings, World Bank, Washington, DC.

———. 2014b. *Republic of Congo— Enhancing Efficiency in Education and Health Public Spending for Improved Quality Service Delivery for All: A Public Expenditure Review of the Education and Health Sectors*. Washington, DC: World Bank. http://documents. worldbank.org/curated/en/2014/06/19755695/republic-congo-enhancing-efficiency -education-health-public-spending-improved-quality-service-delivery-all-public -expenditure-review-education-health-sectors.

———. 2014c. *Mozambique—Public Expenditure Review: Addressing the Challenges of Today, Seizing the Opportunities of Tomorrow*. Public Expenditure Review (PER). Washington, DC: World Bank. http://documents.worldbank.org/curated/en /677921468275102771/Mozambique-Public-expenditure-review-addressing -the-challenges-of-today-seizing-the-opportunities-of-tomorrow.

———. 2015a. "Brief: Decentralization and Intergovernmental Relations Global Solutions Groups." World Bank, Washington, DC. http://www.worldbank.org/en/topic /governance/brief/decentralization-and-intergovernmental-relations-global-solutions -groups.

———. 2015b. *Global Economic Prospects: Having Fiscal Space and Using It*. World Bank Flagship Report. Washington, DC: World Bank. http://www.worldbank.org/content /dam/Worldbank/GEP/GEP2015a/pdfs/GEP15a_web_full.pdf.

———. 2015c. *Madagascar—Public Expenditure Review Education and Health*. Washington, DC: World Bank. http://documents.worldbank.org/curated/en/2016/04/2484144 -public-expenditure-review-education-health.

———. 2016. *World Development Report 2016: Digital Dividends*. Washington, DC: World Bank. http://www-wds.worldbank.org/external/default/WDSContentServer /WDSP/IB/2016/01/13/090224b08405ea05/2_0/Rendered/PDF/World0developm 0000digital0dividends.pdf.

CHAPTER 4

Key Investments to Build the Foundations of Human Capital

Abstract

The foundations of human capital are set early in life, with long-lasting effects in adulthood and in the next generation. Investing early in health, nutrition, early childhood development, and basic education helps to set those foundations and thus yields high returns. Early investments are subject to fewer efficiency trade-offs, and the cognitive and psychosocial skills acquired in early life enable further strong health, learning, and full participation in society at a lower cost. Poverty and exposure to conflict are major risks in early life through the deprivations and stress they cause to children and adults. Cash transfers can sustain household consumption in the short run and the uptake of human development services, which may improve household welfare, in the long run. While some interventions show promising results at the pilot stage, scaling them up requires qualitative shifts, stronger coordination, and innovative delivery systems, entailing new part-nerships between levels of government and with nonstate actors.

The Foundations of Human Capital

The New Evidence on Early Development

The period between the first few days of pregnancy and two years of life (the first 1,000 days) is intense for both physical and cognitive development. Children are expected to grow, on average, 50 centimeters in utero, 24 centimeters in their first year of life, and 12 centimeters in their second year, after which growth slows down until adolescence. Language, vision, and hearing start forming in the womb, and development peaks in the first two years. Some capabilities linked to social functioning, such as habitual responses and emotional control, are also in peak development in those 1,000 days (figure 4.1). During this period, children need good nutrition and become more sensitive to infections and biological programming.[1] At that time, they depend totally on others for nutrition, care, and

Figure 4.1 Early Brain Development Sets the Basis for Many Skills

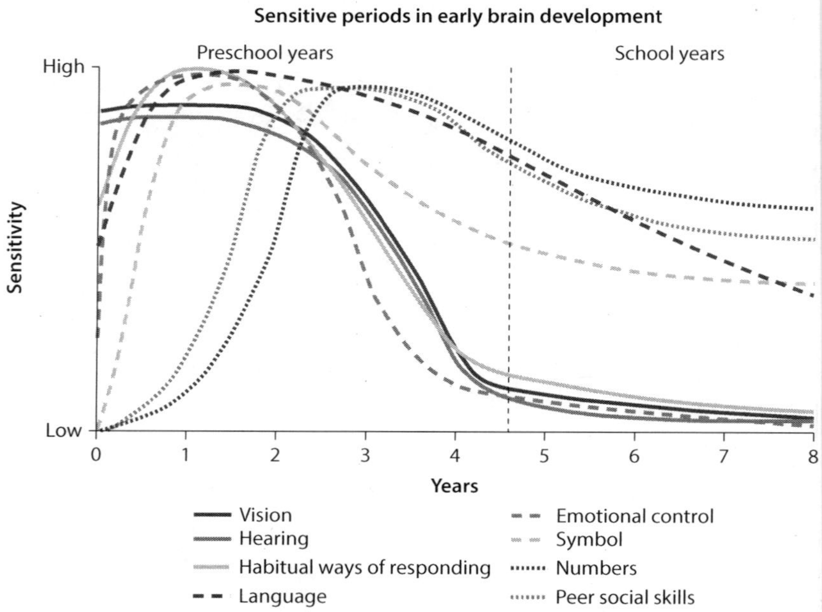

Sensitive periods in early brain development

Sources: Developed by the Council for Early Child Development (Early Years Study 1999; Nash 1997; National Research Council and Institute of Medecine 2000).

social interactions. For this reason, the environment that their caregivers provide is a key factor in their development.

During this period, malnutrition has multiple apparent and insidious consequences: it affects growth, morbidity, intelligence quotient (IQ)–type intelligence, and mortality.[2] Undernutrition translates into small-for-gestational-age, stunting (inadequate length or height-for-age, a symptom of chronic undernutrition), and wasting (inadequate weight-for-height, a symptom of acute undernutrition). Inadequate growth—the visible symptom—hides invisible symptoms, which include impaired brain development and immune system. Undernutrition can affect the hard-wiring of the brain, through malfunctions in the coating of the nerves (myelination) and the formation of connections between neural cells (synapses) (Yusuf 1992). Micronutrient deficiencies, linked to the quality of children's diet, may affect development in other silent ways. Vitamin A deficiency can cause night blindness and is a risk factor for increased severity of infections, which leads to increased mortality. Vitamin B12 deficiency can cause involuntary muscle movements, apathy, and cerebral atrophy. Iron deficiency is associated with fetal and child growth failure, lower cognitive development in children (Georgieff 2007; Nyaradi and others 2013), lower physical activity and productivity in adults, and increased maternal mortality. Zinc deficiency is associated with stunting and higher incidences of diarrhea and pneumonia. Iodine deficiency affects cognitive development and reduces IQ. Joint effects of fetal growth restriction, suboptimum breastfeeding, stunting, wasting, and deficiencies of vitamin A and zinc cause 45 percent of child deaths—3.1 million deaths annually, of which at least 1.5 million are in Africa (*The Lancet* 2008, 2013; Black and others 2013).

With cumulative exposure to developmental risks and shocks, including poverty, disparities widen and trajectories become more firmly divergent as children grow up. In Africa, children in poor families acquire cognitive skills more slowly than children in rich households, and the gap widens with age, which means that children from these groups do not start school on an equal footing (Filmer and Fox 2014). This slower acquisition (figure 4.2) results from poor nutrition, but also from poor stimulation and care, and has cumulative effects if no intervention takes place (similar patterns are found in other parts of the world, such as in Latin America and the Caribbean, as shown by Schady and others 2015). It is an important component of the intergenerational transmission of inequality (Torche 2011).

Conversely, a young brain is remarkably plastic and can repair itself after nutrient repletion during sensitive periods. Since rapid growth and brain development occur during the first 1,000 days, this period is particularly sensitive to deficiencies in diet, but also particularly responsive to interventions, such as the ones described in this chapter. Adolescence is also a sensitive and significant developmental period, with another bout of linear growth and of brain structural reorganization and cognitive maturation.

Early Life Conditions and Their Long-Term and Intergenerational Consequences

Early life conditions have a disproportionate influence on the formation of adult human capital, understood in terms of height, skills (cognitive, noncognitive), and capabilities (health, social functioning) (Friedman and Sturdy 2011; Victora and others 2010). Following retarded intrauterine growth, rapid growth falters in the first 24 months (figure 4.3). The rates in Africa and South Asia are particularly high, and limited catch-up occurs between ages 2 and 4. Cognitive ability, socioemotional competence, and sensory-motor development all affect school preparedness and subsequent school performance.

The nature–nurture interactions that shape human development start very early, and some risk factors that children face from conception are linked to the conditions that their families face. These risks include intrauterine growth restriction (11 percent of births) due to maternal malnutrition and stress, stunting (approximately one-third of children younger than 5 years of age), iron deficiency (one-fourth to one-third of children under age 4), and iodine deficiency (one-third of the population worldwide). Maternal depression (which affects one-sixth of postpartum mothers) can impair bonding between mother and infant (Bernard Van Leer Foundation, 2009). Inadequate cognitive stimulation also affects child development.

Evidence from Brazil, Guatemala, India, the Philippines, and South Africa (Victora and others 2008) shows that poor fetal growth or stunting in the first two years of life leads to irreversible damage, including shorter adult height,

Figure 4.2 Cognitive Skills Increase Slowly, Especially for the Poorest Children: Proportion of Children Who Can Carry Out Basic Cognitive Tasks

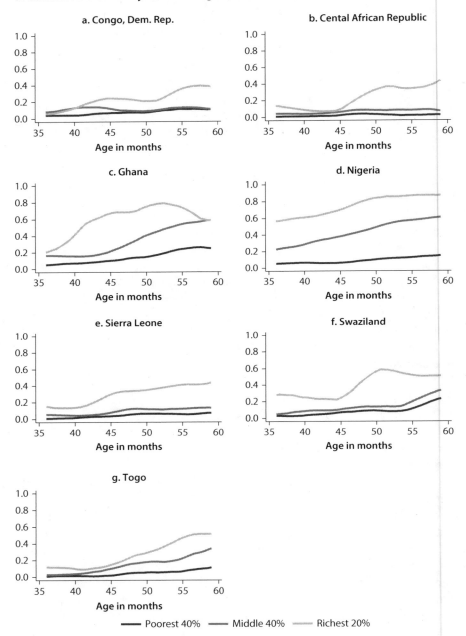

Source: Based on MICS 4 data.

Note: Panels show proportion of children who can perform two of the following three tasks: identify or name at least 10 letters of the alphabet; read at least four simple, popular words; know the name and recognize the symbols of the numbers from 1 to 10.

Figure 4.3 After 24 Months of Age, Stunted Children Have Little Catch-Up Growth

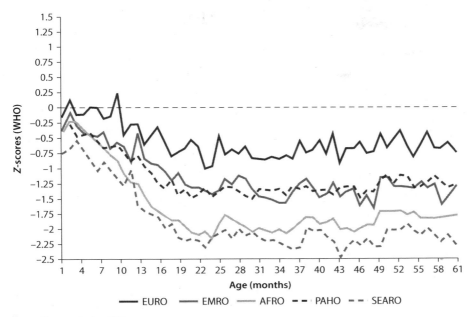

Source: Victora and others 2010.

Note: Mean height-for-age Z scores by age, relative to the World Health Organization standard, by region. EURO refers to the following countries in Europe and Central Asia: Armenia, Kazakhstan, Kyrgyzstan, Moldova, Mongolia, Montenegro, and Turkey; AMRO refers to the following countries in Latin America: Bolivia, Brazil, Colombia, Dominican Republic, Guatemala, Haiti, Honduras, Nicaragua, and Peru; EMRO refers to the following countries in Middle East and North Africa: Egypt, Jordan, Morocco, and Yemen; SEARO refers to the following countries in South and East Asia: Bangladesh, Cambodia, India, and Nepal; AFRO refers to the following countries in Africa: Benin, Burkina Faso, Cameroon, Central African Republic, Chad, Comoros, Cote d'Ivoire, Congo, Eritrea, Ethiopia, Gabon, Ghana, Guinea, Kenya, Lesotho, Liberia, Madagascar, Malawi, Mali, Mauritania, Mozambique, Namibia, Niger, Nigeria, Rwanda, Senegal, Tanzania, Uganda, Zambia, and Zimbabwe.

lower schooling attainment, reduced adult income, and decreased birthweight of offspring. Children who are undernourished in the first two years of life and who put on weight rapidly later in childhood and in adolescence are at high risk of chronic diseases related to nutrition (high glucose concentrations and blood pressure, and harmful lipid profiles). However, rapid gain in weight or length in the first two years of life does not seem to increase the risk of chronic disease, even in children with poor fetal growth. Height-for-age at two years is the best predictor of human capital. Stunted children have poorer performance in school (reduction in test scores equivalent to two years of schooling). With the assumption that every year of schooling is equivalent to an increase of 9 percent in adult annual income, Grantham-McGregor and others (2007), *The Lancet* (2007, 2011) estimated a loss in adult income of between 22 and 30 percent. Women who were undernourished in infancy are more likely to face risky pregnancies and give birth to low-birthweight children.

Many aspects of fetal growth influence long-term health, and children who experienced malnutrition in utero and in their early years are also more at risk of chronic diseases, such as type 2 diabetes, abdominal obesity, hypertension, and cardiovascular disease (Alderman 2011; Dover 2009; Torche 2011). For example, children in utero during the Dutch famine of 1944–45 have increased risk of chronic disease and mental illness in middle age and a greater loss of attention and cognitive ability than the general population as they age further. Children with fetal exposure to the Biafra famine of 1967–70 face increased risk of diabetes and hypertension. One possible explanation is linked with adaptation to nutritional stress in the womb (Barker hypothesis). The signal derived from limited nutrients in utero leads to an adaptation in which the child becomes particularly efficient at conserving resources. However, should that individual be subsequently confronted with a resource-rich environment, this maladapted response, or mismatch, would contribute to overnutrition and increased the risk of chronic disease.

While the long-term effects of growth failure are severe, interventions such as nutritional supplementation and basic medical care in the early years have a strong potential to improve outcomes over the life course. A long-run longitudinal study in Guatemala (Hoddinott and others 2011) provides additional evidence on the long-term effects of malnutrition, including on body size, adult fitness, wages, and type of employment (box 4.1). Participants who had received nutritional supplementation (a high-protein energy drink with multiple micronutrients) and free preventive and curative medical care (including community health workers, trained midwives, immunization, and deworming) were less likely to be stunted.

Box 4.1 The Consequences of Early Childhood Growth Failure over the Life Course in Guatemala

Growth failure in early life in rural Guatemala, as measured by height-for-age and stunting at 36 months, has potential effects on a wide range of domains in adulthood: education, marriage, fertility, health, wages and income, and poverty and consumption. Participants in a nutrition supplementation trial between 1969 and 1977 were interviewed again between 2002 and 2004.

Participants who were stunted at 36 months of age left school earlier and had lower grade attainment; they also had significantly worse results on tests of reading and vocabulary and nonverbal cognitive ability 35 years later. They made worse marriage matches—that is, they married people with lower schooling attainment. Women had 1.86 more pregnancies and were more likely to experience stillbirths and miscarriages. No link was found with greater risks of cardiovascular or other chronic disease.

Individuals who were not stunted earned higher wages and were more likely to hold higher-paying skilled jobs or white-collar jobs. They were 34 percentage points less likely to live in a poor household. A 1 standard deviation increase in height-for-age was associated with an increase in men's hourly wage of 20 percent, an increase in women's likelihood of operating their own business of 10 percentage points, and an increase in per capita consumption of households where the participants lived of nearly 20 percent.

Sources: Hoddinott and others 2011, Calderón and Hoddinott 2011.

The double burden of malnutrition—coexistence of high rates of undernutrition and increasing rates of overweight and obesity—is becoming a public health problem in Africa. In many countries, obesity is rising faster than stunting is declining. Some children younger than 5 years of age are becoming overweight; more than 7 percent in Africa and up to 17 percent in Southern Africa (Provo 2013). Countries also are witnessing concurrent increases in being overweight and obesity with changes in dietary patterns linked to urbanization, especially among adolescent girls and women (figure 4.4) (Popkin, Adair, and Ng 2012; Kimani-Murage 2013, for rural South Africa; Keding and others 2013, for Tanzania; UNFPA 2014). In Ghana, in 2008, 9.3 percent of women were obese and 8.6 percent were underweight. In Tanzania, in 2014, 11.4 percent of women were obese and 10.4 percent were underweight. In both countries, obesity rates were higher in urban areas. Obesity in pregnancy may also threaten the welfare of the next generation, as maternal hyperglycemia or diabetes increases the risk of diabetes for their offspring. The double burden may exist within households, with obese mothers and undernourished children, especially in urban areas in Benin, Ghana, and South Africa (Maxwell and others 2000).

Similarly, early patterns of attachment and bonding are key for children to develop self-confidence, conflict resolution skills, and character traits such as conscientiousness, perseverance (being able to delay gratification), sociability (and empathy), and curiosity. These skills can be learned and reinforced, but they depend on the family and caregiving environment. Maternal depression, which leads to increased stress in utero and after birth, may increase anxiety in infants. Toxic stress, linked to poverty, affects family environment.[3] Prolonged activation of the stress response systems can disrupt the development of brain architecture and other organ systems and increase the risk for stress-related disease and

Figure 4.4 Malnutrition Imposes a Double Burden

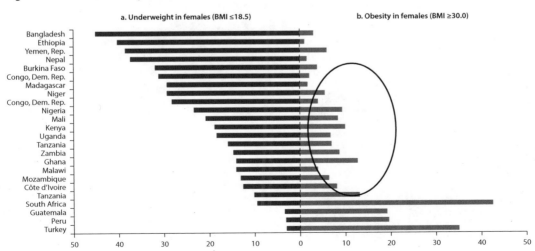

Source: WHO Global Database on Body Mass Index 2013. Data from the most recent year.
Note: BMI = body mass index.

From Mines and Wells to Well-Built Minds • http://dx.doi.org/10.1596/978-1-4648-1005-3

cognitive impairment well into the adult years. Scarcity affects parenting attention (Banerjee and Mullanaithan 2008; Mullanaithan and Shafir 2013), quality of care, schooling decisions, and children's capacity to learn. In Canada, childhood traumas are associated with adult chronic illness through poor immune functioning and poor cardiovascular and mental health; socioeconomic status functions as a potential buffer (Mock and Arai 2011; see figure 4.5). In Chile and Lebanon, Torche (2011) and Torche and Shwed (forthcoming) found that exposure to an earthquake and to bombings during the first semester of pregnancy is linked to a higher prevalence of low birthweight and cognitive impairment, especially in low-income families.

Character skills ("soft skills")—such as conscientiousness, perseverance, sociability, and curiosity—are as important as pure cognitive skills to success at school and in the workplace. They rival IQ in predicting educational attainment, labor market success, health, and criminality. They can be acquired and modified with age and instruction. The foundation for these early skills (1) depends heavily on the quality of nurturing (Snellman, Silva, and Putnam 2015); and (2) provides the basis on which additional skills can be learned (Heckman and Kautz 2013). To succeed in society, people need both cognitive and character skills. While both are malleable to different degrees at different ages, inequalities among families in parenting and a lack of support for schoolchildren are key determinants of inequalities later in life.

Failure to develop those foundational skills is costly and difficult to compensate for later in life. It can lead to long-term, difficult-to-reverse effects on educational attainment, health, fertility, earnings, and engagement in risky activities and crime. These problems are costly for both individuals and society (Heckman

Figure 4.5 Childhood Trauma Is Associated with Chronic Illness in Adulthood and Mediated through Mental Health and Income

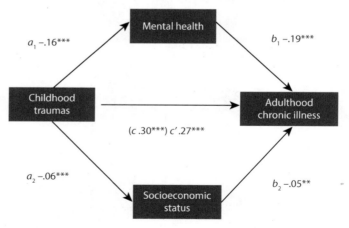

Source: Mock and Arai 2011.
Note: The value in parentheses is the unstandardized regression coefficient for the association between childhood traumas and adulthood chronic illness before the addition of self-rated mental health and socioeconomic status to the model; n = 9,301.
$**p < .01; ***p < .001.$

From Mines and Wells to Well-Built Minds • http://dx.doi.org/10.1596/978-1-4648-1005-3

and Masterov 2007; Naudeau and others 2008). Linguistic and cognitive delays accumulate quickly in preschool children; Paxson and Schady (2007) have shown that, while children at age 3 in Ecuador have similar vocabularies, by age 6, children in poorer households have a poorer age-adjusted vocabulary, while those in richer households have a richer vocabulary. A similar pattern develops with maternal schooling; by age 6, children whose mothers have not completed primary school have a poorer age-adjusted vocabulary than those whose mothers have completed secondary school. There is a similar, but less clear, pattern with paternal schooling (figure 4.6). One potential explanation is that children in poorer households or with less educated mothers tend to be spoken to less, and the speech they hear may be poorer in vocabulary and in sentence complexity (Fernald and Hidrobo 2011).

Figure 4.6 Gaps in Vocabulary Widen among Ecuadorian Children Ages 36–72 Months According to the Wealth of Their Households and Their Mother's Schooling

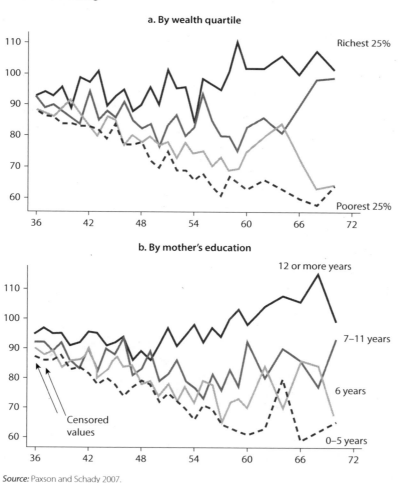

Source: Paxson and Schady 2007.

In summary, early life conditions have long-term consequences for human development:

- Early life nutrition matters for brain development and adult health (diabetes, high-blood pressure, and mental health).
- Early life stimulation provides the basis for IQ-type intelligence (prior to age 3, which solidifies around adolescence) and character skills (which are more malleable), and
- Providing the foundation early is easier and cheaper.
- Multiple skills are necessary to succeed in life. Character skills take longer to develop than cognitive skills, but both skills matter for productivity and productive inclusion in society.
- Long-term undernutrition in infancy is linked with worse marriage matches, and women who are stunted face more and higher-risk pregnancies. Children of malnourished mothers face higher risks of chronic diseases such as diabetes. In contrast, girls' education is associated with decreased undernutrition. In resource-rich countries where the demographic transition is at an early stage, investments in prenatal care, children's health, and girls' education can help to accelerate the transition between quantity and quality of children and stimulate the positive feedback loop between decreased fertility and investment in human capital.

Toxic stress linked with living in poverty has lasting effects through its effects on family environments (limited attention, parenting quality), so children who have grown up in poverty are more likely to experience dropping out of school, low productivity, and a low income and to contribute to the intergenerational transmission of poverty (Grantham-McGregor and others 2007). In addition, poor families have fewer resources to deal with acute stress (natural and human-made disasters), so the consequences of short-term shocks at sensitive periods have long-term repercussions for children's development. In resource-rich countries, both types of stress are prevalent, given high poverty rates and risks of conflict, so investing early to improve the family environment has potentially high returns.

Interventions to Strengthen the Foundations of Human Capital

The early years of life are a period of both great vulnerability and great opportunity to invest in human capital. Failure to invest early is costly and difficult to compensate for later in life (Walker and others 2011). A range of interventions can strengthen the foundations of human capital, notably those that promote better nutrition, maternal and child health, early childhood development, and basic education. The earlier the intervention, the higher are both the probability of preventing and reversing the damage and the long-term payoff. Investing early is effective, minimizes efficiency trade-offs (figure 4.7), and helps to break the intergenerational transmission of poverty.

Interventions to strengthen the foundations of human capital are sound investments with very high rates of return. No one has conducted a global cost-benefit analysis of nutrition interventions (World Bank 2010), but individual interventions

Figure 4.7 Investing Early, While the Brain Is Growing, Pays Off

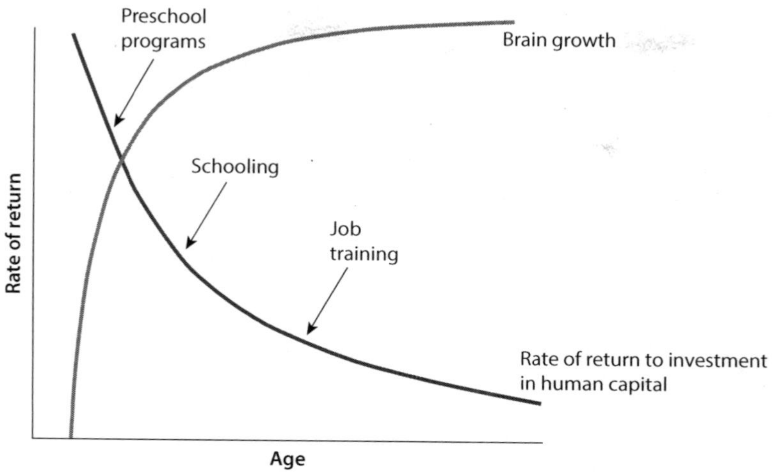

Source: Heckman and Carneiro 2003.

Table 4.1 Per Capita Costs of Nutrition Interventions Are Very Low

Intervention	Annual per capita cost (US$)
Breastfeeding promotion	0.30–4.00
Vitamin A supplements	0.20
Therapeutic zinc supplements	0.47 (10 days)
Deworming (school age)	0.32–0.49
Iron supplement	10–50
Folate fortification	0.01
Iron fortification of staples	0.10–0.12
Salt iodization	0.05

Sources: Horton, Alderman, and Rivera 2008; Horton and others 2010.

have consistently shown low costs per capita benefit-cost ratios greater than 2:1 (table 4.1). Rates of return for behavioral interventions range from 5:1 to 67:1 for the promotion of breastfeeding, from 4:1 to 43:1 for vitamin A supplementation, 30:1 for salt iodization, and from 3:1 to 60:1 for deworming. The newer evidence on the long-term benefits of improved nutrition in utero and in the first two years of life may mean that the returns are larger still. New delivery approaches—such as multimicronutrient powders (*sprinkles*), therapeutic foods (*plumpy nut*), and better social marketing—also make implementation more effective. In addition, because the determinants of malnutrition lie in several sectors (access to clean water, adequate maternal and child health services, and access to and the availability of nutritious foods), a multisectoral approach builds on the synergies. Continued investments in nutrition-specific interventions to avert maternal and child under-nutrition and micronutrient deficiencies through community engagement and delivery strategies that can reach poor segments of the population at greatest risk can make a great difference. If this improved access is linked to nutrition-sensitive approaches—that is, women's empowerment, agriculture, food systems, education, employment, social protection, and safety nets—they can greatly accelerate progress in countries with the highest burden of maternal and child undernutrition and mortality (Bhutta and others 2013; Ruel and others 2013).

Investments in early childhood development (ECD) have also shown significant and long-lasting benefits to enhance school readiness and related educational outcomes, improve physical and mental health, reduce reliance on the health care system, and reduce involvement in high-risk behavior (Naudeau and others 2011). In the United States, participants in a high-quality active learning preschool program (High/Scope Perry Preschool) had higher rates of high school completion (71 vs. 54 percent for the control group), higher monthly earnings (29 vs. 7 percent earned more than US$2,000 per month), and higher rates of homeownership (36 vs. 13 percent for the control group at age 27 years). Participants in a full-time quality child care program (Abecederian Project) were less likely to smoke, use marijuana, or become teenage parents than nonparticipants. These kinds of effects are especially important in resource-rich countries where poverty and fertility levels and risks of conflict are high. In terms of lifetime earnings only, Engle and others (2011) computed a global benefit-cost ratio of 17.6:1 for increasing preschool enrollment (figure 4.8).

As an integrated system for human capital formation, interventions in nutrition, health, and early education have mutually reinforcing and cumulative effects. Well-nourished, healthy children who have received adequate care and stimulation are better prepared to enter school and succeed. The skills that children develop early form the basis for future learning and labor market success (Heckman and Kautz 2013). Nutrition feeds the brain and builds the body, stimulation sparks the mind, love and protection buffer the negative effects of stress and adversity (Lake and Chan 2015), and good schools provide cognitive

Figure 4.8 Early Child Nutrition and Education Interventions Have Positive Benefit-Cost Ratios

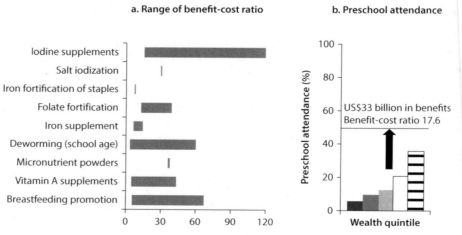

Sources: For nutrition interventions, Horton, Alderman, and Rivera 2008; for preschool attendance, Engle and others 2011.

and social learning to enable people to succeed in the workplace. For these reasons, the three main priorities for interventions are ensuring that mothers and their children are healthy, that children are prepared for school, and that they learn what they need to succeed in the workplace and outside. These interventions build on each other's synergies, and multisectoral approaches and system building are key to harnessing these synergies and accelerating the effects.

The rest of this section discusses some of the key interventions in each of these domains. For each priority, we summarize the risks, the interventions to address them, and some of the evidence on their effects.

Ensuring Healthy Mothers and Babies

Many African countries did not reach the Millennium Development Goals (MDG) of reducing the proportion of people who suffer from hunger as measured by the proportion of underweight children (MDG1), reducing child mortality (MDG4), or improving maternal health by reducing maternal mortality and ensuring universal access to reproductive health (MDG5). For the SSA countries for which information is available (map 4.1), only Ghana, Liberia, Malawi, Mauritania, Mozambique, Rwanda, Swaziland, and Tanzania were on track to reach MDG1 in 2011. For MDG4, the 11 countries with the highest child mortality rates were Angola, the Central African Republic, Chad, Côte d'Ivoire, the Democratic Republic of Congo, Guinea, Mali, Niger, Nigeria, and Sierra Leone—all emerging or resource-rich countries—and Guinea-Bissau. In terms of MDG5, the countries with maternal mortality ratios greater than 1 per 100 live births were Angola, Cameroon, Chad, the Democratic Republic of Congo,

Map 4.1 SSA Countries Made Slow Progress toward MDGs 1, 4, and 5, 2011

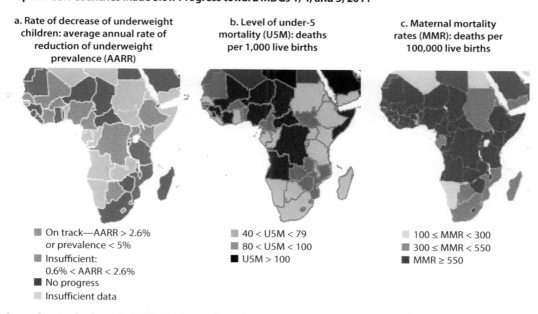

a. Rate of decrease of underweight children: average annual rate of reduction of underweight prevalence (AARR)

b. Level of under-5 mortality (U5M): deaths per 1,000 live births

c. Maternal mortality rates (MMR): deaths per 100,000 live births

- On track—AARR > 2.6% or prevalence < 5%
- Insufficient: 0.6% < AARR < 2.6%
- No progress
- Insufficient data

- 40 < U5M < 79
- 80 < U5M < 100
- U5M > 100

- 100 ≤ MMR < 300
- 300 ≤ MMR < 550
- MMR ≥ 550

Sources: For rates of underweight, UNICEF 2013; for rates of mortality, UNICEF and others 2014.

Guinea-Bissau, Liberia, Nigeria, Niger, and Sierra Leone—all emerging or resource-rich countries—and Burundi, Malawi, and Rwanda.

The first steps to guarantee that children are healthy is that their mothers are healthy and do not die. In SSA, maternal undernutrition, severe anemia, tuberculosis, malaria, and human immunodeficiency virus / acquired immunodeficiency syndrome (HIV/AIDS) increase the risks of maternal death. Orphans face heightened challenges in terms of both physical and mental health. As mentioned, maternal undernutrition is linked to intrauterine growth restriction and low birthweight; maternal stress and depression are also linked to low birthweight, stunting, and insecure attachment in their offspring.

Interventions to strengthen maternal and child health include providing prenatal care during pregnancy, adequate birth and emergency preparedness and skilled care during childbirth, and proper care and support in the weeks after childbirth; preventing teenage pregnancy; promoting breastfeeding; providing complementary feeding; and managing childhood illnesses.

First, it is important to provide prenatal care during pregnancy, adequate birth and emergency preparedness and skilled care during childbirth, and proper care and support in the weeks after childbirth. The goal is to provide four comprehensive visits during a normal pregnancy, including iron and folate supplementation and multinutrients, as needed, to ensure a low-risk pregnancy and adequate weight for the baby. Overall coverage of births by a skilled attendant remains at 46.5 percent in SSA; a lack of skilled care contributes to more deaths by hemorrhage (one-third of deaths), perinatal infections (one-tenth of deaths), and hypertension (one-fifth of deaths). Fee abolitions and results-based financing have helped to increase coverage in Burundi and Rwanda (Africa Health Forum 2013). A low birthweight (weight less than 2.5 kilograms) reflects the poor health and nutrition status of mothers and yields long-term nutritional and health consequences for the children. Interventions to address it include the following:

- Provide affordable (free or low-cost) health and nutrition services (such as those described here) through different mechanisms, including insurance schemes, social safety net programs, and government provision.
- Prevent or treat maternal infections, including prophylaxis for and treatment of malaria and testing for and management of syphilis and other sexually transmitted infections.
- Provide iron folate supplementation for all pregnant women.
- Provide counseling and support for increased dietary intake (quality and quantity) during pregnancy, reduced maternal workload, prevention and treatment of anemia, decreased indoor air pollution, reduced tobacco consumption, avoidance of gender violence, and planning for contraception after delivery.
- Provide maternal supplements of balanced energy and protein for pregnant women facing food shortages.

Second, preventing teenage pregnancy is essential. Africa has the highest rate of teenage pregnancies, with Niger topping the list (51 percent of women ages

20–24 years reporting a birth before age 18 years). Interventions upstream to support secondary schooling for girls include the recruitment of female teachers (Baird and others 2009), provision of sanitation facilities in school, and provision of cash transfers (Baird and others 2011; Duflo and others 2006; Lindert and others 2007), fee waivers, stipends, fellowships, and in-school health interventions, including access to information and contraceptives. Cash transfers may also have effects on sexual debut and age at marriage (Baird and others 2010, for Malawi; Handa and others 2014, for Kenya). Workforce initiatives to support the school-to-work transition for adolescent girls, such as the Adolescent Girls Initiative, are important too. This is an important step, especially in resource-rich countries, which are still in the early stages of demographic transition from high fertility and mortality to low fertility and mortality. Improving prenatal care and child health as well as girls' education can help to accelerate the transition and promote a virtuous cycle of investments in human capital.

Third, it is key to promote breastfeeding. Effective transmission of infant and young child feeding messages through multiple communication channels, lactation management training for health workers in the field and in the hospital, and community outreach (home visits by midwives) have made it possible to increase exclusive breastfeeding in Sri Lanka (World Bank 2013). A high-level political commitment and a culture supportive of breastfeeding also likely contribute.

Fourth, complementary feeding is needed to foster catch-up growth before age 2. Growth can falter significantly in the first 18 months of life, and weaning is a critical moment in that trajectory. Complementary feeding, together with adequate child-feeding practices and management of infections, are essential to avoid significant growth faltering. Complementary feeding needs to be timely and adequate in terms of amount, frequency, and consistency. The foods need to be prepared in a safe manner and given in an adequate way, with active, responsive feeding emphasizing the relationship with the child.

Fifth, it is essential to manage childhood illnesses. Integrated management of childhood illnesses combines improved management of childhood illness with aspects of nutrition, immunization, and other important disease prevention and health promotion activities. The objectives of this approach are to reduce deaths and the frequency and severity of illness and disability and to contribute to improved growth and development. Developed by the World Health Organization and the United Nations Children's Emergency Fund, the strategy includes three main components: (1) improvements in the case management skills of health staff through the provision of locally adapted guidelines on the integrated management of childhood illnesses and through activities to promote their use; (2) improvements in the health system required for the effective management of childhood illness; and (3) improvements in family and community practices. Specific challenges include addressing the prevalence of diarrhea and the administration of therapeutic zinc, the prevalence of acute respiratory infections, and the treatment of malaria.

To deliver these services, many African countries are seeking to complement center-based care with community health providers. These providers can perform a range of basic services from prenatal care to growth monitoring, management of diarrhea, instructions about proper hygiene and feeding practices, malaria pro-phylaxis, access to contraception, and even management of maternal depression. Similarly, community-based nutrition interventions such as those in Senegal hold much promise for improving child nutrition (box 4.2).

Accelerating the progress in nutrition will require effective, large-scale nutrition-sensitive programs that address key underlying determinants of nutrition and enhance the coverage and effectiveness of nutrition-specific interventions (Ruel and others 2013). These include investments in agriculture, social safety nets,

---

Box 4.2 Community-Based Growth Promotion Programs

Honduras, Jamaica, Madagascar, Nigeria, Senegal, Tanzania, and some states in India use a strat-egy of community-based growth promotion, which incorporates some of the key Scaling-Up Nutrition interventions and strengthens knowledge and capacity at the community level.

Such strategies have proven effective in improving mothers' knowledge of child nutrition, atti-tudes, and practices; in boosting family demand for health care; and in reducing undernutrition. Successful, large-scale child growth promotion programs in these countries achieved sharp declines in child malnutrition in the first five years, with a more gradual rate of decline in moder-ate and mild undernutrition after that. The community basis allows practitioners to address mul-tiple causes of malnutrition, with a focus on women and on children under age 2.

Leading interventions include nutrition education or counseling. These interventions often accompany child growth monitoring, offer advice on maternal care services during pregnancy, promote exclusive breastfeeding and appropriate and timely complementary feeding, encour-age health and childcare practices, and make referrals to health centers. Some programs have provided micronutrient supplements for pregnant mothers and children, as well as immuniza-tion and related services.

Program experiences highlight the importance of three elements: female community work-ers as service delivery agents; regular monitoring of child growth (weight), paired with coun-seling and communication with the mother by a well-trained agent who benefits from regular supervision in weighing, recording, and counseling; and well-designed, culturally appropriate, and consistent nutrition education to promote specific nutrition practices. The challenges relate to agent training, support, and motivation; barriers faced by beneficiary mothers in implementing recommended behavioral changes; and the high costs of food supplementation.

In Senegal, the national nutrition program adopted community-based approaches, targeted the "first 1,000 days," implemented systematic nutrition screening, and delivered interventions using a network of well-supervised nongovernmental organizations (Linnemayr and others 2008). Over the years, the program added bed net distribution, community management of acute undernutrition and food fortification, and, most recently, a cash transfer initiative. Prenatal care increased from one-third to two-thirds, exclusive breastfeeding for the first six months doubled to 58 percent, and correct use of bed nets more than doubled to 59 percent. The rate of stunting in 2005 was only 59 percent of that in 1990. Similarly, the rate of being underweight in 2005 was 65 percent of that in 1990.

Source: World Bank 2013.

early child education, and parenting. Ways to enhance the nutrition sensitivity of programs include improving targeting, using conditions to stimulate participation, strengthening nutrition goals and actions, and optimizing women's nutrition, time, physical and mental health, and empowerment. Nutrition-sensitive programs can help to scale up nutrition-specific interventions and to create a stimulating environment in which young children can grow and develop to their full potential.

Resource-rich countries face a specific set of challenges in protecting their nascent and growing human capital from potential public health problems that have accompanied the discovery of natural resources, including tuberculosis, HIV/AIDS, infectious diseases, and gender-based violence as well as occupational health issues in the mining sector. Box 4.3 summarizes some of these local economic effects and interventions to limit the negative effects of mining.

Box 4.3 Mineral Wealth and the Protection of Human Capital

While, in theory, local resource booms could stimulate an increase in local incomes if the sector has enough local backward linkages, the effects on education and health are potentially less benign. Environmental pollution and work-related injuries can reduce the benefits. The magnitude of the negative effects are in part, related to the quality of local institutions to enforce air and water quality regulations or safety oversight.

Large-scale mining and mineral processing can generate significant amounts of air pollutants. Mining also can release industry-specific pollutants—such as cyanide, mercury, and heavy metals—which have cumulative effects on the quality of soil and water sources. Environmental pollution has important health consequences and can affect school and cognitive development as well as agricultural productivity. In Northern Chile, children living near a deposit of mineral waste have a higher concentration of lead in their blood and worse school results. A review of 44 countries showed increased stunting in children and anemia among young women within 5 kilometers of mines. In Ghana, gold production is associated with decreased agricultural productivity within 20 kilometers of the mines. Decreased agricultural productivity may undermine women's ability to provide food and water for their family and increase their workload.

The often harsh living conditions for miners in small-scale mining as well as in large-scale mining, along with the lack of information and education about prevention, can contribute to a high prevalence of HIV/AIDS and other communicable diseases among miners and their families. Also, work-related injuries and health risks—lung cancer, for example—reduce miners' life expectancy and often put families in particularly precarious situations. In addition, a transient male workforce can bring increased alcohol use, sex workers, and violence to communities, which can affect women's safety.

The closing of noneconomic mines has added to poverty, especially in mono-industry communities and mineral-dependent regions. In addition to the loss of jobs among the local population, essential public goods and services originally provided by the mining company—transportation and water, for example—have ceased to be delivered, with particularly harmful effects on the poor and other vulnerable groups.

Source: Aragon and others 2015: Chuhan-Pole and others 2015; Loayza and Rigolini 2016.

Ensuring School Readiness

The skills that children develop in their first years of life provide the foundations for their future learning and labor market success. ECD enhances a child's ability to learn, work with others, be patient, and develop other skills on which to build formal learning and social interactions in the school years and beyond. In resource-rich countries, ECD is potentially a key factor in helping children to manage conflicts and develop patience, which will serve them as adults. ECD also ensures that children stay in school, an important ingredient in decreasing risky behaviors in adolescence. Across all countries, children in the highest income quintile are more than twice as likely to attend preschool as those in the lowest quintile. They are also more likely to benefit from higher-quality stimulation at home.

The most promising interventions include parenting interventions and center-based care and early education. Engle and others (2007, 2011) systematically reviewed studies and identified the benefits from various "ECD" interventions. In all cases, effects are larger for children from disadvantaged situations. Results seem stronger for small programs than for scaled-up programs.

- *Parenting interventions* promote parent–child interaction to improve responsiveness in infants and child feeding, increase attachment, and encourage learning, book reading, play activities, positive discipline, and problem solving related to child development. Parenting education and support can be delivered through home visits, community groups, regular clinic visits, and media. These interventions can improve children's cognitive and psychosocial development. Effects are larger when there are systematic curricula and training opportunities for childcare workers and parents and when there are active strategies to show and promote caregiving behaviors—practice, role play, or coaching to improve parent–child interaction.
- *Preschool care, childcare, and daycare* can be formal (linked to schools or offered by private providers with a fixed classroom) or nonformal and community-based (with few or no professionally trained teachers and locally adapted sites). These interventions usually improve children's cognitive functioning, readiness for school, and school performance. Effects are larger for high-quality programs, whether formal or nonformal.

Other promising interventions try to create opportunities for changes through the environment by tackling poverty and using the media. As mentioned, cash transfer programs can help parents to provide for their children's needs and provide incentives for parents to invest in their children's human capital. Very few evaluations have assessed cognitive and language skills, but those that have (Ecuador, Mexico, and Nicaragua) have found small positive effects. As television and radio ownership increases, educational programming (content that is educational, nonviolent, and designed for young children) may help to improve child development (Engle and others 2011; Naudeau and others 2011).

Interventions are most effective when they are both multisectoral—they address the health, nutrition, early stimulation, and learning needs of young children—and integrated (Grantham-McGregor and others 2007). This is not always possible during countries' early engagement with ECD—hence the importance of constructing a policy framework that can raise the visibility of a nation's vision and goals for young children, clarify the respective responsibilities of different government agencies, and provide critical guidance for public and private investments (Naudeau and others 2011).

Ensuring Relevant Learning and Quality Basic Education

Sub-Saharan Africa has made great strides toward achieving universal primary enrollment (from 60 to 78 percent between 2000 and 2012), but rapid population growth and conflicts pose a big challenge to maintaining this progress. Armed conflicts—particularly in resource-rich countries—and other emergencies are keeping too many children out of school. For example, in the conflict-affected province of Nord Kivu in the Democratic Republic of the Congo, almost one in two children of primary school age from the poorest households had never been to school in 2010, compared with one in four in the province of Kasaï-Oriental (United Nations 2014). In addition, the early incidence of dropping out is higher in resource-rich countries, and poor, rural girls are more likely not to complete their primary education (figure 4.9), which is an important determinant of early childbearing. Reasons for early dropouts include being over-age for grade level

Figure 4.9 The Early Dropout Rate Is Still Too High in SSA: Educational Attainment of Population 25 Years of Age and Older

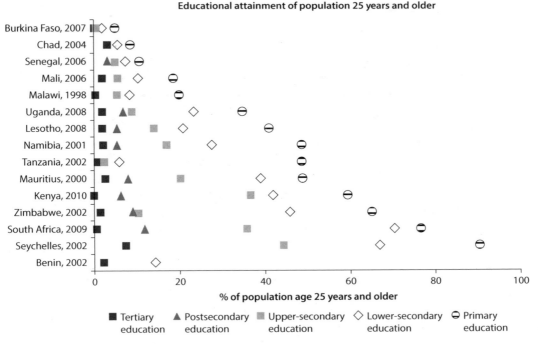

Source: Huebler (2012).

From Mines and Wells to Well-Built Minds • http://dx.doi.org/10.1596/978-1-4648-1005-3

(due to late entry or repetition), distance between home and school, household poverty, need to combine work and study, and opportunity costs. In total, 43 million children are out of school in Sub-Saharan Africa, of whom 56 percent are girls.

Quality of schooling remains an issue, with high rates of absenteeism among teachers (discussed in chapter 3), poor infrastructure, and poor-quality textbooks and teaching methods. As a result, the potential learning gains from schooling—cognitive and psychosocial—elude many pupils and place them at further disadvantage in the transition from school to the labor market. Similar to noncognitive skills, cognitive skills such as literacy and numeracy form the foundation for acquiring higher-order and technical skills later in life, whether through more formal education, training, or on-the-job learning. Basic cognitive skills are necessary for learning more advanced concepts, and better foundational skills lower the costs of additional investments (Filmer and Fox 2014).

Key interventions include education for all, training teachers to improve their academic qualifications and pedagogical skills, smaller classes and groupings by levels, and accountability. Curricular reforms to focus on competencies (basic numeracy and literacy skills, noncognitive skills) are key to increasing learning and responding to the demands of employers. Teaching approaches that are more interactive and group based may facilitate the acquisition of both cognitive and behavioral skills, for instance (box 4.4). Complementary interventions to ensure that girls stay in school and to improve learning for all include the following:

- Hiring female teachers
- Building separate latrines for girls or maintaining clean, accessible latrines for all children
- Promoting school health interventions such as deworming, and
- Promoting parents' participation in school through school committees or volunteer activities.

Box 4.4 What Types of Interventions Improve Student Learning?

The literature on what improves learning in schools is vast, but systematic literature reviews have been conducted to identify the types of interventions that are most effective in improving learning outcomes for students. Probably tens of thousands of articles have been published on factors affecting student learning. Even when one restricts the literature to rigorous impact evaluations conducted in developing countries, the number of studies remains large. Fortunately, several literature reviews have recently been conducted to synthesize the messages from this literature (Conn 2014; Glewwe and others 2014; Kremer, Brannen, and Glennerster 2013; Krishnaratne, White, and Carpenter 2013; McEwan 2015; Murnane and Ganimian 2014). Evans and Popova (2015) assessed whether these various reviews provide similar messages regarding what does and does not improve learning outcomes in developing and especially low-income countries. In total, the six reviews identified 227 rigorous studies measuring the impact of various interventions on learning outcomes

box continues next page

Box 4.4 What Types of Interventions Improve Student Learning? *(continued)*

in developing countries. A bit more than half (134) were random control trials (RCTs). The others were quasi-experimental studies. As noted by Evans and Popova (2015), there is quite a bit of divergence in the recommendations made by the studies, for at least two reasons:

- *Different samples.* Only three studies were included in all six reviews, and 70 percent of the studies were included in only one review. The reviews had different selection criteria (for example, considered RCTs only or only studies for Africa), but also different search methodologies and levels of comprehensiveness.
- *Different categories and interpretations.* The same programs were classified in different ways in the various reviews, and interpretation of "success" varied depending on the criteria used.

Despite the divergence in findings, the literature reviews point to some common sets of interventions that are likely to improve learning. Evans and Popova (2015) suggest that three types of interventions tend to be recommended across multiple reviews: (1) pedagogical interventions that match teaching to individual student learning levels; (2) individualized, repeated teacher training that is associated with a specific method or task; and (3) accountability-boosting interventions. Specific interventions in each of these three broad areas have proven successful (table B4.4.1). This does not mean that other interventions cannot be successful or are not required, but there seems to be a consensus about the effectiveness of these interventions in the various reviews.

Table B4.4.1 Interventions with Some Consensus on Effectiveness in the Literature Reviews

Area of intervention	Specific interventions
Pedagogical interventions that match teaching to individual student learning levels	1. Assign students to separate classes based on initial ability so that teachers can focus instruction at the level of learning of individual students (Duflo and others 2011) [4 reviews] 2. Use mathematics software to help students to learn at their own pace (Banerjee and others 2007) [5 reviews]; by contrast, distributing computers does not, by itself, lead to gains 3. Train teachers to use an initial reading assessment and then continually assess student performance (Piper and Korda 2011) [2 reviews]
Individualized and repeated teacher training associated with a specific method or task	1. Train teachers and provide them with regular mentoring to implement early grade reading instruction in local language (Lucas and others 2014) [3 reviews] 2. Combine student reading groups with in-school supervisors to provide ongoing guidance to group leaders (Cabezas and others 2011) [2 reviews] 3. Teach teachers to use storybooks and flash cards (He and others 2009) [1 review]; by contrast, similar programs introduced without teacher preparation tend to be less effective (He and others 2008) [3 reviews]
Accountability-boosting interventions	1. Provide teachers with incentives to be present in school (Duflo and others 2012) [4 reviews] and to perform (Muralidharan and Sundararaman 2011) [3 reviews]; but design the incentives to improve learning, while reducing the risk of strategic countervailing teacher responses (Glewwe and others 2009) [5 reviews] 2. Supplement civil service teachers with locally hired teachers on short-term contracts (Duflo, Hanna, and Ryan 2012) [4 reviews]; (Banerjee and others 2007) [5 reviews]

Source: Box contributed by Quentin Wodon, based on Evans and Popova (2015).

From Mines and Wells to Well-Built Minds • http://dx.doi.org/10.1596/978-1-4648-1005-3

Education systems have scope for developing skills other than cognitive skills. Increased attention to imparting behavioral skills through schooling may take several forms, including modes of instruction as well as the modeling of appropriate behaviors, including teachers' behavior, in the school environment. First, school success itself increases self-esteem and confers a greater sense of self-determination, as shown in research among high school and college graduates in the United States. Second, the way that teaching and learning are delivered may influence behavioral skills. Teaching approaches that encourage participation, group activities, and exploration instill different mind-sets among students than approaches that emphasize rote learning. Third, the experience of education and the habits learned in school matter. Students' exposure to an environment where teachers are absent 20 percent of the time with little consequence (box 3.2) will likely instill a sense that punctuality (one of the skills that some employers say they are seeking) is not important (Filmer and Fox 2014).

Technical and vocational education and training (TVET) has the potential to help youth in the school-to-work transition, given the levels of high school dropouts and the demands of the labor market for midlevel technical skills as countries urbanize and develop more industry and services (box 4.5). However, TVET is not fully geared to the needs of either job seekers or employers in most African countries. Issues of curriculum, quality, participation of employers, and costs are pervasive. In resource-rich countries, this mismatch could be a short-term bottleneck to providing technicians for the extractive industries and a longer-term bottleneck to helping workers to move from one sector to another as countries diversify their economy.

The benefits of investing across health, nutrition, early childhood development, and education accrue to individuals, generations, and countries. For each individual, synergies occur between health, nutrition, and education, and early skills form the foundation for acquiring new skills at a lower cost. Empowering women and involving men in positive ways are key for the next generation. Between 1970 and 1995, an increase in female education was associated with an increase in farm productivity and a 43 percent decrease in undernutrition (figure 4.10). In contrast, early marriage and maternal mortality were

Box 4.5 The Role of Technical and Vocational Education and Training

Formal TVET runs parallel to general schooling at the secondary or tertiary level and meets the need for intermediate or advanced technical skills. Entry requirements often include having completed primary or secondary school. Therefore, participants in formal TVET have substantially more schooling than participants in other forms of postschool training.

In Nigeria, technical colleges at the secondary level produce craftsmen and master craftsmen, focusing on traditional technical vocations (electricians, vehicle mechanics, and masons).

box continues next page

Box 4.5 The Role of Technical Vocational Education and Training (*continued*)

At the tertiary level, vocational institutions (polytechnics) produce technicians, professionals, and engineers. In Rwanda, technical secondary schools prepare students to enter the labor market at roughly the same level as an upper-secondary-school graduate. Vocational training centers prepare basic education graduates or dropouts to enter the labor market.

Several types of nongovernmental entities also provide technical and vocational training, including for-profit private institutes and firms, which provide 35 percent of the training across Africa (Mingat, Ledoux, and Rakotomalala 2010). Compared with public institutes, private training providers tend to focus on "light" vocational skills—such as business, commercial, and service skills—possibly owing to the high fixed costs of providing more industry-oriented sorts of skills. Private providers in Uganda, for instance, focus on office qualifications and various business skills that require only limited investment. Private providers also tend to be concentrated in specific regions—often those with larger populations and greater demand for training (Ghana and Zambia are examples).

Source: Filmer and Fox 2014.

Figure 4.10 Girls' Completion of Secondary School Is Associated with Less Stunting

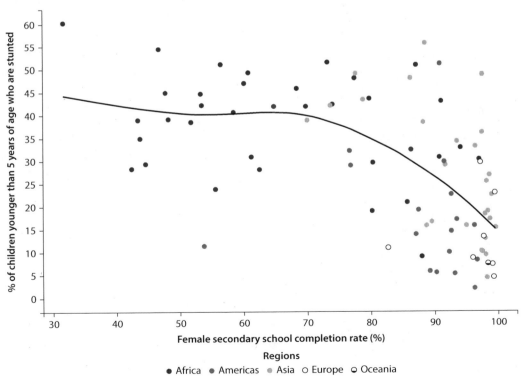

Source: World Bank 2014.

From Mines and Wells to Well-Built Minds • http://dx.doi.org/10.1596/978-1-4648-1005-3

associated with an increase in stunting (World Bank 2014). Maternal education has multiple protective effects: it is associated with less maternal depression; better child nutritional status; a better quality of the childrearing environment through family planning (birth spacing), knowledge about ECD, and higher educational aspirations; and an ability to access and benefit from human development interventions. Positive involvement of fathers is also associated with higher educational aspirations and less exposure to violence. Undernutrition taxes 3–4 percent of gross domestic product annually in Sub-Saharan Africa (World Bank 2013). Human capital is at the core of broad-based growth, as East Asian countries have demonstrated.

The Role of Cash Transfers in Increasing Demand for Health and Education Services

This chapter has identified key points of entry for building human capital at the youngest ages. This section turns to the demand side and focuses on the types of interventions that aim to increase the use of services. It examines, in particular, various types of cash transfers that have been deployed in many parts of the world (Fiszbein and others 2009) and that are increasingly being discussed in the context of natural-resource-rich countries in SSA (for example, in Tanzania), sometimes in the form of direct dividends.

Since the first generation of evidence on cash transfers in Latin America in the 1990s, similar programs have been increasingly adopted and evaluated in Sub-Saharan Africa. Latin American cash transfer programs have traditionally focused on the dual goals of reducing current and future poverty by conditioning cash receipt on compliance with certain education- and health-related activities (conditional cash transfers, CCTs). In contrast, cash transfer programs in Africa tend to focus on either combating chronic poverty and food insecurity or easing the effects of shocks such as droughts on vulnerable populations (Del Ninno and Mills 2015; Garcia and Moore 2012), through the provision of often unconditional transfers (UCTs). However, in practice, while many UCTs do not impose explicit conditions, they often carry strong social messaging (that is, labeling), which is likely to affect recipients' behavior, notably with respect to health and education. Indeed, a review of achievements in Africa (Evans and Popova 2014) showed that cash transfers increase school enrollment, attendance, test scores, and grade completion significantly and have positive effects on health and nutrition (box 4.6).

Cash transfer programs increase demand for health and education services through two pathways: an income effect, and an effect of the conditions or accompanying measures. Demand for education increases with income (see the discussion on inequalities in chapter 1). The additional income provided by cash transfers may enable households to resolve barriers such as informal fees, transportation, uniforms, and supplies. It may also compensate households for some of the opportunity cost of the lost child labor, especially as children enter their teenage years.

Box 4.6 Cash Transfers in Sub-Saharan Africa: What Do They Achieve?

As the number of cash transfer programs in Africa has grown, so too has the quality of evidence about their effectiveness. Since 2008, 21 cash transfer programs have been rigorously evaluated across 14 SSA countries, consisting of 16 RCTs and 5 quasi-experimental studies. Of these 21 cash transfer programs, 15 are UCTs, 3 are CCTs, and 3 have both unconditional and conditional arms.

Between them, these impact evaluations provide evidence from both resource-rich and non–resource-rich SSA countries that cash transfers improve many outcomes, including consumption, income, education, health, and nutrition measures. In terms of consumption, 13 of 16 evaluations found that total (food and nonfood) consumption increased as a result of the transfer, 2 found no significant impact, and 1 found that cash transfers decreased expenditures on a specific consumption item, while increasing spending or remaining constant on other items. Moreover, consumption of temptation goods, such as alcohol and tobacco, does not increase as a result of receiving cash transfers (Evans and Popova 2014). Fewer evaluations reported effects on income and poverty reduction, but 4 of the 7 that did found significant improvements and none found the opposite.

Almost all programs for which education outcomes are reported were found to increase either student attendance, enrollment, test scores, or grade completion significantly. Similarly, of 19 evaluations reporting cash transfer effects on either health or nutrition, 15 found a significant positive impact, while the remainder found an insignificant positive impact. A new wave of evaluations also found that cash transfers can decrease risky sexual behavior and HIV/AIDS prevalence.

Both UCTs and CCTs alike produce significant positive effects on education, health, and nutrition. Among three programs with both UCT and CCT arms, CCTs tended to produce larger education effects (in Malawi), particularly for marginalized children (in Burkina Faso). CCTs were more effective in improving health center visits for children in Burkina Faso, but UCTs were more effective at improving mental health for adolescent girls in Malawi.

Overall, a small but highly valuable amount of experimental and quasi-experimental evidence from diverse countries and program modalities across the region found that cash transfers—both conditional and unconditional—have been effective at improving many facets of human development and are now showing promise for tackling new issues specific to the region.

Source: This box was contributed by Anna Popova and David Evans.

When services are available, the basic premise of CCTs is that healthier and better-educated workers will get better jobs and be able to afford more education for their children, breaking the vicious circle of intergenerational poverty. First-generation programs placed a high emphasis on enrollment and attendance, especially in primary and lower-secondary school. Programs are now experimenting with promoting transitions from primary to secondary school, and secondary school completion (Mexico). Others are linking cash transfers with preschool attendance (the Philippines) and growth monitoring (pilot in Bangladesh).

To reach young children and areas where services are not fully available, cash transfer programs have adopted a range of strategies, including strong social messaging, communications for behavior change, and community-based interventions to promote parenting practices, early stimulation, nutrition, health, and sanitation practices through peer-to-peer learning (using positive deviant households to show others how they can change their behavior). These approaches had positive effects in Nicaragua (Macours, Schady, and Vakis 2012). Evaluations of first-phase pilot programs are under way in Burkina Faso, Djibouti, and Niger.

Going to Scale with ECD and Cash Transfers

Education and basic health services are typically already provided on a large scale. However, many of the other types of services discussed in this chapter have not gone to scale, although they show promising returns at the pilot level. Some that have gone to scale have shown lackluster results since (a) economies of scale did not materialize and (b) coordination costs increased. In addition, if unit costs are high, budget constraints may cause partial implementation of the intervention package or limit coverage. However, a few programs are testing innovative ways to keep costs low and quality acceptable as they scale up.

Providing Early Childhood Development and Education Services at Scale

Based on the experience of countries such as Cambodia, the Arab Republic of Egypt, El Salvador, Indonesia, Mexico, Mozambique, Turkey, and Senegal, Naudeau and Holland (2014) and Bernal, Sirali, and Naudeau (2015) identified a three-pronged strategy to scale up ECD interventions to reach the 0–6 years age group:

- *Leverage existing health, nutrition, and education services.* At health facilities, providing training for providers, materials for parents, and play materials for children helps to transmit key messages about ECD. If community health workers visit families regularly, they can discuss and monitor nutrition and parenting during their visits. Indonesia and Mexico are also strengthening school preparedness by supporting volunteers who teach groups of parents or children in community structures.
- *Leverage the capacity of nonstate actors.* Partnerships can be leveraged with civil society organizations (as the Mozambican government is doing with Save the Children to expand the successful preschool pilot; Martinez, Nadeau, and Pereira 2012), the private sector (to provide basic health and early childhood care and education, especially in poor urban areas), and communication channels (to expand educational programming that is age-appropriate and nonviolent).
- *Use cash transfers to promote ECD.* Cash transfers can be used to encourage access to services (when available) and changes in behavior regarding parenting practices with the support of civil society organizations.

Scaling-Up Cash Transfers

Based on the experience of countries such as Brazil, Ethiopia, Ghana, Kenya, and South Africa, several strategies to scale up cash transfers in Africa seem promising:

1. *Earmark sources of funds.* Earmarking some of the resources for health and education may increase the amount of resources, signal ownership of the programs to donors, and foster sustainability by integrating the programs in the national budget (Ethiopia, Kenya, Tanzania).
2. *Leverage local government capacity and nonstate actors for local implementation.* In SSA, targeting is often devolved to local governments and communities, while the delivery of complementary interventions is subcontracted to nongovernmental organizations and other partners (Niger).
3. *Promote a systems approach with common tools and improved coordination.* A common registry of poor and vulnerable households and a common payment mechanism are important tools for minimizing duplications and gaps in coverage and fostering coordination with health and education providers at the local level. Complementary actions targeting girls' education (fellowship, boarding facilities) and female economic empowerment (Zambia) or workfare (Ethiopia and Tanzania) can also integrate effects at the household level.
4. *Leverage information and communication technologies.* Mobile and electronic payments have high institutional and setup costs but may increase efficiency in the medium term. Sending text messages with human development content may nudge behavior changes and reach households in remote locations at a lower cost.

Conclusions

This chapter has sought to make the case for investing in the foundations of human capital by summarizing the evidence on early life conditions and their effects in adulthood and between generations. It has also shown that investments in health, nutrition, early childhood development, and basic education are complementary and mutually reinforcing. Early cognitive and psychosocial skills provide the basis for learning further skills at a lower cost. The chapter argues that investing early is cheaper and smarter, as the returns are very high and the equity and efficiency trade-offs are minimal. After windows of opportunity close, remediation is more expensive even if the brain retains learning capacity throughout life. To reap maximum benefits, quality of services is key. Cash transfers can help to overcome some barriers to accessing existing services, and they can also be combined with behavior change interventions, focusing on feeding practices and ECD. Some countries in Africa are taking these interventions to scale with innovative homegrown partnerships and implementation processes.

Annex 4A: Cash Transfer Programs in Africa

Country	Program name	CCT or UCT	Education	Health and nutrition	Consumption	Income and poverty reduction	Evaluation
Random control trials							
Burkina Faso[a]	Nahouri Cash Transfers Pilot Project	CCT and UCT	CCT: +; UCT: +				Akresh, de Walque, and Kazianga 2013a
				CCT: +; UCT: (+)			Akresh, de Walque, and Kazianga 2013b
Democratic Republic of Congo[a]	Concern Worldwide Cash Transfer and Vouchers Program	UCT		(+)	+	(+)	Aker 2013
Kenya	GiveDirectly Unconditional Cash Transfers Program using M-Pesa	UCT	(+)	(−) & +	+	(+) & (−)	Haushofer and Shapiro 2013
	Kenya Cash Transfer Program for Orphans and Vulnerable Children	UCT		+	+		Kenya CT-OVC Evaluation Team 2012a
			+				Kenya CT-OVC Evaluation Team 2012b
			Primary: (+); secondary: +	+	+	+	Ward and others 2010
				+	+	+	Zezza, de la Brière, and Davis 2010
Lesotho	Child Grants Programme	UCT	+	+	+		Daidone, Davis Dewbre, and Covarrubias 2015
						+	Filipski, Thome, Taylor and Davis 2015
Malawi	Mchinji Social Cash Transfer Pilot Scheme	UCT		+	+		Miller, Tsoka, and Reichert 2011
			+	+	+		Miller, Tsoka, and Reichert 2008

table continues next page

Annex 4A *(continued)*

Country	Program name	CCT or UCT	Education	Health and nutrition	Consumption	Income and poverty reduction	Evaluation
					+		Zezza, de la Brière, and Davis 2010
	Social Cash Transfer Scheme	UCT	+				Covarrubias, Davis, and Winters 2012
	Zomba Cash Transfer Program	CCT and UCT	2 years after program: dropouts CCT: +; schoolgirls CCT: (+); schoolgirls UCT: (+)	2 years after program: dropouts CCT: (+); schoolgirls CCT: (+); schoolgirls UCT: (+)			Baird and others 2015
			+	+			Baird, de Hoop, and Ozler 2013
			CCT: +; UCT: (+)				Baird, McIntosh, and Ozler 2011
			Round 1: +; round 2: −				Baird and others 2010
			+				Baird, McIntosh, and Ozler 2009
Niger[a]	Concern Worldwide's UCT using Zap m-money platform	UCT		+			Aker and others 2016
Nigeria[a]	Kano Conditional Cash Transfer Program	CCT	+				Sabarwal and Habyarimana 2015
Tanzania[a]	TASAF CCT Pilot Program	CCT	+	(+)	Most items (+) and (−), except insurance: +; other flours: −		Evans, Hausladen, Kosec, and Reese 2014
							Packel and others 2012
	RESPECT trial	CCT	+				
Uganda	Youth Opportunities Program	UCT	+		+	+	Blattman, Fiala, and Martinez 2013
	WFP Cash Transfers to UNICEF-supported ECD centers	UCT	+	+			Gilligan and Roy 2013

table continues next page

Annex 4A (continued)

Country	Program name	CCT or UCT	Education	Health and nutrition	Consumption	Income and poverty reduction	Evaluation
Zambia[a]	Child Grants Programme	UCT	+		+		Handa, Natali, and others 2015
				(+) and (−)			Handa, Peterman, and others Tembo 2016
				(+) and (−)	+		Seidenfeld and others 2014
			+				Seidenfeld and others 2015
Zimbabwe[a]	Diocese of Mutare Community Care Program	CCT and UCT	CCT: +; UCT: +	CCT: +; UCT: +			Robertson and others 2013
Quasi-experimental studies							
Ethiopia	Productive Safety Net Programme	UCT			(+)	(+)	Sabates-Wheeler and Devereux 2010
	Productive Safety Nets Programme and Household Asset Building Programme	UCT and PW		+	+		Berhane and others 2011
Ghana[a]	Livelihood Empowerment Against Poverty	UCT	+		(−)		Handa and others 2013
South Africa	South African Child Support Grant	UCT		+			Aguero, Carter, and Woolard 2008
	Old-Age Pension Program	UCT		Girls: +; boys: (+)			Duflo 2003
			Male pensioner: +; female pensioner: (+)				Edmonds 2006

Note: CCT = conditional cash transfer; UCT = unconditional cash transfer; WFP = World Food Programme; UNICEF = United Nations Children's Fund; ECD = early childhood development PW = public works; + = a significant positive result, − = a significant negative result, (+) = an insignificant positive result; (−) = an insignificant negative result.

a. Resource-rich country.

Notes

1. Biological programming is the process by which exposure to a stimulus (positive or negative) during a critical period of development can change the predisposition to developing disease with long-term consequences for health status. During a critical period for a nutrient, if that nutrient is in adequate supply, an irreversible change in the brain structure and function can occur. An example is the a lack of folic acid in the first few weeks of pregnancy, which can lead to neural tube defects (spina bifida).

2. Malnutrition includes undernutrition and overnutrition. Undernutrition results from insufficient quantity and quality of food intake, a high burden of infections and poor care practices, compounded by low access to health and social services. It translates into small-for-gestational-age, stunting (low height-for-age, a measure of chronic undernutrition), wasting (low weight-for-height, a measure of acute undernutrition), being underweight (low weight-for-age), and micronutrient deficiencies (vitamins A, calcium, iron, and zinc in particular). Overnutrition results in being overweight (body mass index (BMI) [weight (kg)/height squared (meters)] greater than 25) and obesity (BMI greater than 30).

3. Toxic stress response can occur when a child experiences strong, frequent, or prolonged adversity—such as physical or emotional abuse, chronic neglect, caregiver substance abuse or mental illness, exposure to violence, and the accumulated burdens of family economic hardship—without adequate adult support.

References

Africa Health Forum. 2013. "Results-Based Financing for Health." Brief, World Bank, Washington, DC.

Aguero, Jorge, Michael Carter, and Ingrid Woolard. 2007. "The Impacts of Unconditional Cash Transfers on Nutrition: The South African Child Support Grant." International Poverty Center, Working Paper 39, Brasília.

Aker, Jenny. 2013. "Cash or Coupons? Testing the Impacts of Cash versus Vouchers in the Democratic Republic of Congo." Center for Global Development, Working Paper 320, Washington, DC.

Aker, Jenny, Rachid Boumnijel, Amanda McClelland, Niall Tierney, and others. 2016. "Payment Mechanisms and Anti-Poverty Programs: Evidence from a Mobile Money Cash Transfer Experiment in Niger." *Economic Development and Cultural Change* 65 (1).

Akresh, Richard, Damien de Walque, and Harounan Kazianga. 2013a. "Alternative Cash Transfer Delivery Mechanisms: Impacts on Routine Preventative Health Clinic Visits in Burkina Faso." NBER Africa Project, University of Chicago Press, Chicago, IL.

———. 2013b. "Cash Transfers and Child Schooling: Evidence from a Randomized Evaluation of the Role of Conditionality." Mimeo.

Alderman, Harold. H., ed. 2011. *No Small Matter. The Impact of Poverty, Shocks, and Human Capital Investments on Early Childhood Development.* Washington, DC: World Bank.

Aragón, Fernando M., Punam Chuhan-Pole, and Bryan C. Land. 2015. "The Local Economic Impacts of Resource Abundance: What Have We Learned?" Policy Research Working Paper 7263, World Bank, Washington, DC.

Baird, Sarah, Ephraim Chirwa, Craig McIntosh and Berk Özler. 2010. "The Short-Term Impacts of a Schooling Conditional Cash Transfer Program on the Sexual Behavior of Young Women." *Health Economics* 19 (S1): 55–68.

Baird, Sarah, Ephraim Chirwa, Craig McIntosh, and Berk Özler. 2015. "What Happens Once the Intervention Ends? The Five-Year Impacts of a Cash Transfer Experiment in Malawi." 3ie Final Grantee Report, International Initiative for Impact Evaluation, New Delhi, India.

Baird, Sarah, Jacobus Joost de Hoop, and Berk Özler. 2013. "Income Shocks and Adolescent Mental Health." *Journal of Human Resources* 48 (2): 370–403.

Baird, Sarah, Craig McIntosh, and Berk Özler. 2009. "Designing Cost-Effective Cash Transfer Programs to Boost Schooling Among Young Women in Sub-Saharan Africa." Policy Research Working Paper 5090, World Bank, Washington, DC.

———. 2011. "Cash or Condition: Evidence from a Randomized Cash Transfer Program." *Quarterly Journal of Economics* 126 (4): 1709–53.

Banerjee, Abhijit, Shawn Cole, Esther Duflo, and Leigh Linden. 2007. "Remedying Education: Evidence from Two Randomized Experiments in India." *Quarterly Journal of Economics* 122 (3): 1235–64.

Banerjee, Abhijit, and Sendhil Mullanaithan. 2008. "Limited Attention and Income Distribution." *American Economic Review: Papers and Proceedings* 98 (2): 489–93.

Berhane, Guush, John Hoddinott, Neha Kumar, and Alemayehu Seyoum Taffesse. 2011. "The Impact of Ethiopia's Productive Safety Net and Household Asset Building Program." Final report, International Food Policy Research Institute, Washington, DC.

Bernard Van Leer Foundation. 2009. "Family Stress: Safeguarding Young Children's Care Environment: Early Childhood Matters." Bernard Van Leer Foundation, Hague, Netherlands.

Bernal, Raquel, Yasemin Sirali, and Sophie Naudeau. 2015. "Early Child Development: What Does It Cost to Provide It at Scale" (blog). Brookings Institution, Washington, DC. https://www.brookings.edu/blog/education-plus-development/2015/01/20/early-childhood-development-what-does-it-cost-to-provide-it-at-scale/.

Black, Robert, Cesar G. Victora, Susan P. Walker, Zulfiqar A. Bhutta, Parul Christian, Mercedes de Onis, Majid Ezzati, Sally Grantham-McGregor, Joanne Katz, Reynaldo Martorell, Richard Uauy, and the Maternal and Child Nutrition Study Group. 2013. "Maternal and Child Undernutrition and Overweight in Low-Income and Middle-Income Countries." *The Lancet* 382 (9890): 427–51.

Bhutta, Zulfiqar A., Jai K. Das, Arjumand Rizvi, Michelle F. Gaffey, Neff Walker, Susan Horton, Patrick Webb, Anna Lartey, Robert E. Black, and *The Lancet* Nutrition Interventions Review Group, the Maternal and Child Nutrition Study Group. 2013. "Evidence-Based Interventions for Improvement of Maternal and Child Nutrition: What Can be Done and at What Cost?" *The Lancet* 382 (9890): 452–77.

Blattman, Christopher, Nathan Fiala, and Sebastian Martinez. 2013. "The Economic and Social Returns to Cash Transfers:Evidence from a Ugandan Aid Program." Report, Columbia University, New York.

Cabezas, Veronica, Jose Cuesta, and Francisco Gallego. 2011. "Effects of Short-Term Tutoring on Cognitive and Noncognitive Skills: Evidence from a Randomized Evaluation in Chile." Working Paper, Pontifica Universidad Católica de Chile, Santiago.

Calderón, Maria. C., and John Hoddinott. 2011. "The Inter-Generational Transmission of Cognitive Abilities in Guatemala." Research Department Publications 4722, Inter-American Development Bank, Research Department, Washington, DC.

Chuhan-Pole, Punam, Andrew L. Dabalen, Bryant C. Land, Aly Sanoh, Gregory Smith, Anja K. Tolonen, Fernando Aragón, Carl M. E. Andersson, Ola D. Hall, Karl A. Kotsadam, Michael Lewin, and Niklas Olaon. 2015. *Africa Socio-Economic Impacts of Mining on Local Communities*. Washington, DC: World Bank. http://www-wds.worldbank.org /external/default/WDSContentServer/WDSP/AFR/2015/07/31/090224b083041372 /4_0/Rendered/PDF/Socioeconomic00ommunities0in0Africa.pdf.

Conn, Katharine M. 2014. "Identifying Effective Education Interventions in Sub-Saharan Africa: A Meta-Analysis of Rigorous Impact Evaluations." Columbia University, New York.

Covarrubias, Katia, Benjamin Davis, and Paul Winters. 2012. "From Protection to Production: Productive Impacts of the Malawi Social Cash Transfer Scheme." *Journal of Development Effectiveness* 4 (1) 50–77.

Daidone, Silvio, Benjamin Davis, Joshua Dewbre, and Katia Covarrubias. 2015. "Lesotho's Child Grant Programme." 24-Month Impact Report on Productive Activities and Labour Allocation. Lesotho Country Case Study Report. FAO, Rome.

Del Ninno, Carlo, and Bradford Mills. 2015. *Safety Nets in Africa: Effective Mechanisms to Reach the Poor and Most Vulnerable*. Washington, DC: World Bank.

Dover, George J. 2009. "The Barker Hypothesis: How Pediatricians Will Diagnose and Prevent Common Adult-Onset Diseases." *Transactions of the American Clinical and Climatological Association* 120: 199–207.

Duflo, Esther. 2003. "Grandmothers and Granddaughters: Old-Age Pensions and Intrahousehold Allocation in South Africa." *World Bank Economic Review* 17 (1): 1–25.

Duflo, Esther, Pascaline Dupas, Michael Kremer, and Samuel Sinei. 2006. "Education and HIV/AIDS Prevention: Evidence from a Randomized Evaluation in Western Kenya. Policy." Policy Research Working Paper 4024, World Bank, Washington, DC.

Duflo, Esther, Pascaline Dupas, and Michael Kremer. 2011. "Peer Effects, Teacher Incentives, and the Impact of Tracking: Evidence from a Randomized Evaluation in Kenya." *American Economic Review* 101 (5).

———. 2012. "School Governance, Teacher Incentives, and Pupil-Teacher Ratios: Experimental Evidence from Kenyan Primary Schools." NBER Working Paper 17939, National Bureau of Economic Research, Cambridge, MA.

Duflo, Esther, Rema Hanna, and Stephen P. Ryan. 2012. "Incentives Work: Getting Teachers to Come to School." *American Economic Review* 102 (4): 1241–78.

Early Years Study. 1999. "Reversing the Real Brain Drain." Final Report, Ontario Children's Secretariat, Toronto, Ontario, Canada.

Edmonds, Eric. 2006. "Child Labor and Schooling Responses to Anticipated Income in South Africa." *Journal of Development Economics* 81 (2): 386–414.

Engle, Patrice, Maureen M. Black, Jere R. Behrman, Meena Cabral de Mello, Paul J. Gertler, Lydia Kapiriri, Reynaldo Martorell, Mary Eming Young, and the International Child Development Steering Group. 2007. "Strategies to Avoid the Loss of Developmental Potential in More Than 200 Million Children in the Developing World." *The Lancet* 369 (9557): 229–42.

Engle, Patrice L., Lia. Fernald, Harold H. Alderman, Jere R. Behrman, Chloe O'Gara, Aisha Yousafzai, Meena Cabral de Mello, Melissa Hidrobo, Nurper Ulkuer, Ilgi Ertem, and Selim Iltus. 2011. "Strategies for Reducing Inequalities and Improving Developmental Outcomes for Young Children in Low and Middle Income Countries." *The Lancet* 378 (9799): 1339–53.

Evans, David, Stephanie Hausladen, Katrina Kosec, and Natasha Reese. 2014. *Community-Based Conditional Cash Transfers in Tanzania: Results from a Randomized Trial.* Washington, DC: World Bank.

Evans, David, and Anna Popova. 2014. "Cash Transfers and Temptation Goods: A Review of Global Evidence." Policy Research Working Paper 6886, World Bank, Washington, DC.

———. 2015. "What Really Works to Improve Learning in Developing Countries? An Analysis of Divergent Findings in Systematic Reviews." Policy Research Working Paper 7203, World Bank, Washington, DC.

Fernald, Lia, and Melissa Hidrobo. 2011. "Effect of Ecuador's Cash Transfer Program (Bono de Desarrollo Humano) on Child Development in Infants and Toddlers: A Randomized Effectiveness Trial." *Social Science and Medicine* 72 (9): 1437–46.

Filipski, Mateusz, Karen Thome, J. Edward Taylor, and Benjamin Davis (2015). Effects of Treatment Beyond the Treated: A General Equilibrium Impact Evaluation of Lesotho's Cash Grants Program. *Agricultural Economics* 46 (3015): 227–43.

Filmer, Deon, and Louise Fox. 2014. *Youth Employment in Sub-Saharan Africa.* Africa Development Forum. Washington, DC: Agence Française de Développement and World Bank.

Fiszbein, Ariel, Norbert Schady, Francisco Ferreira, Margaret Grosh, Niall Keleher, Pedro Olinto, and Emmanuel Skoufias. 2009. *Conditional Cash Transfers: Reducing Present and Future Poverty.* Washington, DC: World Bank.

Friedman, Jed, and Jennifer Sturdy. 2011. "The Influence of Economic Crisis on Early Childhood Development: A Review of Pathways and Measured Impact." In *No Small Matter: The Impact of Poverty, Shocks, and Human Capital Investments in Early Childhood Education,* edited by Harold Alderman. Human Development Perspectives. Washington, DC: World Bank.

Garcia, Marito, and Charity M. T. Moore. 2012. *The Cash Dividend: The Rise of Cash Transfer Programs in Sub-Saharan Africa.* Washington, DC: World Bank.

Georgieff, Michael K. 2007. "Nutrition and the Developing Brain: Nutrient Priorities and Measurements." *American Journal of Clinical Nutrition* 85 (Suppl.): 614S–20.

Gilligan, Daniel O., and Shalini Roy. 2013. "Resources, Stimulation, and Cognition: How Transfer Programs and Preschool Shape Cognitive Development in Uganda." Annual Meetings, Agricultural and Applied Economics Association, Washington, DC, August 4–6.

Glewwe, Paul, Michael Kremer, and Sylvie Moulin. 2009. "Many Children Left Behind? Textbooks and Test Scores in Kenya." *American Economic Journal: Applied Economics* 1 (1): 112–35.

Glewwe, Paul W., Eric A. Hanushek, Sarah D. Humpage, and Renato Ravina. 2014. "School Resources and Educational Outcomes in Developing Countries: A Review of the Literature from 1990 to 2010." In *Education Policy in Developing Countries,* edited by Paul Glewwe. Chicago, IL: University of Chicago Press.

Grantham-McGregor, Sally, Yin B. Cheung, Santiago Cueto, Paul Glewwe, Linda Richter, Barbara Strupp, and the International Child Development Steering Committee. 2007. "Developmental Potential in the First Five Years for Children in Developing Countries." *The Lancet* 369 (9555): 60–70.

Handa, Sudhanshu, Carolyn Tucker Halpern, Audrey Pettifor and Harsha Thirumurty. 2014. "The Government of Kenya's Cash Transfer Program Reduces the Risk of Sexual Debut among Young People Age 15–25." PLoS ONE 9(1): e85473.

Handa, Sudhanshu, Luisa Natali, David Seidenfeld, Gelson Tembo, and Zambia Cash Transfer Evaluation Team. 2015. "The Impact of Zambia Unconditional Child Grant on Schooling and Work.Results from a Large Scale Social Experiment." UNICEF Office of Research, Working Paper WP 2015-01, Florence.

Handa, Sudanshu, Michael Park, Robert O. Darko, Isaac Osei-Akoto, Benjamin Davis, and Silvio Diadone. 2013. "Livelihood Empowerment against Poverty Impact Evaluation." Carolina Population Center, University of North Carolina.

Handa, Sudanshu, Amber Peterman, David Seidenfeld, and GelsonTembo. 2015. "Income Transfers and Maternal Health: Evidence from a National Randomized Social Cash Transfer Program in Zambia." *Health Economics* 25 (2): 225–36.

Haushofer, Johannes, and Jeremy Shapiro. 2013. "Household Response to Income Changes: Evidence from an Unconditional Cash Transfer Program in Kenya." Paper, Massachusetts Institute of Technology, Boston.

Hazin, Adriano N., J. G. Bezerra Alves, and Ana Rodrigues Falbo. 2007. "The Myelination Process in Severely Malnourished Children: MRI Findings." *International Journal of Neuroscience* 117 (8): 1209–14.

He, Feng, Leigh Linden, and Margaret McLeod. 2008. "How to Teach English in India: Testing the Relative Productivity of Instruction Methods with Pratham English Language, Education Program." Report Columbia University, New York.

He Feng, Leigh Linden, and Margaret McLeod. 2009. "A Better Way to Teach Children to Read.Evidence from a Randomized Control Trial. Mimeo, 42 pp., Columbia University, New York.

Heckman, James J., and Pedro Carneiro. 2003. "Human Capital Policy." IZA Discussion Paper 821, Institute for the Study of Labor, Bonn, Germany. http://ssrn.com /abstract=434544.

Heckman, James J., and Tim Kautz. 2013. "Fostering and Measuring Skills: Interventions that Improve Character and Cognition." NBER Working Paper 19656, National Bureau of Economic Research, Cambridge, MA. http://www.nber.org/papers/w19656.

Heckman James J., and Dimitri V. Masterov. 2007. "The Productivity Argument for Investing in Young Children." *Review of Agricultural Economics* 29 (3): 446–93.

Hoddinott, John, John Maluccio, Jere R. Behrman, Reynaldo Martorell, Paul Melgar, Agnes R. Quisumbing, Manuel Ramirez- Zea, Aryeh D. Stein, and Kathryn M. Yount. 2011. "The Consequences of Early Childhood Growth Failure over the Life Course." IFPRI Discussion Paper 01073, International Food Policy Research Institute, Poverty, Health and Nutrition Division, Washington, DC.

Horton, Susan, Harold Alderman, and Juan Rivera. 2008. "Hunger and Malnutrition." Copenhagen Consensus 2008 Challenge Paper, Copenhagen Consensus Center, Tewksbury, MA.

Horton, Susan, Meera Shekar, Christine McDonald, Ajay Mahal, and Jana K. Jana. 2010. *Scaling Up Nutrition: What Will It Cost?* Washington, DC: World Bank. https:// openknowledge.worldbank.org/handle/10986/2685.

Huebler, Friedrich. 2012. "Educational Attainment in Sub-Saharan Africa." International Education Statistics. Accessed at http://huebler.blogspot.com/2012/02/ssa.html.

Keding, Gudrun, John M. Msuya, Brigitte L. Maass, and Michael B. Krawinke. 2013. "Obesity as a Public Health Problem among Adult Women in Rural Tanzania." *Global Health Science and Practice* 1 (3): 359–71. http://dx.doi.org/10.9745/GHSP-D-13 -00082.

Kenya CT-OVC Evaluation Team. 2012a. "The Impact of the Kenya Cash Transfer Program for Orphans and Vulnerable Children on Household Spending." *Journal of Development Effectiveness* 4 (1): 9–37.

———. 2012b. "The Impact of the Kenya Cash Transfer Program for Orphans and Vulnerable Children on Household Spending." *Journal of Development Effectiveness* 4 (1): 38–49.

Kimani-Murage, Elizabeth W. 2013. "Exploring the Paradox: Double Burden of Malnutrition in Rural South Africa." *Global Health Action* 6: 19249.

Kremer, Michael, Connor Brannen, and Rachel Glennerster. 2013. "The Challenge of Education and Learning in the Developing World." *Science* 340 (6130): 297–300.

Krishnaratne, Shari, Hoard White, and Ella Carpenter. 2013. "Quality Education for All Children? What Works in Education in Developing Countries." 3ie Working Paper 20, International Initiative for Impact Evaluation, New Delhi, India.

Lake, Anthony, and Margaret Chan. 2015. "Putting Science into Practice for Early Child Development." *The Lancet* 385 (9980): 1816–17.

Lindert, Kathy, Anja Linder, Jason Hobbs, and Bénédicte de la Brière. 2007. "The Nuts and Bolts of Brazil's Bolsa Família Program: Implementing Conditional Cash Transfers in a Decentralized Context." Social Protection Working Paper 0709, World Bank, Washington, DC.

Linnemayr, Sebastian, Harold Alderman, and Abdoulaye Ka. 2008. "Determinants of Malnutrition in Senegal: Individual, Household, Community Variables, and Their Interaction." *Economics and Human Biology* 6 (2): 252–63.

Loayza, Norman, and Jamele Rigolini. 2016. "The Local Impact of Mining on Poverty and Inequality: Evidence from the Commodity Boom in Peru." *World Development* 84 (C): 219–34.

Lucas, Adrienne M., Patrick McEwan, Moses Ngware, and Moses Oketch. 2014. "Improving Early Grade Literacy in East Africa: Experimental Evidence from Kenya and Uganda." *Journal of Policy Analysis and Management* 33: 950–76.

Macours, Karen, Norbert Schady, and Renos Vakis. 2012. "Cash Transfers, Behavorial Changes and Cognitive Development in Early Childhood: Evidence from a Randomized Control Experiment." IDB Working Paper IDB-WP-301, Inter-American Development Bank, Washington, DC.

Martinez, Sebastian, Sophie Naudeau, and Vitor Pereira. 2012. "The Promise of Preschool in Africa: A Randomized Impact Evaluation of Early Childhood Development in Rural Mozambique." Save the Children and the World Bank, Washington, DC.

Maxwell, Daniel, Carol Levin, Margaret Armar-Klemesu, Marie T. Ruel, Saul Morris, and Clement Ahiadeke. 2000. "Urban Livelihoods and Food and Nutrition Security in Greater Accra, Ghana." IFPRI Research Report 112. International Food Policy Research Institute, Washington, DC.

McEwan, Patrick. 2015. "Improving Learning in Primary Schools of Developing Countries: A Meta-Analysis of Randomized Experiments." *Review of Educational Research* 20 (10): 1–42.

Miller, Candace, Maxton Tsoka, and Kathryn Reichert. 2008. "Impact Evaluation Report: External Evaluation of the Mchinji Social Cash Transfer Pilot." Center for International Health and Development, Boston University School of Public Health, Boston, MA; and The Centre for Social Research, University of Malawi, Zomba, Malawi.

Miller, Candace, Maxton Tsoka, and Kathryn Reichert. 2011. "The Impact of the Social Cash Transfer Scheme on Food Security in Malawi." *Food Policy* 36 (2): 230–8.

Mingat, Alain, Blandine Ledoux, and Ramahatra Rakotomalala. 2010. "Developing Post-Primary Education in Sub-Saharan Africa: Assessing the Financial Sustainability of Alternative Pathways." Africa Human Development Series. World Bank, Washington, DC.

Mock, Steven E., and Susan M. Arai. 2011. "Childhood Trauma and Chronic Illness in Adulthood: Mental Health and Socio-Economic Status as Explanatory Factors and Buffers." *Frontiers in Psychology* 1 (January 31): 246.

Mullanaithan, Sendhil, and Eldar Shafir. 2013. *Scarcity: Why Having Too Little Means So Much*. New York: Macmillan.

Muralidharan Kharthik, and Venkatesh Sundararaman. 2011. "Teacher Performance Pay: Experimental Evidence from India." *Journal of Political Economy* 119: 39–77.

Murnane, Richard J., and Alejandro Ganimian. 2014. "Improving Educational Outcomes in Developing Countries: Lessons from Rigorous Evaluations." NBER Working Paper w20284, National Bureau of Economic Research, Cambridge, MA.

Nash, J. Madeleine. 1997. "Fertile Minds." *Time* (special report), February, 49–56.

National Research Council and Institute of Medicine. 2000. *From Neurons to Neighborhoods: The Science of Early Childhood Development*. Committee on Integrating the Science of Early Childhood Development, edited by J. P. Shonkoff and D. A. Phillips. Board on Children, Youth, and Families, Commission on Behavioral and Social Sciences and Education. Washington, DC: National Academy Press.

Naudeau, Sophie, Wendy Cunningham, Mattias K. Lundberg, and Linda McGinnis. 2008. "Programs and Policies That Promote Positive Youth Development and Prevent Risky Behaviors: An International Perspective." *New Directions for Child and Adolescent Development* 122 (Winter): 75–87.

Naudeau, Sophie, and P. A. Holland. 2014. "How Can Countries Devise Low-Cost Approaches to Offering ECD Services Sustainably." Education Global Practice Note: Development Challenges and Solutions. World Bank, Washington, DC.

Naudeau, Sophie, Naoko Kataoka, Alexandria Valerio, Michelle J. Neumann, and Leslie K. Elder. 2011. *Investing in Young Children: An Early Childhood Development Guide for Policy Dialogue and Project Preparation*. Directions in Development, Human Development. Washington, DC: World Bank.

Nyaradi, Anett, Jianghong. Li, Siobhan Hickling, Jonathan Foster, and Wendy H. Oddy. 2013. "The Role of Nutrition in Children's Neurocognitive Development, from Pregnancy through Childhood." *Frontiers in Human Neuroscience* 7 (March 26): 1–16.

Packel, Laura, William H. Dow, Damien de Walque, Zachary Isdahl, and Albert Majura. 2012. "Sexual Behavior Change Intentions and Actions in the Context of a Randomized Trial of a Conditional Cash Transfer for HIV Prevention in Tanzania." World Bank Policy Research Working Paper, World Bank, Washington, DC.

Paxson, Christina, and Norbert Schady. 2007. "Cognitive Development among Young Children in Ecuador: The Roles of Wealth, Health and Parenting." *Journal of Human Resources* 42 (1).

Piper, Benjamin, and Medina Korda. 2011. "EGRA Plus: Liberia. Program Evaluation Report." Research Triangle International, NC.

Popkin, Barry M., Linda S. Adair, and Shu W. Ng. 2012. "Global Nutrition Transition and the Pandemic of Obesity in Developing Countries." *Nutrition Review* 70 (1): 3–21.

Provo, A. M. 2013. "Toward Sustainable Nutrition for All: Tackling the Double Burden of Malnutrition in Africa." *Sight and Life* 27 (3): 40–48.

Robertson, Laura, Phyllis Mushati, Jeffrey W Eaton, Lovemore Dumba, Gideon Mavise, Jeremiah Makoni, Christina Schumacher, Tom Crea, Roeland Monasch, Lorraine Sherr, Geoffrey P Garnett, Constance Nyamukapa, and Simon Gregson. 2013. "Effects of Unconditional and Conditional Cash Transfers on Child Health and Development in Zimbabwe: A Cluster-Randomized Trial." *The Lancet* 381 (9874): 1283–92.

Ruel, Marie T., Harold Alderman, and the Maternal and Child Nutrition Study Group. 2013. "Nutrition-Sensitive Interventions and Programmes: How Can They Help to Accelerate Progress in Improving Maternal and Child Nutrition?" *The Lancet* 392 (9891): 536–51.

Sabarwal, Shwetlena, and James Habyarimana. 2015. "Kano Conditional Cash Transfer Program for Girls' Education." Impact Evaluation Report, World Bank, Washington, DC.

Sabates-Wheeler, Rachel, and Stephen Devereux. 2010. "Cash Transfers and High Food Prices: Explaining Outcomes on Ethiopia's Productive Safety Net." Future Agricultures Consortium Working Paper 004.

Schady, Norbert, Jere Behrman, Maria Caridad Araujo, Rodrigo Azuero, Raquel Bernal, David Bravo, Florencia Lopez-Boo, Karen Macours, Daniela Marshall, Christina Paxson, and Renos Vakis. 2015. "Wealth Gradients in Early Childhood Cognitive Development in Five Latin American Countries." *Journal of Human Resources* 50 (2): 446–63.

Seidenfeld, David, Leah Principe, Sudhanshu Handa, and Laura Hawkinson. 2015. "The Impact of an Unconditional Cash Transfer on Early Childhood Development: The Zambia Child Grant Program." Paper, American Institutes for Research, Bethesda, MD.

Seidenfeld Davis, Sudhanshu Handa, Gelson Tembo, Michelo S, Harland Scott C, and Leah Prencipe. 2014. "The Impacts of an Unconditional Cash Transfer on Food Security and Nutrition: The Zambia Child Grant Program." Institute of Development Studies (IDS), Special collection on child nutrition in Zambia.

Shonkoff, Jack, and Deborah Phillips, eds. 2000. "From Neurons to Neighborhoods: The Science of Early Child Development." National Academies Press.

Snellman, Kaissa, Jennifer M. Silva, and Robert D. Putnam. 2015. "Inequity Outside the Classroom: Growing Class Differences in Participation in Extra-Curricular Activities." *Voices in Urban Education* 40: 7–14.

The Lancet. 2007. "Series on Child Development in Developing Countries." *The Lancet,* January 6. http://www.thelancet.com/series/child-development-in-developing -countries-2.

———. 2008. "Series on Maternal and Child Nutrition." *The Lancet,* January 16. http://www .thelancet.com/series/maternal-and-child-nutrition.

———. 2011. "Series on Child Development in Developing Countries." *The Lancet,* September 23. http://www.thelancet.com/series/child-development-in-developing -countries-2.

———. 2013. "Series on Maternal and Child Nutrition." *The Lancet,* June 6. http://www .thelancet.com/series/maternal-and-child-nutrition.

Torche, Florencia 2011. "The Effect of Maternal Stress on Birth Outcomes: Exploiting a Natural Experiment." *Demography* 48 (4): 1473–91.

Torche, Florencia, and Uri Shwed. Forthcoming. "The Hidden Cost of War: The Effect of Prenatal Exposure to Armed Conflict." Institute of Human Development and Social Change, New York University, New York.

United Nations. 2014. "The Millennium Development Goals Report." United Nations, New York.

UNFPA (United Nations Population Fund). 2014. *State of World Population 2014: The Power of 1.8 Billion—Adolescents, Youth, and the Transformation of the Future.* New York: UNFPA.

UNICEF (United Nations Children's Fund). 2013. "Improving Child Nutrition: The Achievable Imperative for Global Progress." UNICEF, Paris.

UNICEF, World Health Organization (WHO), World Bank, and United Nations (UN). 2014. "Levels and Trends in Child Mortality: Report 2014." World Bank, Washington, DC.

Victora, Cesar G., Linda Adair, Caroline Fall, Pedro Hallal, Reynaldo Martorell, Linda Richter, and Harshpal Singh Sachdev. 2008. "Maternal and Child Undernutrition: Consequences for Adult Health and Human Capital." *The Lancet* 371 (9609): 340–57.

Victora, Cesar G., Mercedes de Onis, Pedro C. Hallal, Monika Blössner, and Roger Schrimption. 2010. "Worldwide Timing of Growth Faltering: Implications for Interventions." *Pediatrics* 125 (3): e473–80.

Walker, Susan P., Theodore D. Wachs, Sally Grantham-McGregor, Maureen Black, Charles A. Nelson, Sandra L. Huffman, Helen Naker-Henningham, Susan M. Chang, Jena D. Hamadani, Betsy Lozoff, Jullie M. Meeks Gardner, Christine A. Powell, Atif Rahman, and Linda Richter. 2011. "Inequality in Early Childhood: Risks and Protective Factors for Early Child Development." *The Lancet* 378 (9799): 1325–38.

Ward, Patrick, Alex Hurrell, Aly Visram, Nils Riemenschneider, Luca Pellerano, Clare O'Brien, Ian MacAuslan, and Jack Willis. 2010. "Cash Transfer Program for Orphans and Vulnerable Children (CT-OVC): Kenya-Programme Operational and Impact Evaluation, 2007–2009, Final Report." Oxford Policy Management, Oxford.

World Bank. 2010. *What Can We Learn From Nutrition Impact Evaluations? Lessons from a Review of Interventions to Reduce Child Malnutrition in Developing Countries.* Washington, DC: World Bank, Internal Evaluations Group.

———. 2013. "Improving Nutrition through Multi-Sectoral Approaches: Guidance Notes for World Bank Task Team Leaders." World Bank, Washington, DC.

———. 2014. *Education for All Report.* Washington, DC: World Bank.

Yusuf, Harun. K. M. 1992. *Understanding the Brain and Its Development: A Chemical Approach.* Singapore: World Scientific Publisher.

Zezza, Alberto, Bénédicte de la Brière, and Benjamin Davis. 2010. "The Impact of Social Cash Transfers on Household Decision-Making and Development." Paper presented at the African Economic Conference, Tunis.

Environmental Benefits Statement

The World Bank Group is committed to reducing its environmental footprint. In support of this commitment, we leverage electronic publishing options and print-on-demand technology, which is located in regional hubs worldwide. Together, these initiatives enable print runs to be lowered and shipping distances decreased, resulting in reduced paper consumption, chemical use, greenhouse gas emissions, and waste.

We follow the recommended standards for paper use set by the Green Press Initiative. The majority of our books are printed on Forest Stewardship Council (FSC)–certified paper, with nearly all containing 50–100 percent recycled content. The recycled fiber in our book paper is either unbleached or bleached using totally chlorine-free (TCF), processed chlorine–free (PCF), or enhanced elemental chlorine–free (EECF) processes.

More information about the Bank's environmental philosophy can be found at http://www.worldbank.org/corporateresponsibility.